Praise for *Tapping Into Ultimate Success*

"So many motivational books just talk about how to achieve success.
Tapping Into Ultimate Success *actually shows you, step-by-step,*
how to remove the obstacles that are blocking your success."

— Hale Dwoskin, *New York Times* best-selling
author of *The Sedona Method*

"To be perfectly honest, I didn't get how this process would
help me, since I'm a more practical person. I didn't get it until
I experienced it firsthand using Jack and Pamela's techniques.
It was fast, easy, and profound. I was able to eliminate a lifelong
issue, and I immediately had evidence that life was different."

— Marcia Wieder, CEO, Dream University

"For those who have spent years trying to create success, but
are unsatisfied with their results, this book is a gold mine of
answers. No one does success like Jack Canfield, and ***Tapping Into***
Ultimate Success *is sure to be a resource for years to come."*

— Fabrizio Mancini, president, Parker Chiropractic College

"Meridian Tapping fans will find the book extremely valuable,
because it presents a new approach to tapping that brings forth the
creative side of our selves, rapidly and with striking results. This book
makes an impressive contribution to the field of self-development."

— Patricia Carrington, Ph.D., author of *Multiply the Power of EFT*

"It was time that someone got inside the 'why' success doesn't
happen easily for most people. Jack Canfield, one of the leading
voices for success in the world, has teamed up with Pamela Bruner
and brought some astonishing new answers for those who have been
asking 'Why not me?' ***Tapping Into Ultimate Success*** *delivers*
a resounding, 'Yes, you can—and here's how!'"

— Lisa Nichols, *New York Times* best-selling author of *No Matter What!*

"We know that limiting beliefs are the #1 reason that people don't
take action to achieve success. Now, ***Tapping Into Ultimate Success***
shows you exactly how to remove those limiting beliefs, so you can
take action powerfully and effectively. Congratulations to Jack and
Pamela for creating a work that shares a new perspective on success."

— Bob Proctor, best-selling author of *You Were Born Rich*

"Finally, a book that tells us not just what to do, but exactly how to do it, and why we haven't been able to do it before. **Tapping Into Ultimate Success** is a guidebook for creating new levels of success in all areas of your life."

— Cynthia Kersey, best-selling author of
Unstoppable and *Unstoppable Women*

"If you know what you have to do, but you're struggling to do it, you will find a practical—yes, it really works—solution in **Tapping Into Ultimate Success.** Jack Canfield combined his success principles with Pamela Bruner's brilliant understanding of tapping into an easy-to-read, easy-to-apply system. And, yes, the book is filled with inspiring stories and great examples—it wouldn't be Jack without them."

— Pete Bissonette, president, Learning Strategies Corporation

"Jack Canfield charmed the world with his **Chicken Soup for the Soul** stories and inspired us with **The Success Principles.** Now he's teamed up with another top success coach to bring us the how-to behind his work. This is the piece that will enable you to say yes to all your dreams."

— Paul Scheele, author of *PhotoReading* and *Natural Brilliance*

"This is a very good book written by very good people. As a guy who used to think my body existed to carry my brain around, and who has only recently come to understand how many patterns that interfere with the experience of happiness and success are locked in our bodies, this book is a revelation! Tapping works. Buy this book. Do the process. You will be grateful you did. Highly recommended."

— Stewart Emery, speaker, educator, and best-selling
author of *Success Built to Last*

"Here is your opportunity to drink deeply of the profound wisdom of one of the real wise ones, my lifetime friend and mentor, Jack Canfield. Read, assimilate, and apply what Jack is sharing, and your life and lifestyle will start improving at once!"

— Mark Victor Hansen, co-author of *Chicken Soup for the Soul*

TAPPING
INTO ULTIMATE SUCCESS

TAPPING

INTO ULTIMATE SUCCESS

HOW TO OVERCOME ANY OBSTACLE
AND SKYROCKET YOUR RESULTS

Jack **Canfield** &
Pamela **Bruner**

HAY HOUSE, INC.
Carlsbad, California • New York City
London • Sydney • Johannesburg
Vancouver • Hong Kong • New Delhi

First published and distributed in the United Kingdom by:
Hay House UK Ltd, 292B Kensal Rd, London W10 5BE. Tel.: (44) 20 8962 1230;
Fax: (44) 20 8962 1239. www.hayhouse.co.uk

Published and distributed in the United States of America by:
Hay House, Inc., PO Box 5100, Carlsbad, CA 92018-5100. Tel.: (1) 760 431 7695 or
(800) 654 5126; Fax: (1) 760 431 6948 or (800) 650 5115. www.hayhouse.com

Published and distributed in Australia by:
Hay House Australia Ltd, 18/36 Ralph St, Alexandria NSW 2015. Tel.: (61) 2 9669
4299; Fax: (61) 2 9669 4144. www.hayhouse.com.au

Published and distributed in the Republic of South Africa by:
Hay House SA (Pty), Ltd, PO Box 990, Witkoppen 2068. Tel./Fax: (27) 11 467
8904. www.hayhouse.co.za

Published and distributed in India by:
Hay House Publishers India, Muskaan Complex, Plot No.3, B-2, Vasant Kunj,
New Delhi – 110 070. Tel.: (91) 11 4176 1620; Fax: (91) 11 4176 1630.
www.hayhouse.co.in

Distributed in Canada by:
Raincoast, 9050 Shaughnessy St, Vancouver, BC V6P 6E5. Tel.: (1) 604 323 7100;
Fax: (1) 604 323 2600

Copyright © 2012 by Jack Canfield and Pamela Bruner

The moral rights of the authors have been asserted.

Cover design: Shelley Noble • *Interior design:* Tricia Breidenthal
Interior illustrations: David Babb

The authors of this book do not dispense medical advice or prescribe the
use of any technique as a form of treatment for physical, emotional, or medical
problems without the advice of a physician, either directly or indirectly. The
intent of the authors is only to offer information of a general nature to help you
in your quest for emotional and spiritual well-being. In the event you use any of
the information in this book for yourself, which is your constitutional right, the
authors and the publisher assume no responsibility for your actions.

This EFT®-oriented book is provided as a good faith effort to expand
the use of tapping and tapping-related techniques in the world. It represents the
ideas of the authors and does not necessarily represent those of Gary Craig, the
founder of EFT®.

This book is for educational purposes only. While impressive results have
been reported with tapping and energy technologies, the field is still considered
experimental. Given that, nothing in this book should be construed as a promise of benefits or guarantee of any results.

A catalogue record for this book is available from the British Library.

ISBN 978-1-84850-929-0

Printed and bound in Great Britain by CPI Group (UK) Ltd, Croydon, CR0 4YY.

*This book is dedicated to
all those who have the courage
to overcome their fears and limiting
beliefs and create meaningful
and fulfilling lives.*

CONTENTS

FOREWORD

I read this book cover to cover, and when I finished . . . I was really frustrated.

No, not the usual kind of frustration with a book, like when it has a bad ending or you feel you've wasted hours of your life. I was frustrated because it was so *good.*

All I kept thinking was, *Why couldn't I have read this book ten years ago?* It would have likely meant that I didn't feel so frustrated, anxious, stressed, or overwhelmed. It would have meant more money, better relationships, more successful business ventures, and a lot more.

Oh, well. Such is life.

The good news is that my frustration didn't last long, and what set in was a deep excitement for what this book is. . . .

You hold in your hands the potential for *real* change in your life. If you've spent countless hours reading, studying, attending success seminars, and the like, and have yet to see the results you desire, it's likely that you're missing a critical piece to the puzzle. That critical piece—generally understood as the concept of releasing resistance, limiting beliefs, past traumas, negative emotions, and so forth—is covered brilliantly in this book.

You're probably aware of some of the habits and patterns that have stopped you in the past, but don't know a practical way to release them. You can talk about your fear of failure until you're blue in the face, dissecting it from every angle, talking to coaches and counselors about it and so forth; but unless you bring in a tool that clears that fear, the way tapping does, you're not going to get anywhere.

The exciting thing is that with tapping, you *can* go some-where, and *fast*. The results I've seen with tapping in the last eight years I've been studying it have been nothing short of ex-traordinary. Some of the results border on miraculous, and some might deem them a miracle if they didn't understand the inherent power of the body to heal and to let go of limiting beliefs, fears, and negative emotions.

Besides being known for his wild success with the *Chicken Soup for the Soul* series, Jack Canfield is also known as "America's Suc-cess Coach." His life and his accomplishments at all levels—finan-cial, emotional, and societal—have been so stunning that it only makes sense to pay attention to what he has to say, so we can try to replicate his results.

In this book, he's teamed up with Pamela Bruner, a leader in the burgeoning field of tapping and energy psychology, to bring you a book that is highly relevant to your life and your challenges—and perhaps most important, a book that will deliver *results*.

That's the exciting thing about combining Jack Canfield's proven success principles with a powerful tool like tapping: the result is not something that you'll sit around and passively think about, or "will" yourself to implement. The result is a guidebook that will take you step-by-step, in order to create dramatic positive change and results in your life.

And want to know what is maybe the best part? You only have to go about 30 pages deep into this book to experience tapping and have a positive result.

Once you have that experience—once you know deep down that you have discovered a tool that will finally make all your dreams come true, that will relieve you of past limiting beliefs, negative emotions, and everything else that is holding you back—the rest of the journey through the book promises to be an exhilarating adventure.

So get started today, even if it is just 30 pages at first. Experi-ence tapping and the power of the success principles to change your life!

— **Nick Ortner,**
Executive Producer, *The Tapping Solution*

INTRODUCTION

With so many great teachings in the world, why aren't more people successful?

There is a multitude of books, videos, and audios on spiritual principles, universal laws, and success concepts. There are motivational speeches and workshops, retreats and seminars, but achieving success is still a struggle for so many. While the ideas presented are inspiring and often motivating, applying them is where so many get stuck.

Just having the map won't get you to the destination. Just knowing what to do isn't enough. Humans are designed with protective mechanisms that often interfere with goal achievement, and as a result, millions are frustrated in their attempts to go from where they are to where they want to be.

This book and DVD are designed to bridge that gap.

Although people have always had ways to overcome obstacles to success, the older methods are tedious and require months or years of hard labor, intense concentration, and dogged perseverance. Newer, cutting-edge techniques are emerging that enable you to move from upset to calm, from fear to confidence, and from stopped to successful in a fraction of the time—weeks, days, or even minutes!

Tapping (short for Meridian Tapping) is one of these techniques. We'll be describing exactly what tapping is and how to do it in the next chapter; but first, we want to share what you can expect by reading this book and following these teachings.

Tapping is being successfully used around the world for issues as varied as fears, phobias, post-traumatic stress disorder (PTSD), food cravings, and chronic pain. By using this simple technique, you can take years off your journey to personal power and accomplishment by transforming the beliefs and emotions that cause self-doubt, self-sabotage, procrastination, and so much more.

We've both used tapping to increase the money we make (Pamela used it to build a million-dollar business in less than three years), but that's only the beginning. We've also used it to deepen our relationships, turn around limiting beliefs, and reduce the fears and anxieties that naturally occur when playing a big game . . . and we've helped many others to do the same.

Tapping was originally developed as a way to remove negative emotions only, and this is certainly valuable. However, just removing the negative without replacing those emotions or beliefs with new, positive feelings and ideas is only completing half the job. In order to achieve ultimate success, you need to experience uplifting emotions and install empowering beliefs. The tapping processes described in this book and DVD will show you how to do exactly that.

We've chosen to illustrate how these tapping techniques can be used to overcome obstacles to success by working with the principles outlined in the book *The Success Principles* by Jack Canfield and Janet Switzer. However, you can use these techniques to overcome any obstacle or limitation that keeps you from creating success in your life, no matter how you define "success"! Further, although this book refers heavily to these success principles, it has been written to stand alone. (And please note that the principles are presented in an order that allows for the most logical flow of the tapping techniques, not in the numeric order of the previous book.)

◎

This book is arranged in nine chapters to make it as easy as possible to learn the techniques. We use what Pamela calls the "stone soup" method of teaching, based on the old folktale "Stone Soup":

> A traveler came to a very poor village and asked for some food, but was told that there was no food to be had. He smiled and said that would not be a problem, as he had a stone that would create a wonderful soup, just by cooking the stone! A pot full of water was brought, and the traveler carefully took a wrapped bundle from his pack. He then unwrapped a large gray stone and placed it in the pot.
>
> As the water heated, the traveler would taste the soup and exclaim that it was cooking beautifully. At one point he said, "Ah, it's heavenly! It's truly wonderful as it is. However, if just a scrap of onion were added, it would be even better!" The villagers realized that they had a few onion peelings, and threw them in the pot with the stone.
>
> After a few more minutes of stirring and tasting, the traveler said, "It's just delightful. Almost perfect! However, if there were just a few bits of carrot, oh, how incredible it would be." The villagers managed to locate a few bits of carrot, and added them to the pot.
>
> And so it went. The traveler would declare the soup to be delicious, but allowed that it would be even better with the addition of this or that small ingredient. In a very short time, a fragrant pot of soup was created, in a village whose people believed that they had no food.

Even the simplest tapping techniques introduced here will give you powerful results. As you add additional elements to your array of tapping skills, you'll be giving yourself a tremendous resource to use in many different areas of your life. As we teach each technique, we'll introduce a powerful success principle and the resistance that you might encounter when you try to implement that principle, and then demonstrate how you can use tapping to remove the resistance. You'll also read many case studies of clients who have used these techniques to skyrocket their results.

~~DON'T READ THIS BOOK!~~

~~Did we get your attention? Great!~~

More accurately, we'll say: don't *just* read this book. We certainly hope you find this book to be motivating and inspiring. However, more fundamental and important than that, this book is meant to inform and teach. In easy-to-follow steps you'll learn a powerful set of techniques that will allow you to achieve your dreams and goals. Like any tool, it has to be used in order to work. So read, enjoy, and more important, *do* the work in this book.

Here's how to use this book and DVD:

Get a notebook or journal, or create a file on your computer if you prefer to work that way. You'll need someplace to capture your notes as you go through the book, so you can track your progress. You'll want to do this to see, and celebrate, how much you're going to accomplish. It's easy to discount the progress you've made if there isn't a record of where you've come from and the work that you've done. Keep your record. It doesn't have to be fancy or neat, but it needs to be written down.

Throughout the book, you'll be given exercises and Action Steps. *It is vitally important that you do these.* If you just read the book without doing them, it may be inspiring, but you won't get all of the tremendous results that are possible. Practice the techniques by doing the exercises and Action Steps, and you'll be amazed at how much freedom and transformation you can achieve. In order to support you in completing your work, you can download a PDF of all the Action Steps as a workbook at **www.TappingInto UltimateSuccess.com**.

There is a Chapter Checklist at the end of each chapter, designed as a self-check. If you can agree with all the statements and correcly answer all the questions, you'll be able to get the most out of the chapters that follow.

We start with basic information about tapping and why it works. Then you'll learn the simplest form of the technique, which you can use immediately to start removing your obstacles to success. You can learn and experiment with these life-changing tools within a very short time after you pick up the book! In the rest of the second chapter, "Removing Fears," we address fears and add a couple of additional steps to make the tapping process that much more powerful and flexible.

In Chapter 3, "Overcoming Limiting Beliefs," we explore how limiting beliefs are formed, along with the process for transforming them into empowering beliefs. Then in Chapter 4, "Foundations for Success," we explore the most important principles that can bring you phenomenal results, and how to overcome obstacles that may stop you from living those powerful ideas. In Chapter 5, "Accelerating Success," we explore even more creative tapping techniques, and see how to apply them to implement the principles that will bring you ultimate success.

In Chapter 6, "Healing the Past," you'll learn an exciting new technique that can break the power of old, damaging memories. In Chapter 7, "Creating the New You," you'll begin creating your own tapping routines to create the visions and achieve the goals you've always desired. In Chapter 8, "Creating New Habits for Success," we'll look at how you can put much of your work on autopilot, so you're moving ahead more easily. You'll also start creating more of your own tapping routines that you can use to empower all areas of your life. In Chapter 9, "Financial Success," we'll look at the common blocks to creating wealth in your life and how to overcome them.

In order for you to locate key points more easily, we've used the following conventions:

- Lists of ideas or thoughts will be marked with regular bullets.

- Tapping phrases will be marked with diamond-shaped bullets.

- Sections labeled "Tapping Tips" contain hints that will increase the effectiveness of your tapping.

- Tapping techniques are capitalized, as are words or phrases that originated in other works on tapping.

- Success stories are set in gray boxes. You can read them as examples as well as for inspiration.

The companion DVD demonstrates many of the techniques in the book. You can use the DVD to see us apply these techniques in unscripted demonstrations, and you'll see for yourself the extraordinary transformation that can occur with tapping. Just viewing the DVD, and tapping along with us as you watch, can have a powerful effect.

Learning something new takes time, whether it's a team sport, a musical instrument, or a new technique for freedom and success. Creating ultimate success—success on your terms, as you define it—takes attention and effort, but it doesn't have to take struggle. You can learn the basics of this technique in only a few minutes. As you continue to delve into the work, you'll be able to handle complex emotions, challenging situations, and lifelong limiting beliefs with more and more ease. It's worth the time.

Your ultimate success, and results that you can only barely imagine now, are within your reach. It is our intention that this work helps you step into your success powerfully, and more fully than you ever have before.

— **Jack Canfield and Pamela Bruner**

A NEW TECHNIQUE FOR CREATING SUCCESS

If you're like us, you want to create success in your life. You want to achieve your goals, create and maintain a certain lifestyle, have great relationships, enjoy vibrant physical health, and feel happy and joyful.

In 2004, the book *The Success Principles* was written to help you do just that, and it's one of the most powerful and complete books on how to achieve success ever written. So why haven't all the readers of the book achieved those kinds of results in every area of their lives?

Certainly, many people *have* achieved outstanding results using the success principles, but others struggle to implement the ideas presented in the book. If you're one of them, perhaps you've experienced success in one arena, but find another area of your life isn't looking the way you'd like it to be.

"Ultimate Success" is not just success in one area. It's not having only financial success, yet having poor relationships. It's not just having good relationships, while your health suffers. And ultimate success does not mean focusing only on the areas of your life that are working and ignoring those parts in which you feel helpless. Ultimate success is success in *all* areas. It's not just the achievement of your goals; more important, it's the ability to remove any obstacle that comes up as you pursue those goals. When the journey becomes a path of mastery, ease, and exciting challenge rather than struggle, suffering, and insurmountable obstacles, *that* is ultimate success.

This book and DVD program were written to help you achieve ultimate success. We'll explore the resistance, blocks, and barriers that keep you from living the success principles, and give you an exciting new technique—tapping—to remove those blocks. Once you're able to remove your negative emotions and overcome your limiting beliefs, you will be able to achieve success in a powerful new way. You'll get from where you are to where you want to be more quickly and more easily than you ever imagined.

On this journey, we'll look at the following:

- Why change is challenging, and what to do about it

- The new, cutting-edge energy techniques, and why they are so effective

- How to remove negative emotions that keep you from taking action

- An understanding of belief systems, and how to change them

- Specific suggestions for overcoming blocks to implementing each of the success principles

In the end, if you take the actions described in the book and do the exercises provided, you'll find yourself able to remove negative emotions and install positive ones, shift limiting beliefs that don't serve you and create new empowering beliefs, and take action in areas where you were stagnant before. With those new abilities, you will be able to create the success you desire . . . in *every* area of your life.

If you haven't read the Introduction, go back now and read it. It contains important information about how to use the book and DVD, which will greatly increase the enjoyment and value you get from them.

WHY CAN'T I EASILY MAKE CHANGES IN MY LIFE?

We often say that we want to make changes in our lives. You may want to make more money, lose weight, get a new or better relationship, start a new career, or take up a new hobby. Yet change can seem so hard. Why is there so much struggle around change?

The reason lies in the fact that the mind is divided into two parts: literally, two hemispheres. One part is responsible for rational, conscious thought and processes ideas sequentially, using language. The other part is emotional and processes ideas simultaneously, using pictures.

The emotional, subconscious mind is far more powerful than the rational, conscious mind. It is capable of processing more information, controls approximately 95 percent of the thoughts you think and the actions you take each day, and is motivated by the pull of pleasurable rewards and the push of negative emotions.

◎

If you think of the emotional mind as an elephant and the rational mind as the rider, you can understand the challenge of change. The rider can control the elephant, as long as the elephant doesn't have any strong desires about the direction in which it moves. If the elephant doesn't want to go, however, the rider has very little chance of forcing it.[1]

Studies have shown that when you attempt to use willpower to create change, success is very limited. Willpower has been proven to be an exhaustible resource.[2] The more you use up in one area, the less you have for another area. So if you're trying to start a new business and lose weight at the same time, relying on will-power alone to accomplish tasks in both of these areas will probably not succeed.

The concept of the conflict between the elephant and the rider (the rational and the emotional) goes back thousands of years, to the teachings of Buddha, Plato, and the Bible. Many different techniques and approaches have been used since then to get the rider and the elephant to work together, usually based on trying to tame the elephant to obey the will of the rider.

The emotional, subconscious elephant experiences fear, anger, sadness, anxiety, and a host of other negative emotions when pursuing goals. This isn't a moral failing or a sign of weakness; it's the way that the brain is wired. The subconscious was designed by evolution to protect us from danger. However, this part of the brain isn't good at distinguishing between what is actually physically dangerous, like a saber-toothed tiger chasing you, and what is only emotionally dangerous, like rejection or failure. Because of this, these emotional deterrents keep you from taking action and achieving your goals. Also, limiting beliefs can keep the elephant paralyzed, not knowing that success is possible.

The reason why so many people fail to achieve success is that the elephant is averse to the actions that need to be taken. To make tasks much easier, you need to have the elephant motivated to move in a certain direction. At the very least, the elephant needs to be neutral and not resisting the rider.

Some approaches to create change have included:

1. **Changing the goals,** or attempting to reduce the power of the emotional desires. Philosophies of nonattachment take this approach. If you don't want anything—if you have no desires—then your elephant is easier to control.

2. **Creating disincentives for actions that move you away from the goal.** If the elephant thinks that an action comes with a terrible consequence, it might

be dissuaded from the action. This approach has very limited success.

3. **Attempting to strengthen the control of the rider.** This is actually an emotional approach, disguised as a rational one. By creating an identity of toughness and control, the rider seems stronger. In fact, the elephant has bought into feeling good about "being a tough guy," and becomes easier to control because of the rewards of honoring the identity. We'll talk more about honoring identity in a later chapter.

4. **Creating habits.** When an activity becomes habitual, it doesn't require the attention of the rider anymore, and requires much less effort. Creating the habit, though, can take considerable effort.

All of these approaches work for some people, to some degree. But because the emotional elephant is so much stronger, it makes far more sense to reduce the resistance—the negative emotions—to moving in the direction of your goals.

If you could reduce those negative emotions and change your limiting beliefs to empowering ones, your success would be much easier.

That's where the tapping techniques come in.

WHY TAPPING WORKS

When tapping was first used in the 1970s, tapping theory was based on the energy meridians of acupuncture (which is where its full name, Meridian Tapping, comes from). It was thought that clearing those energy meridians would clear a disruption in the body's energy system, and so remove negative emotions.

However, we have a new understanding based on recent scientific studies. It has been discovered that the brain does not become fixed by one's early adult years, but rather, it can be changed at any age. New neural connections can always be formed. Unfortunately, this can work against us. When we experience a trauma or something that triggers a negative emotion, we create neural pathways that support re-triggering that negative emotion. (As an example, if you have an experience that causes you to believe that people are mean or dangerous, you will look for evidence to support this belief and ignore evidence to the contrary.) We also create pathways that support limiting or disempowering beliefs that we may have created in the moment of a trauma. This process of creating pathways is so fast, in fact, that Nobel Prize winner Eric Kandel says we can double the neural connections for a given thought pattern in only one hour!

We can be grateful to Sigmund Freud for giving us an understanding of the significance of the unconscious mind. However, he was unfortunately incorrect when he said, "Insight produces change." Conditions like phobias and PTSD exist because the brain creates a feedback loop that builds and enhances neural pathways. As we'll see later in the book, experiences throughout life create fears and limiting beliefs that become hardwired into the brain. This occurs in all human beings, not just those who suffer significant trauma. In order to transform yourself, you must interrupt the feedback loop that is creating these patterns.

Simply understanding your fears and limiting beliefs, however, usually does not give you the ability to overcome them. Consider a person with a fear of flying: He may know *consciously* that flying is safer than driving in a car. Nevertheless, this doesn't prevent his *subconscious* mind from creating certain symptoms every time he boards an aircraft.

Now, recall an experience that made you angry or upset. If you continue to think about it, even if you try to ignore it, you're building more and more neural pathways of stress and upset. The fact that this process gets stronger over time makes it even more essential that we interrupt the process of creating these negatively based neural connections, because any negative emotion or limiting belief will only get worse over time, not better.

Tapping interrupts this process. Tapping sends signals to the brain to react with calm, not with fear or upset. It has been proven to dramatically reduce cortisol levels. This in turn reduces stress. Any time you think about something upsetting, whether it's an action that you're about to take or a disturbing memory, tapping helps to neutralize the upset you feel.

Dawson Church, author of *The Genie in Your Genes* and multiple studies on the effectiveness of EFT tapping, says:

> Tapping creates a piezoelectric charge that travels through the connective tissue along the path of least electrical resistance. When a traumatic memory is recalled, along with the awareness of the site in the body that holds the primary memory of the trauma, tapping introduces a message of safety to the body that is not congruent with the emotionally arousing memory.[4]

Tapping was developed by drawing on traditions from psychology, kinesiology, and more. Pioneers in these fields include Roger Callahan, John Diamond, George Goodheart, Francine Shapiro, Patricia Carrington, and Gary Craig. Most people who now work in tapping began their work by learning EFT, of which many variations exist. Much of what is in this book is based on Gary Craig's original EFT and the innovations later added by Dr. Patricia Carrington. However, the terms used to describe the tapping techniques in this book are ours, unless otherwise noted. In this book, we'll use the term *tapping*, unless we're specifically talking about a technique that is part of the original EFT as defined by Gary Craig.

The advantages of tapping are numerous:

- It's simple enough that anyone can do it, even children!
- It's noninvasive.
- It requires no special equipment or location.
- It's much faster than most other techniques.
- It's flexible enough to adapt to any situation or issue.

- You can do tapping by yourself.*
- Tapping will work even if you are skeptical. So try it!

*Tapping is a wonderful self-help technique. However, if you're working on deep trauma, abuse, or any other serious issue, we suggest the help of a tapping practitioner. To find a tapping practitioner, see "Next Steps" at the end of the book for more information.

GET STARTED TAPPING

(**Note:** If you are very familiar with tapping or EFT, you may want to skim through or skip this part.)

In order for the tapping to be most effective, we want to tap on certain electrically sensitive points. These are some of the same points that have been used in acupuncture for 5,000 years, which we call *acupoints*. Although there are hundreds of acupoints, tapping works with less than 20.

We'll introduce the points little by little in this work, so you can learn them a few at a time. Once you've tried tapping a few times, the points will become second nature.

Please familiarize yourself with the following illustration. These are the eight main points that we'll be using our tapping routines:

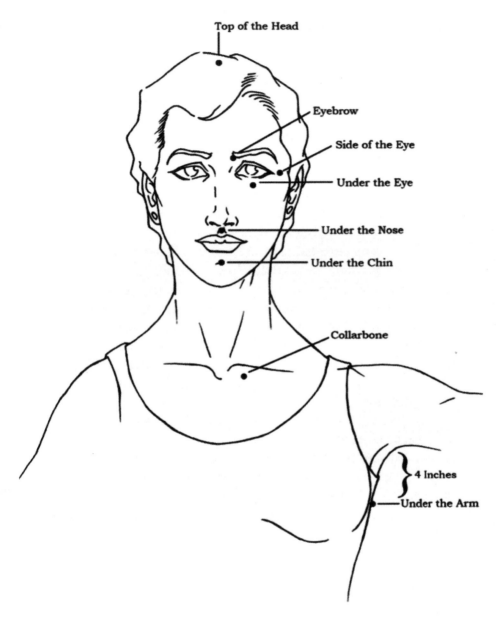

Although some of the points are shown on just one side of the body, they are on both sides. So, for example, there is a single point at the the top of the head, but there are two eyebrow points:

one at the start of the right eyebrow just above the nose, and the other at the start of the left eyebrow.

Tapping was originally taught one-sided; you tap with either hand, on either side of the body. Most people tap with their dominant hand. Some people choose to tap with both hands when there are two points. For example, the right hand would tap the right eyebrow point, and the left hand would tap the left eyebrow point simultaneously. Then at the chin point, only one hand is used.

We recommend you start tapping with one hand on just one side of the body, using whichever hand is most comfortable for you. When you are more familiar with tapping, you can experiment with using both hands, and see if you prefer that.

Using your index and middle finger, you'll tap each one of the points approximately five to seven times before moving on to the next point. (Since you'll often be speaking while you tap, don't worry about accurate counting. If you tap more or less times than five to seven, that's okay.) You have completed a "round" of tapping when you've tapped on each of the eight points. Watch the video so that you're clear on the points, but don't worry much about precision.

Tap lightly, but firmly. This isn't massage, so tapping with force isn't necessary. If you can't tap a particular point due to an injury, just skip that point. Unlike acupuncture, tapping is a very forgiving process. One reason it is common to tap using both the index finger and the middle finger together is that you're tapping a fairly large area with both fingers on any particular spot. (Refer to the DVD for more clarity on this.)

MEASURING THE PROGRESS OF TAPPING

When you tap, you'll want to keep track of your progress on each issue. To do that, we use a scale called the "SUDS" scale. **SUDS** stands for Subjective Units of Distress. When you first begin to work on an issue such as a fear, one of the first questions you'll ask yourself is, "How intense is this emotion?" using a scale of 0–10. Zero means "no intensity," the emotion isn't present, while ten means "extreme intensity."

The important thing to remember about the SUDS scale is that it *is* subjective. It's your measure of how angry, fearful, or upset you are. Therefore, there are no right or wrong answers. What's right is what's true for you in the moment.

You can also use the SUDS scale to measure your intensity when you think of a past event. Are you upset about something that happened last week or last year? How upset are you? Is the emotion really anger or is it something else, like sadness? Also, be sure to distinguish between how you felt about an event *then,* and how you feel about that same event *now.* Your intensity may be lower or higher. With the SUDS scale, you want to evaluate how you feel *now* about the event.

Establishing a number rating for the intensity of the emotion allows you to measure your progress in reducing that intensity after a round (or several rounds) of tapping.

◎

Since you've got the initial tapping points, let's use what you've learned to remove some of the fears and discomforts you may be experiencing in your life. You're now ready to start using the simple, powerful technique of tapping to bring about positive transformation!

ACTION STEP: GET STARTED TAPPING

Watch the first section of the DVD, which includes the tapping points.

Tap all the points so that you're familiar with the location of each point.

Practice using the SUDS scale. Think about an event in the last week that was upsetting or frightening. When you think about it now, on a scale of 0–10, how intense is that emotion? (Remember, the scale is subjective, so there are no right or wrong answers.) However, being able to tune in to your emotions and notice their intensity will enable you to clear your obstacles to success.

CHAPTER CHECKLIST

I know what the eight tapping points are.
I understand how to use the SUDS scale.

◎ ◎ ◎

REMOVING FEARS

WHY DO WE HAVE SO MUCH FEAR?

Fear is perhaps the most pervasive emotion human beings experience. In fact, we've been programmed for fear as a survival mechanism.

Fifty thousand years ago, survival depended on avoiding danger, and remembering the signals of life-threatening situations. If you remembered which valley had the saber-toothed tiger in it, you were more likely than your carefree companions to live longer. Fear was an emotion that would increase your life expectancy, so humans evolved with fear.

In today's society, this programming doesn't serve us as well as it once did. Our fears, which would originally be triggered only in true fight-or-flight situations, are now constantly aroused by the stresses of everyday life. Fears include perceived threats to safety, identity, and community approval. The fear of losing community approval has led to problems ranging from teenage peer pressure and hazing to such extremes as the genocides perpetrated in Nazi Germany and in Rwanda.

For some people, fear is paralyzing, while for others, it's just uncomfortable. Some individuals even regard fear as a challenge, and step in the direction of it. If you can do this, or operate in spite of your fear, you can accomplish a great deal more in life.

EXPERIENCE YOUR FEAR AND TAKE ACTION ANYWAY (SUCCESS PRINCIPLE 15)

In the past, this "feel the fear and do it anyway" philosophy, or trying to talk yourself out of being scared, was the best option. Yet fear isn't a rational response. While we may have rational concerns or reasons for it, the fear itself comes from a completely different part of the brain that is usually not responsive to logical arguments. Sometimes these fears are so severe that they are categorized as phobias, including fear of heights, fear of public speaking, fear of open spaces or closed spaces, and more. These same fears can also occur in less intense versions.

Fears can hinder your success, even if they aren't as strong as phobias.

Fear doesn't have to be a phobia to affect our success. A fear of networking can keep a business professional from success. A fear of asking someone for a date can keep a person single and lonely. You may not even be aware of your fear—you may instead see it more as "discomfort" or "disliking" some activity. Most people are very good at procrastinating when it comes to an activity that triggers fear, and then claiming they are too busy to take action.

It is possible to reduce or eliminate fear using tapping. This next exercise is the first step in learning to use tapping for your ultimate success.

TAPPING TECHNIQUE: SIMPLE TAPPING

Read through the five steps in the Simple Tapping process. You'll then get a chance to try Simple Tapping on your own issue.

STEP 1: IDENTIFY YOUR FEAR

Although you may think that you have a fear of networking, or of asking someone for a date, those aren't actually your fears. Your fears are what you imagine will happen when you do those things.

Example: *I'm afraid to go to the networking event.*
Why? *Because I imagine that my mind will go blank and I'll look foolish.*
True fear: *I'm afraid I'll look foolish.*

Example: *I'm afraid to ask Sally for a date.*
Why? *Because I imagine she'll say no and I'll be embarrassed.*
True fear: *I'm afraid I'll be embarrassed.*

Write down your fear. If you have more than one, write them all down.

STEP 2: MEASURE YOUR LEVEL OF FEAR

You'll want to do this so that you can be aware of any change in intensity. Sometimes tapping works so quickly and effectively that something that you rate as a 10 in intensity may be a 4 several minutes later. Therefore, unless you've previously measured your level of fear, you can be unaware of the progress you've made.

On the 0–10 SUDS scale, with 10 being the most intense, measure your fear. Remember, SUDS stands for Subjective Units of Distress, so there is no right or wrong number here, only what you perceive. Let the first number that comes to mind be okay. If you find it very challenging to assign a number to the intensity of your fear, you may try picturing how big it is using your hands to visually measure its width. Is it the size of a beach ball, a basketball, or a baseball?

Some people have a tendency to push away their emotions. For example, if you were told as a child not to cry, you may not be in touch with your feelings. If you believe that negative emotions like anger are wrong, you may not want to allow yourself to feel anger. However, tuning in to your emotions and tapping is the quickest way to clear them, so allow yourself to feel whatever is there. (**Note:** the only exception to this is if you're working on very severe trauma. In that case, consult a tapping practitioner for advanced tools to clear this type of traumatic emotion.)

Next to your fear, write down its intensity.

STEP 3: TAP ON YOUR FEAR

We'll use the tapping points we outlined in the last chapter. Begin by tapping on the top of the head, and state your fear. Don't just say the words; allow yourself to fully feel the fear that you're naming. (One exception: If you're feeling overwhelming fear or intensity, please read "Tapping Tip: Turning Down the Intensity," which appears later in this chapter.) Tap the next point, the eyebrow point, and state your fear again, again focusing not just on the words but on the feeling of fear. Continue to tap on the remaining points, stating your fear as you tap on each point.

We'll call each of the phrases that you say *Reminder Phrases* since they remind you to focus on your issues. You can repeat the same words each time you tap, or you can change them as you focus on the fear. The exact words aren't important; what's important is that you're tuned in to your emotion. The words are just a focus for your feelings, so don't worry about whether they are "right."

Once you've tapped on each of the eight points, you've completed one "round." The following is an example of Reminder Phrases you might say as you go through two rounds of tapping:

* ❖ *Top of the Head: I'm afraid to ask Sally for a date.*
* ❖ *Eyebrow: I'm afraid she'll say no, and I'll be embarrassed.*
* ❖ *Outside of Eye: I'm afraid she'll say no, and I'll be embarrassed.*

- ❖ **Under the Eye:** *I'll be embarrassed.*

- ❖ **Under the Nose:** *I'll be <u>so</u> embarrassed if she says no.*

- ❖ **Chin:** *I'll be mortified if she says no.*

- ❖ **Collarbone:** *How will I ever be able to look her in the eye if she says no?*

- ❖ **Under the Arm:** *I'll be so embarrassed.*

- ❖ **Top of the Head:** *I'll be so embarrassed.*

- ❖ **Eyebrow:** *I'm so afraid that she'll say no.*

- ❖ **Outside of Eye:** *It's embarrassing to think about.*

- ❖ **Under the Eye:** *I'll be embarrassed.*

- ❖ **Under the Nose:** *How will I survive if she says no?*

- ❖ **Chin:** *I don't know if I can ask.*

- ❖ **Collarbone:** *I'll be so embarrassed if she says no.*

- ❖ **Under the Arm:** *I'll be so embarrassed.*

You can tap more than two rounds, if you prefer.

STEP 4: EVALUATE YOUR FEAR

Take a deep breath, and measure your fear again. A number of possibilities may have occurred.

— **Your intensity may have increased.** This happens sometimes when you tune in to the fear and really allow yourself to feel it, rather than push it away. Tuning in to the emotion is a good thing, and the quickest way to get results during tapping. If your intensity did increase, you did a good job of tuning in. Immediately begin tapping again, and continue until you feel the fear lessen.

— **Your intensity may have decreased.** Write down your new number, or indicator of intensity. If it's still above a zero, repeat the tapping routine.

— **Your intensity may have stayed the same.** This can happen when you're not actually tuned in to the feeling. If you're not tuned in, you can't clear it, so you may want to attempt to more closely identify the feeling. (There are other issues that can also interfere with reducing intensity, and we'll be exploring those in upcoming chapters.) You may also just need to persevere, so tap several more rounds and see if you notice any change. If not, proceed to the next exercise. You'll learn much more about tapping in the upcoming chapters that will help you zero in on the issues.

— **Your feeling may have shifted.** Perhaps instead of feeling embarrassed, you now feel angry at the thought of Sally saying no to you. Or you may have a new thought such as *Everyone always says no to me.* When this happens, you have often cleared, or at least diminished, your original fear to the point that a new issue has become more important. A new feeling or thought is an entirely new issue, so return to Step 1 and repeat the process, even if the emotion is anger now, not fear.

— **Your fear may feel as though it is still intense, but may begin to feel fuzzy or distant.** Some people describe it as being "behind a screen." Continue to tap, and the intensity will usually fade.

STEP 5: NOTICE YOUR CHANGES

As your fear subsides, you may notice your beliefs changing. For instance, you might begin to believe that it is less likely that Sally will say no to you. Or you may feel that it is equally likely that she will say no, but no longer feel embarrassed at that thought. You might even start to feel proud of yourself for being willing to ask her out on a date, regardless of her response.

The goal is to get the fear to a 0, and clear any other negative emotions that may be in the way of you taking action (see the next Tapping Tip for more information). We'll talk in upcoming chapters about additional techniques to support your belief changes.

TAPPING TIP: CLEARING THE ENTIRE ISSUE

The situation described in Step 4 as "your feeling may have shifted" is known as a "change of aspect." *Aspect* is the term used to refer to the different details, emotions, and thoughts that can make up an event that you're trying to clear.

For example, fear of flying may be composed of the following:

- Fear of takeoff

- Fear of landing

- Fear of confined spaces

- Fear of being in the air

- Fear of too many people

- Fear of being out of control

   . . . and more.

In order to adequately eliminate a fear of flying, any of these aspects that are present have to be dealt with. Fortunately, tapping is such a fast modality that this needn't be overwhelming. (See Joe's story in Chapter 6, "Healing the Past," for a tapping session involving fear of flying.)

It's important to be aware of all of the various aspects of an issue when you're tapping, otherwise you may not be aware of the progress you're making. Even if the entire situation isn't cleared yet, each different thought or emotion that you clear about a particular issue is a victory.

TAPPING TIP: THE APEX PROBLEM

Because shifts in thoughts and feelings brought about by powerful techniques such as tapping can be so sudden and dramatic, people sometimes discount the changes that have occurred. This is what Roger Callahan named the "apex problem," which describes people's tendency to explain an unusual event in terms that make sense to them, even if those terms aren't accurate. In other words, after using tapping to reduce a fear, some individuals will say, "Well, I guess it wasn't that bad a fear after all," because it is reduced so quickly . . . despite the fact that they had previously rated the fear as very intense.

Another part of the apex problem is that because tapping is unusual, and may be outside of your experience and comfort zone, you may credit the change that occurred to something other than tapping, such as, "I guess I just talked myself out of the fear." Be aware of the tendency to do this as you work through these techniques.

This is a good reason to write down your feelings, particularly the intensity you perceive before you begin tapping. Once you become accustomed to the results that you get with tapping, the apex problem becomes less of an issue. However, it's always a good idea to keep track of the progress that you've made in clearing your resistant emotions, so you can celebrate it.

TAPPING TIP: TURNING DOWN THE INTENSITY

If you have a memory that feels too intense, you don't have to fully feel the fear as you begin tapping on it. Instead, you can imagine how intense the fear would be, without delving into it completely, and tap on that. You could imagine locking your fear in a box, and visualize tapping on the fear that you have locked in the box. These are somewhat more advanced techniques, and this type of creative tapping will become more familiar to you as you proceed through this book. Once you've taken the edge off the fear by either tapping on how intense you *imagine* the fear to be, or tapping on the fear locked away in a box, you will be able to allow the lessened fear to surface and clear it with Simple Tapping. If you have a serious emotional trauma that you're trying to clear, we recommend getting the support of a tapping practitioner.

Don't worry, removing your fears doesn't mean removing ordinary caution. Removing a fear of heights doesn't mean that you'll immediately go walking on the edge of a skyscraper. Removing your fears will make you more able to take healthy risks such as asking for things that you want, trying new experiences, and attempting new endeavors.

SUCCESS STORY

Pamela writes: I worked with Dee briefly at a conference. She had a fear of asking questions and sharing in the breakout sessions that were being held, but she knew that was holding her back from getting the most out of the event.

I asked her what she was most afraid of. She said, "I'm afraid of having everyone look at me. I just want to sink into the floor." She reported her SUDS level for this fear was an 8.

I instructed her in tapping each point and told her to repeat after me (we did this round twice):

- ❖ *Top of the Head: I'm so afraid to have everyone look at me.*

- ❖ *Eyebrow: I'm so afraid to have everyone look at me.*

- ❖ *Outside of Eye: I just want to sink into the floor.*

- ❖ *Under the Eye: I'm so afraid to have everyone look at me.*

- ❖ *Under the Nose: I just want to sink into the floor.*

- ❖ *Chin: I'm so afraid to have everyone look at me.*

- ❖ *Collarbone: I just want to sink into the floor.*

- ❖ *Under the Arm: I'm so afraid to have everyone look at me.*

I asked her if her fear was still at a level 8. She said no, it seemed the strangest thing, but she felt much calmer, and her fear was now at a level 4.

I asked if the fear was the same; in other words, was it still a fear of everyone looking at her? She reported that her fear was now that she would stumble over her words, and look foolish. This is a "change of aspect." I decided to continue using Simple Tapping, and instructed her to repeat after me.

- ❖ *Top of the Head: I'm afraid I'll stumble over my words.*

- ❖ *Eyebrow: I'm afraid I'll look very foolish.*

- ❖ *Outside of Eye: I'm afraid I'll stumble over my words.*

- ❖ *Under the Eye: I'm afraid I'll look very foolish.*

- ❖ *Under the Nose: I'm afraid I'll stumble over my words.*

- ❖ *Chin: I'm afraid I'll look very foolish.*

- ❖ *Collarbone: I'm afraid I'll stumble over my words.*

- ❖ *Under the Arm: I'm afraid I'll look very foolish.*

When we finished that round, Dee said that her fears were seeming pretty silly to her. She said, "So what if I stumble over my words? As long as I get my question answered, that's what's important."

I asked her if her fear was now at a 0. She said it was a 1 or 2, but she thought she could handle that since it was so much better. I asked her if she thought there was any benefit to anyone else if she shared a comment or asked a question. She said, "Of course! I always benefit from other people's questions, so they probably benefit from mine."

I asked her to tap one more round, speaking her fears just as she had done in the previous rounds, but thinking of someone she might help with her question or comment. She did that, and reported that she was no longer afraid to speak up at the conference. She said, "This is a minor miracle! I've never liked speaking up in a group of people I didn't know!"

ACTION STEP: PUTTING SIMPLE TAPPING INTO ACTION

Complete the following statements in your journal or workbook.

The fear I choose to work on is:
My initial SUDS level of this fear is:
After tapping, my new SUDS level is:
Additional aspects of this fear that I discovered include:
During this exercise, I noticed:

If you don't fully succeed in reducing your fears, don't despair. There is a lot more to learn and experience about tapping, and you'll become much more adept with practice.

FEAR OF FAILURE AND FEAR OF SUCCESS

Many people talk about a fear of failure, and it's an issue you can use tapping techniques to alleviate. However, in order for tapping to be effective, you have to be tapping on a specific thought and emotion.

Remember the example of "I'm afraid to ask Sally for a date"? The real fear was "I'm afraid I'll be embarrassed." Similarly, a fear of failure is too broad a description to be effective in a tapping routine. You need to look at what lies beneath the fear of failure. Here's how.

When you feel a fear of failure, ask yourself:

1. What do I fear will happen—what does "fail" mean?

2. What would it mean if that happened?

3. How will I feel if that happens?

For example, perhaps you are writing your first book, and find yourself worried about finishing it. Maybe you believe that no publisher will take it, or that you'll be unable to sell any copies yourself. You identify this as a fear of failure. So you apply the questions:

— What do I fear will happen? I'm afraid that I'll put a lot of work into this and it won't be appreciated. I'm afraid the book will be criticized if it is read, but that few people will read it. I'm afraid no publisher will ever want it.

— What would it mean if that happened? It would mean that I'm a terrible writer. It would mean that I'm a failure. It would mean that I can't make money doing what I love to do.

— How will I feel if that happens? I'll feel depressed, rejected, and hurt. I'll be sad that I can't share my work, and angry that no one will give me a chance.

It's easy to see with a list like this that fear of failure can create a huge impression in the subconscious mind! This is an imaginative list of worries. It's also a wonderful way to uncover the deeper fears you need to tap on.

Remember aspects? All of the statements that answer the first two questions are different aspects of this fear of failure, and need to be cleared. Some of them may only have an intensity of 2 or 3, but they still need to be cleared in order to eliminate the fear of failure. In order to do that, let's expand on what we've learned about tapping so far.

ACTION STEP: REMOVING FEAR OF FAILURE

Identify a project or activity that you have a fear of failure around. Ask yourself these three questions, and keep these answers for tapping exercises throughout the book.

What do I fear will happen?
What would it mean if that happened?
How will I feel if that happens?

TAPPING TECHNIQUE: ORIGINAL EFT

ADDING A POWERFUL AFFIRMATION

We're going to add another step to our tapping routine to make it even more powerful, and to overcome barriers that may be present to our making a change.

Sometimes Simple Tapping works beautifully, and sometimes we have barriers in the way of clearing our issues. You may have heard the phrase *What you resist, persists.* That is, sometimes a condition called "Psychological Reversal" is present, and Simple Tapping doesn't seem to work.

In order to remove the Psychological Reversal, you'll do two things. First, you'll tap on a new acupoint (the KC point), and second, you'll add an affirmation to eliminate the resistance you may have.

THE ORIGINAL EFT AFFIRMATION

EFT, developed by Gary Craig, starts with a sentence called the setup statement. The setup statement consists of two parts: a statement of your issue known as the Reminder Phrase, followed by this affirmation:

> *I deeply and completely love and accept myself.*

The two are combined in this way:

* ❖ *Even though I* [state your issue], *I deeply and completely love and accept myself.*

Examples include:

* ❖ *Even though I'm really angry at Fred, I deeply and completely love and accept myself.*

* ❖ *Even though I'm afraid that I won't get that promotion, I deeply and completely love and accept myself.*

❖ *Even though I'm sad that I won't be able to go on the trip, I deeply and completely love and accept myself.*

❖ *Even though I'm upset that I'm overweight, I deeply and completely love and accept myself.*

INTRODUCING THE KARATE CHOP (KC) POINT

This point is on the side of the hand opposite the thumb. You'll tap the Karate Chop (KC) point continually while saying your setup statement three times. Then proceed as you would with Simple Tapping, tapping a round of all eight points while repeating your Reminder Phrases.

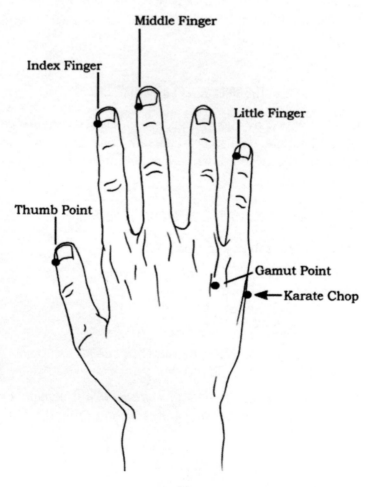

TAPPING TIP: STEALTH TAPPING

The other finger points can be used in a technique called Stealth Tapping. Use them when you want to tap to reduce anxiety or fear in an unobtrusive way, such as when you're in a public place. Some practitioners even like to include them when tapping their usual rounds. However, we won't be routinely using them in this work.

EXERCISE: PUTTING ORIGINAL EFT INTO ACTION

You may want to watch the section of the DVD that covers original EFT before beginning this exercise.

Identify a situation in which you feel upset with yourself. Perhaps you are blaming or criticizing yourself for something. You may want to use your answers from the previous Action Step, "Removing Fear of Failure." Now we will create a setup statement using that incident.

First, state what's upsetting you. This is your Reminder Phrase. Here are possible ways of phrasing it:

❖ *I'm upset with myself for . . .*

❖ *I feel bad that I . . .*

❖ *I was wrong to . . .*

Write down your Reminder Phrase and your SUDS level (your emotional intensity level). Now add the Original EFT Affirmation to the end of your Reminder Phrase, like this:

❖ *Even though* [Reminder Phrase], *I deeply and completely love and accept myself.*

This is your setup statement. Now you're ready to tap!

Start by tapping the Karate Chop (KC) point while saying your setup statement three times. Now begin Simple Tapping: tap each of the eight points at least 5–7 times, repeating your Reminder Phrase once for each point. Do two rounds.

At the end, check your SUDS level again. Do you notice a change in the intensity of your upset? What happened for you as you tapped? Did a new thought come up? Did the intensity remain the same, but the emotion changed (for example, from anger to sadness)?

TAPPING TIP: ROUNDS AND SERIES

In the tapping world in general, the word *round* is used in two different ways. It's used to mean tapping all the points once through, as in Simple Tapping. It is also sometimes used to refer to a setup statement and the multiple rounds done after that statement. However, in this book we'll use the word *round* to describe tapping once through all the points, and use the word *series* to refer to a setup statement and all the rounds that come after that.

SUCCESS STORY

Michael had a big presentation to give at a location he wasn't familiar with. Although he got directions, he found himself lost and realized that he would get to his presentation late. Although his presentation went relatively well, he was very upset that he caused himself the additional stress, and beat himself up over "making a stupid mistake." His SUDS level (level of upset) was a 9, so he started with Simple Tapping. His Reminder Phrases were:

* *What an idiot thing to do!*
* *This presentation was so important—how could I be so stupid?*
* *I feel like an idiot.*
* *This was such a stupid mistake.*

28

After tapping several rounds, he felt calmer and evaluated his new SUDS level at a 6. He decided to create a setup statement with the Original EFT Affirmation, which he repeated three times while tapping the KC point:

- ❖ *Even though I still feel like an idiot for getting lost, I deeply and completely love and accept myself anyway.*

Then he did two more rounds of Simple Tapping, using Reminder Phrases like:

- ❖ *I still feel like an idiot.*
- ❖ *It was a pretty stupid mistake to make.*
- ❖ *I know I won't make <u>that</u> mistake again.*
- ❖ *It wasn't very smart.*

He reassessed his SUDS level and had an intensity of only 3. However, he found that he was still very concerned about making the same mistake again. This was a change of aspect, so he changed the setup statement.

- ❖ *Even though I'm afraid that if I stop feeling stupid about this I'll do it again, I deeply and completely love and accept myself anyway.*

His Reminder Phrases were:

- ❖ *I'm afraid I'll do something else stupid if I let the rest of this upset go.*
- ❖ *I'm afraid I'll blow something else.*

After two more rounds of Simple Tapping, Michael found his intensity was now at a 0. He was focusing more on being proud that he had given a good presentation regardless of his tardiness. He resolved to make a checklist of actions to take before each presentation to ensure that he was as prepared as possible, and felt good about that decision.

TWO WAYS OF BELIEVING

We usually think of the word *belief* as similar to *thought,* so if you ask me what I believe, I can tell you. However, we actually believe things in two different ways.

In the next chapter we'll explore belief change in depth, but we need to make an important distinction in order to understand our emotions, and tap on them more effectively.

1. RATIONAL, CONSCIOUS BELIEFS

These are the beliefs that we are aware of. They are obvious to us, or are discernible with a little bit of inquiry. They are part of our conscious mind.

2. EMOTIONAL, SUBCONSCIOUS BELIEFS

These are beliefs that we may not be aware of. They express themselves as emotional reactions to people or situations, and may elude us when we try to pin them down. Most important, these subconscious beliefs can be in agreement or disagreement with our conscious beliefs.

When the subconscious beliefs, or emotions, are in disagreement with the conscious beliefs, you have emotional discomfort and self-sabotage. This is very common.

It's important to note that belief-change work can be done both when the subconscious and the conscious beliefs agree, and when they don't agree. For example, suppose that you'd like to make more money, but you have a conscious belief that making over $200,000 is wrong, and that no one needs that much money. In order to change that, you'd first go to work on the conscious belief, to create the belief that it was okay to make that much money. Many transformational books and workshops are designed to help you shift conscious beliefs in this way. However, if you still felt uncomfortable with the idea of more money, you'd also need to work on the subconscious or emotional belief.

It's very common to have emotions that disagree with your conscious beliefs. For example, what if you believed consciously that it was fine to make over $200,000, but every time you visualized yourself with that income, you felt uncomfortable? If that's the case, you have a subconscious belief that's sabotaging your conscious belief.

Subconscious beliefs are expressed through emotion. Once we discover and can name a subconscious belief, it's no longer subconscious—it's conscious. Subconscious beliefs and the emotions that they generate are *always* more powerful than conscious beliefs. This is why it's so important to have your conscious beliefs supporting your success, and your subconscious beliefs (your emotions) supporting your success-oriented conscious beliefs.

There are two different ways to approach shifting subconscious beliefs. One, you can bring the subconscious beliefs to the conscious mind by examining your emotions, and the thoughts behind them. Then you can tap on those thoughts that are now conscious rather than subconscious.

Two, you can tap on the negative emotion even if you don't know the thought that's causing it. This is one of the terrific benefits of tapping. Sometimes we don't need to know what the subconscious belief is that is holding us back, we just need to release it.

All of your emotions are based on some thought or belief. Since they are so connected, we'll look at how beliefs and emotions interact, and you can begin to remove any blocks you have to implementing the success principles—or any other life-affirming principle, guideline, or commitment that you may have.

Now we'll add a new, powerful way to do the setup statement to our tapping techniques. The following method helps support your transition from limiting beliefs to more empowering ones.

TAPPING TECHNIQUE: CHOICE STATEMENTS

What if you can't say "I deeply and completely love and accept myself"? For some, the statement may just not feel true.

There are situations in which the Original EFT Affirmation works very well. It's great when you're working on a fear or upset that feels like a failure on your part. In that case, the acceptance phrase can help with removing the negative emotion.

However, there are some situations in which the Original EFT Affirmation doesn't seem to work as well, and we'll want to modify it. It doesn't mean that you can't get the benefits of adding an affirmation to your tapping routine; you just have to modify the affirmation. One way to do this is to use the valuable Choices Trio Method[5] that was developed by leading psychologist and EFT master Dr. Patricia Carrington, and add to it some features that we have developed for your special use here. The use of "Choices" makes life much easier when tapping by allowing you to tap in what you *do* want, in addition to tapping out what you *don't* want.

You will now be using the words *I choose* at the beginning of the affirmation of your setup statement. Instead of saying "I deeply and completely love and accept myself," which may be untrue, you can say "I *choose to* deeply and completely love and accept myself." You always have the ability to make a choice in any moment, so starting your affirmation with *I choose* will often bypass the resistance you might experience with the Original EFT Affirmation.

We'll use the words *I choose* frequently throughout this book in our setup statements, and following Dr. Carrington's example, we'll call these "Choice Statements." We'll be using Choice Statements throughout the rest of this book in many different ways.

If you find even the statement "I choose to deeply and completely love and accept myself" to feel untrue, you can substitute one of these variations:

❖ *I would like to accept myself.*

❖ *I choose to accept myself anyway.*

❖ *I want to find a way to accept myself.*

❖ *I might be open to accepting myself.*

CHOICE STATEMENT—CHOOSING A NEW EMOTION

When you're working to reduce a negative emotion, getting to a SUDS level of 0 can actually be a bit disorienting or confusing. Particularly if you're new to tapping, you may be used to carrying around irritation or anger and letting it slowly defuse over days. What happens when the anger goes away in minutes, or a fear that you've felt for weeks is suddenly gone or drastically reduced?

For some people, this can be disorienting. You'll overcome that by using a Choice Statement to suggest a new, more positive emotion to your subconscious mind.

We find that introducing the Choice Statement works best when your SUDS level is at a 5 or below. There are some exceptions to this rule, but in order to use them effectively, you may want to study the following Choices Trio Method more thoroughly. Then you can ask yourself the question: *If I could choose any emotion in this situation, what would I choose to feel?*

For example, in an earlier section, we were looking at fears connected to finishing a book project, such as: *I'm afraid the book will be criticized.*

If you start with Simple Tapping, you may bring this fear down to a 5 or below. At this point you could introduce a Choice Statement. (Don't try to introduce the Choice Statement until your intensity is at 5 or below. Doing so could lead to suppressing, rather than clearing, the negative emotion.) Suppose you decided that you'd like to feel excitement that your book was arousing attention, or curiosity about the feedback you might receive. You can now construct a Choice Statement with these ideas. Note that you don't need to feel or believe these before you begin tapping. That's what the tapping is for!

Sample Choice Statements using our example could be:

❖ *Even though I'm afraid my book will be criticized, I choose to feel excitement about my book getting attention.*

❖ *Even though I'm afraid my book will be criticized, I choose to be curious about the feedback that I'll receive.*

TAPPING WITH CHOICES

When you use a Choice Statement in your setup statement, you'll also want to use your Choice in your Reminder Phrases— the phrases that you say when you tap the rest of the points.

Here is Patricia Carrington's process called the "Choices Trio," which works very well to remove negative emotions and install positive ones. (Remember that this is done after first using Simple Tapping to decrease the intensity of the negative emotion.) We will also call this the Choices Trio Method.

CHOICES TRIO METHOD

Create a setup statement the same way you did in the original EFT section, combining a Reminder Phrase (the statement of your fear) with a positive affirmation. This time, instead of the affirmation *I deeply and completely love and accept myself,* you'll use a Choice Statement.

State your problem and your Choice Statement three times while tapping the KC point. For example:

❖ *Even though I'm afraid to make that phone call, I choose to feel calm and peaceful.*

❖ *Even though I'm angry at Fred for forgetting our appointment, I choose to feel calm and peaceful.*

1. Tap one round, tapping all the points from the top of the head down to under the arm, using a negative Reminder Phrase, such as:

❖ *I'm afraid.*

❖ *I'm angry.*

34

2. Tap a second round, tapping all the points, using a positive Reminder Phrase based on your Choice Statement, such as:

❖ *I choose to feel calm and peaceful.*

3. Tap a third round, tapping all the points, alternating between the negative phrase and the positive phrase. Be sure to end on a positive phrase. For example:

❖ **Top of the Head:** *I'm afraid.*

❖ **Eyebrow:** *I choose to feel calm and peaceful.*

❖ **Outside of Eye:** *I'm angry.*

❖ **Under the Eye:** *I choose to feel calm and peaceful.*

❖ **Under the Nose:** *I'm afraid.*

❖ **Chin:** *I choose to feel calm and peaceful.*

❖ **Collarbone:** *I'm angry.*

❖ **Under the Arm:** *I choose to feel calm and peaceful.*

(**Note:** The three rounds in the Choices Trio Method are referred to as the negative round, the positive round, and the alternating round.)

EXERCISE: PUTTING THE CHOICES TRIO METHOD INTO ACTION

1. Identify a situation in which you feel fear. Perhaps there is a project you have doubts about, or a difficult person you need to speak to. You may want to phrase it as:

❖ *I'm afraid that . . .*

❖ *I'm anxious about . . .*

This statement is your Reminder Phrase. Write it down, and write down your SUDS level next to it. If your SUDS level is greater than 5, do Simple Tapping to bring down the level. Don't go on to the rest of the exercise until the fear is a 5 or less.

2. When the intensity of your fear is a 5 or less, create a Choice Statement about what you'd like to do or be in this situation, such as:

❖ *I choose to be calm and confident.*

❖ *I choose to proceed with calm expectations.*

❖ *I choose to be open to the possibilities in this situation.*

3. Now, combine your Reminder Phrase and your Choice Statement. This is your setup statement.

❖ *Even though* [my Reminder Phrase], *I choose . . .*

Now you're ready to tap.

4. Tap the Karate Chop (KC) point while saying your setup statement three times.

5. Do three rounds of Simple Tapping, following the Choices Trio Method: Tap the first round while using a negative Reminder Phrase (negative round). Tap the second round using a positive Reminder Phrase based on your Choice Statement (positive round). Then tap a third round while alternating between your negative and positive Reminder Phrases.

6. Assess your SUDS level at the end of this exercise. Do you notice a change in the intensity of your fear? What happened for you as you tapped? Did a new thought come up? Did the intensity remain the same, but did the emotion change? How confident do you now feel about your new Choice?

◎

Next, we'll look at limiting beliefs, how they are created, and how you can use what you've learned so far about tapping and Choices to overcome them.

CHAPTER CHECKLIST

I know what a setup statement is.

I know what a Reminder Phrase is.

I know how to find the Karate Chop (KC) point, and when to use it.

I know the difference between a round and a series.

I know what the SUDS level is, and how to use it.

I know how to create a setup statement using the Original EFT Affirmation and a Choice Statement.

I've done at least one tapping exercise using original EFT.

I know all the steps of the Choices Trio Method and have done at least one tapping exercise using it.

3

OVERCOMING
LIMITING BELIEFS

Although some of what stops us from success is fear, much of it is limiting beliefs . . . and any belief that does not serve you can be changed.

Perhaps you've had some of these thoughts:

- *I can't because . . .*
- *I'm too old.*
- *I'm too young.*
- *I'm too rich.*
- *I'm too poor.*
- *I'm too fat.*
- *I'm too thin.*
- *I'm not smart enough.*

- *I don't have enough experience.*

- *I have too much experience.*

- *I'm not good enough.*

- *I could never do that.*

- *I don't have any talent for that.*

- *I don't have the right connections.*

Most people assume that their limiting beliefs are fact—that they accurately reflect the state of the universe.

According to Carol Dweck, Ph.D., in her book *Mindset: The New Psychology of Success,*[6] your mindset greatly determines your success in life. To discover what kind of mindset you have, read the following sentences and indicate whether you agree or disagree with each:

1. You are a certain kind of person and there is not much that can be done to really change that.

2. No matter what kind of person you are, you can always change substantially.

3. You can do things differently, but the important parts of who you are can't really be changed.

4. You can always change basic things about the kind of person you are.

Don't continue reading until you've noted whether you agree or disagree with these statements.

Now, if you agree with items 1 and 3, you're someone who has a "fixed mindset," and if you agree with items 2 and 4, you have a "growth mindset."

People with a fixed mindset believe that their behavior indicates their basic abilities, and they're not able to change those to any great extent. They tend to avoid risk and failure, because they see an incidence of failure as being indicative of "who they are" (stupid, incapable, inadequate) rather than "something that happened."

On the other hand, if you're a "growth mindset" person, you believe that your abilities are like muscles—they can be built up with practice. If you have a growth mindset, you're more likely to stretch yourself, take risks, accept feedback, and take a long-term view of life.

The good news is that a growth mindset can actually be developed. In a study done with low-income seventh-grade math students, some students were given two hours of generic study-skills training, and others were given two hours of "growth mindset" training—they were taught that their math skills could improve. The math grades of those who received the "growth mindset" training for just two hours significantly improved over the other students.[7]

Do you have a growth mindset or a fixed mindset? If it's fixed, we encourage you to change that. What follows is an example of a possible tapping sequence to change from a fixed mindset to a growth mindset.

EXERCISE: CREATING A GROWTH MINDSET

Setup statements:

* *Even though I believe I was just made this way, I'm open to another possibility.*

* *Even though I believe that I can't really change who I am, what if I could?*

* *Even though I believe that who a person is can't really be changed, I'm willing to look at a new perspective.*

Reminder Phrases:

* *I'm just the way that I am.*

* *I've always been this way.*

❖   *I don't know that I'm capable of changing.*

❖   *If I fail, it means I'm a failure.*

❖   *There's no other way to look at it.*

❖   *It's too dangerous to risk trying something if I might fail.*

❖   *Could I truly fail but not be a failure?*

❖   *Could I learn to overcome the things I can't do now?*

❖   *What if I could be smarter or better if I worked harder?*

❖   *What if I could change the way I am in a powerful way?*

❖   *I'm open to the idea that I am able to change who I am.*

❖   *I could create success even if I fail at first.*

❖   *Failure is a normal part of success. It's how I learn.*

Use the setup statements and Reminder Phrases while tapping rounds using the Choices Trio Method. Note that you may need to tap on the negative phrases repeatedly before you're ready to transition into the positive phrases. You could repeat the first six Reminder Phrases many times, until they no longer ring true, then transition into the final seven phrases.

ACTION STEP: CREATING A GROWTH MINDSET

Evaluate, on a scale of 0–10 (0 being completely untrue, and 10 being completely true), how true the growth mindset statements seem to you.

- No matter what kind of person you are, you can always change substantially.

- You can always change basic things about the kind of person you are.

If you answer less than a 10, do the previous tapping exercise. Start by tapping the Karate Chop point while repeating the setup statement three times. Then do a round of Simple Tapping for each of the Reminder Phrases.

After each series of tapping, pause and reevaluate your level of belief in the growth mindset statements. Repeat this exercise until you completely believe, at a level 10, that you have the ability to change.

◎

In addition to limiting beliefs about yourself, you may have limiting beliefs about the world, such as:

- *It's too hard to make it in this economy.*

- *People in my profession just don't make that much money.*

- *People of my* [race, gender, ethnic background, etc.] *can't get ahead.*

- *People are just mean.*

- *You can't trust anyone.*

- *Men* [or women] *always hurt you.*

- *There's not enough to go around.*

- *Someone always loses.*

These beliefs disempower you, and prevent you from seeing opportunities and possibilities. If a belief doesn't serve you, it can be changed, and tapping is an excellent tool for this change.

First we need to understand the three different kinds of beliefs: empowering beliefs, limiting beliefs, and neutral beliefs.

THREE DIFFERENT TYPES OF BELIEFS

> *It's not the belief that stops you—it's the feeling about the belief that impacts you.*

When you're working with any belief-change system such as tapping, there are three different types of beliefs you'll work with:

1. **Empowering Beliefs**—those that strengthen you and support you in moving in the direction of your success.

   Example: *I am smart, capable, and successful in all I do.*

2. **Limiting Beliefs**—those that weaken you, don't serve you, or stop you from taking action toward your success.

   Example: *I'm not very smart.*

3. **Neutral Beliefs**—those that can be empowering or limiting based on the assumptions beneath them, and the emotions they create.

   Example: *It will rain tomorrow.* (How you feel about this belief determines its effect on you—it's not actually the belief, but the feeling behind it that has power. You may be thinking, *It will rain tomorrow, and we need the rain right now. It's going to be good for the plants and trees.* Or you may be thinking, *It will rain tomorrow, and be cloudy, and that's so depressing. I know I'll get wet on my way to work.*)

With tapping, as with any belief-change system, the objective is to create empowering beliefs and positive emotions and vibrations. It's easy to see that removing limiting beliefs and substituting empowering beliefs will improve the quality of your life and your degree of success. But what about neutral beliefs?

With neutral beliefs, you need to look beneath the belief at the supporting ideas and the emotions around it. So whenever an apparently neutral belief appears during your work, you'll want to ask yourself:

- *What does it mean if this is true?*

- *How do I feel about this?*

- *Do I see this as good or bad?*

- *Why?*

Sometimes neutral beliefs don't serve you. If such a belief is limiting your success or creating an emotion you're uncomfortable with, you'll want to investigate what's beneath it.

REFRAMING YOUR BELIEFS

A *reframe* is a new idea or perspective that allows a reinterpretation of an existing situation or belief.

This term is used in Neuro-Linguistic Programming (NLP). It is based on the idea that we each have frames of reference for our beliefs and actions, so we view, determine, and judge what's possible and appropriate based on these frames of reference. When we *reframe,* or change our frame of reference, we can expand what's possible and have more freedom from negative judgments of ourselves and others.

Beliefs that appear to be neutral but have a limiting belief or negative emotion beneath them can be reframed to have an empowering belief or positive emotion beneath them. For example, suppose you have a belief that if you stop smoking or drinking, the friends you have who do those things will no longer speak to you, and will end the friendship.

This neutral belief of *They won't speak to me if I don't smoke and drink with them* may initially have negative emotions under it, such as fear of loss or sadness. *I'll lose my friends, I'll feel like an outcast,* and *I'll be so lonely* are possible underlying limiting beliefs.

However, you could reframe this neutral belief to have positive thoughts and emotions underneath it. For example: *I'm committed to not smoking and drinking. One of the things that will support me in this commitment is being with people who don't ask me to do these things. Perhaps my friends will support me in this. I could give them the chance to do that. Or maybe I'll make new friends who will support me in my commitments.*

These reframes may appear obvious, but could be difficult to believe, or it may be difficult to become emotionally comfortable with them. Tapping will help with this situation.

Sometimes the reframes will not be obvious at all until the negative emotion has been removed or reduced. New ideas will then begin to occur to you that were not available before. But don't feel that you need to create a reframe before you begin working on a negative emotion. You can tap on the limiting belief or negative emotion, and then add the reframe when it occurs to you.

Introduce reframes into your tapping when your intensity about an issue has dropped to 5 or less. If you're feeling fear, anger, or some other strong emotion at an intensity of 6–10, it may be hard to think clearly enough to create reframes. Do Simple Tapping until your intensity has diminished, then create the reframe.

TAPPING WITH REFRAMES—USING A CHOICE STATEMENT

In the last chapter, we introduced the concept of a setup statement, a statement composed of an acknowledgment of the issue, followed by an affirmation. This setup statement creates the environment for change, and can clear Psychological Reversal. The Original EFT Affirmation, you'll remember, is *I deeply and completely love and accept myself.* Modifications using a Choice Statement include *I choose to accept myself anyway,* and other variations are *I want to find a way to accept myself* or *I'm open to the idea of accepting myself.*

We've also seen how you can use Choices to create other positive emotions, in addition to acceptance. Now let's expand our use of Choices to install powerful reframes.

Up to this point, you've tapped while primarily focused on the negative. Now you'll add more positive statements to your tapping routines. Some people ask whether they can use only positive statements instead of negative statements while tapping. While it's possible to do so, you risk not having effective, complete results. If you begin with positive statements, you may not be focused on the negative emotions enough to clear them, which would keep at least some of them hidden and secretly sabotaging you. Focusing on the negative allows you to completely clear it, and not suppress your emotions, or hide a particular aspect of an issue. Negative emotions then subside.

There is no consensus in the tapping community about why or how positive statements work. One idea is that stating the positive brings up "Yeah, but . . . ," the little voice in your head that disagrees with your positive affirmations. Since you're tapping while that voice is disagreeing, you reduce or eliminate the negative voice.

It does seem to be the case that positive thoughts and feelings become stronger with tapping, but these results are strongest, and most lasting, after the negative emotions have been cleared.

TAPPING TECHNIQUE: OPEN CHOICE STATEMENTS

Sometimes you'd like to create a new, positive choice, but are unsure about what to choose. You may still be feeling some negative emotion around a situation and have trouble imagining a specific choice that seems possible or reasonable. If you're unsure of what to choose, tapping can often stimulate creativity. To do this, create what we call an Open Choice Statement. You can often begin using one of these when your SUDS level is as high as a 7.

An Open Choice Statement creates the space for a solution, without naming a particular solution. It acts as a bridge between Simple Tapping and creating a more specific choice that you may not be ready to make yet. For example:

❖ *Even though I don't know how I can finish this project, I'm open to an exciting new idea.*

❖ *Even though I don't think that I can resolve this situation, I'm open to finding a way to do it.*

❖ *Even though I can't see any way to feel positive about this situation, I'm willing to let the Universe surprise and delight me.*

Using an Open Choice Statement with the Choices Trio Method (the series of tapping with a negative round, a positive round, then an alternating round) is a wonderfully freeing exercise. Often this will drop the intensity of your challenge below a 5, and you'll be flooded with new, creative ideas and positive emotions about handling a situation.

You'll get an opportunity to try this shortly. First, let's discuss Specific Choices.

TAPPING TECHNIQUE: SPECIFIC CHOICE STATEMENTS

Once the intensity of your emotion is at a 5 or below, you can create a positive Specific Choice Statement to install a new belief.

One great way to do this is to ask yourself the following question: *If I could wave a magic wand, what would I love to create in this situation?* (Hint: don't try to change people or situations outside of your control; change yourself or your response to a situation.)

It's most empowering to focus on what's within your area of control, even though you may not believe that you're capable of it yet. Rather than focusing on the event, focus on your desired response, and create a desired positive choice around your response.

Remember E+R=O from *The Success Principles*? That is, Event + Response = Outcome.

For example, don't use: *Even though I'm afraid it may rain tomorrow during our picnic, I choose to know it won't rain.* You can't control the weather. Instead, use: *Even though I'm afraid it may rain tomorrow during our picnic, I choose to have a terrific time anyway.*

Don't use: *Even though I'm afraid I won't get the loan at the bank, I choose to know that I get the loan tomorrow.* Instead, use: *Even though I'm afraid I won't get the loan at the bank, I choose to be confident that I can persevere, and get what I need.*

These types of Choice Statements are Specific Choices, which outline a particular way of being, attitude, or emotion.

TAPPING TIP: GETTING SPECIFIC

Clearing limiting beliefs is a very exciting way to use tapping! It's important to understand how we form these limiting beliefs so that we can transform them in the most effective and efficient way.

Sometimes limiting beliefs can be the result of a single, dramatic incident. Something happens, often in early childhood, and you come to a conclusion such as *I'm not smart* or *I'll never be good enough*. Unfortunately, having made that decision, your mind keeps looking for evidence of that belief, and builds a strong case that it's true. If you've ever tried to change a belief like this in the past, you know how persistent they can be.

In order to effectively clear or change those beliefs, you can't go directly to the belief itself. Think of the belief as the top of a table. The tabletop is held up by many, many legs, each one of which is "evidence" for the belief. If you try to tap on the tabletop, you probably won't get the results that you're looking for. There are just too many legs holding it up.

Instead, you go after the legs of the table. One by one, you begin to reframe or reinterpret the events that are your "evidence" for that belief. The good news is that you don't need to remove all the table legs—only some of them! You may need to only remove 2, or 6, or 11 of them, not the hundreds that you've probably accumulated. When you remove some of the table legs, the belief will just collapse, and you'll be able to install a new belief that serves you.

As we go through the rest of the tapping routines in the book, be sure to create your tapping phrases around specific events or incidents that created a belief.

Here are some examples of taking a general belief and creating specifics to tap on:

Limiting belief: I can't succeed at that new project.
The evidence: I've never done anything that big. I was late with that project I did 3 years ago.

What to tap on:

❖ Even though I was late with that project three years
  ago, and that means that I won't succeed at this one,
  I choose . . .

Limiting belief: I'm not smart enough to make over $100,000.
The evidence: No one in my family has ever done that. I didn't
get good grades in school. I've never made even half of that. I've
made some stupid decisions in my life.
What to tap on:

❖ Even though I got bad grades in school, I'm open to
  the possibility that . . .

❖ Even though I made what seems like a really stupid
  decision about ____, and I feel ____ about that, I
  choose . . .

Note: You can see that this limiting belief about money is
based on a fixed mindset. It's based on the idea that *I'm this way,
and I can't change.* There are multiple items to tap on to clear this.
When the items listed above are cleared, it will be much easier to
change the belief.

TAPPING TECHNIQUE: SOS TAPPING

SOS Tapping is an expansion of the Choices Trio Method that
you've already learned. Instead of just jumping straight into a Specific Choice, we'll work our way into it by using an Open Choice
first. The advantages of this are:

• You bring the Karate Chop point tapping in earlier,
  possibly clearing some psychological resistance.

• You can begin using Open Choices when your
  intensity is as high as a 7.

• You invite creativity and subconscious resources by
  the wording of your Open Choices.

- You release any pressure to make a Specific Choice before you're ready to do so.

Now that you've seen how to create your Choice Statements (both Open and Specific), here's a review of the tapping points. (**Note:** the DVD section with SOS Tapping has more information and examples.)

Use the Karate Chop (KC) point on the side of your hand when you're stating your setup statement. Remember, your setup statement combines your problem or issue with a positive affirmation. For example:

Open Choice:

❖ *Even though I'm afraid I won't get the loan at the bank, I choose to be open to new, exciting possibilities in this situation.*

Specific Choice:

❖ *Even though I'm afraid I won't get the loan at the bank, I choose to be confident that I can persevere, and get what I need.*

Tap on the rest of the points (top of the head, eyebrow, outside of eye, under eye, under nose, chin, collarbone, under arm) when you're saying your Reminder Phrases, either negative or positive. For example:

❖ ***Top of the Head:*** *I'm afraid I won't get the loan at the bank.*

❖ ***Eyebrow:*** *I choose to be confident that I can persevere and get what I need.*

In the rest of the book, we'll use the term **SOS Tapping**, which refers to **S**imple Tapping, **O**pen Choice Statement, **S**pecific Choice Statement. You'll move from Simple Tapping to Open Choice Tapping, and then to Specific Choice Tapping as the intensity of your emotions shifts downward on the SUDS scale.

As you continue tapping through the success principles, you'll see many different examples of positive Choices, both Specific and

Open, and be able to practice creating your own. Let's try this now. (Hint: First watching the part of the DVD that covers SOS Tapping may help you understand and absorb this exercise.)

EXERCISE: PUTTING SOS TAPPING INTO ACTION

Start by identifying a limiting belief that you'd like to change. Then identify one event or incident that is "evidence" for that belief, and the emotion you feel about it.

1. State your fear. This is your Reminder Phrase. You may want to phrase it this way:

- ❖ *I'm afraid that . . .*
- ❖ *I'm anxious about . . .*

2. Note your SUDS level. If your fear level is greater than a 7, do a round of Simple Tapping at this point to bring down the level. Don't go on to the rest of the exercise until the fear is a 7 or less.

3. When the intensity of your fear is a 7 or less, create an Open Choice Statement about what you'd like to do or be in this situation. For example:

- ❖ *I'm open to a new interpretation.*
- ❖ *I'm open to a completely new way to think about this.*
- ❖ *I'm open to a surprising new idea.*

4. Create your setup statement by combining your Reminder Phrase and your Open Choice Statement. (This is an Open Choice setup statement.)

5. Tap the Karate Chop (KC) point while saying your Open Choice setup statement three times.

6. Do three rounds of tapping, following the Choices Trio Method. (You'll repeat your negative Reminder Phrase on the first round, your Open Choice Statement on the second round, and alternate between the two on the third round.)

7. Assess your SUDS level. When the intensity of your fear is a 5 or less, create a Specific Choice Statement about what you'd like to do or be in this situation, such as:

- ❖ *I choose to be calm and confident.*
- ❖ *I choose to proceed with calm expectations.*
- ❖ *I choose to be open to the possibilities in this situation.*

8. Create a new setup statement by combining your Reminder Phrase and your Specific Choice Statement. (This is a Specific Choice setup statement.)

9. Tap the Karate Chop (KC) point while saying your Specific Choice setup statement three times.

10. Do three rounds of tapping, following the Choices Trio Method. (You'll repeat your negative Reminder Phrase on the first round, your Specific Choice Statement on the second round, and alternate between the two on the third round.)

11. Assess your SUDS level again. Do you notice a change in the intensity of your fear? What happened for you as you tapped? Did a new thought come up? Did the intensity remain the same, but did the emotion change? How confident do you now feel about your new choice?

(Although this tapping exercise may seem complex, when you do it several times the steps will flow naturally and easily.)

SUCCESS STORY

Susan, an energy healer, had wanted to write a book for years. However, she had the belief that she just wasn't very good at writing, and this had kept her from even trying to write.

When she decided to work on that belief, she asked herself why she believed that and came up with two reasons. One reason was that she had never done any writing. In fact, she avoided writing anything, even articles about her work or advertising for her business. The other reason was that she had been told by one of her teachers in high school that she couldn't write. The teacher had said, "Some people just aren't born writers, and you're one of them." Although the teacher had gone on to praise Susan's other skills, Susan remembered the comment, and had liked the teacher, and so she believed him.

Susan wasn't angry at the teacher, so she chose to use SOS Tapping to tap on her frustration with her poor writing skills. She reported her SUDS level of frustration was an 8.

She began with Simple Tapping, with the Reminder Phrases:

❖ *I'm so frustrated that I can't write well.*

❖ *I want to write a book!*

❖ *Why do I have to be such a bad writer?*

❖ *This isn't fair.*

After a few minutes of tapping, her frustration level dropped to a 6, and she created an Open Choice setup statement.

❖ *Even though I'm frustrated that I can't write well, I'm open to something new.*

She tapped one round with negative Reminder Phrases, including:

❖ *I'm still frustrated that I can't write well.*

❖ *I still wish I could write beautifully.*

She tapped a second round using her Open Choice Statement and asking questions.

❖ *I'm open to something new.*

❖ *What if I could find another way to handle this?*

❖ *I'm open to a new perspective on this situation.*

She tapped a third round alternating between the negative Reminder Phrases and the Open Choice Statements.

Now her frustration level was down to a 3, and two things had occurred to her. She was now considering whether it would be okay to use a ghostwriter, since she believed that the really important thing was to get her ideas out into the world. She also recognized that she hadn't taken a look at her writing since she was 16 years old, and there was a chance that, with training, she could improve enough to write the book herself. She put one of these ideas in her Specific Choice, and used the other in some of her Reminder Phrases.

❖ *Even though I'm still a little frustrated because I don't think I can write well, I choose to consider that I haven't looked at my writing since I was 16.*

❖ *Even though I'm still a little frustrated because I don't think I can write well, I choose to consider that I've learned lots of things since I was 16—maybe I could learn to write.*

She tapped one round with her negative Reminder Phrase:

❖ *I'm still a little frustrated.*

❖ *I still don't think I can write well.*

She tapped one round with Specific Choices as positive Reminder Phrases.

❖ *I've learned lots of things.*

❖ *I can learn to write.*

❖ *There are many things I didn't do well at 16.*

❖ *I am always learning new things.*

❖ *I could always hire a ghostwriter.*

❖ *I have lots of options.*

At this point, Susan felt that her frustration was at a 0, so she skipped the alternating round. She was excited about the idea of taking a writing course and beginning her book.

EMBRACE CHANGE
(SUCCESS PRINCIPLE 31)

The idea of embracing change is a powerful reframe. Change is something that is scary for most people—we tend to avoid it unless we've initiated it, and even then sometimes we sabotage it. If you're accustomed to your spouse, family, job, home, community, and all of your other familiar environments, then when those environments begin to change, it's not uncommon to feel threatened.

But what if the change actually produced a better circumstance for you? What if it made your life easier or more exciting, or made you stronger and more capable? Even if you don't know whether that will happen, as you see things begin to change, you do have the opportunity to declare that the change will bring you something better, and cooperate with the change to make that happen. Of course, doing this greatly increases the chance that you will be able to perceive and take advantage of the opportunities in the change.

You'll want to keep two things in mind when you're using tapping to embrace change. One is to be specific about what you fear. For example, if your company is being taken over by another company, you could say that you're worried about the takeover. However, for tapping purposes, it would be better to say specifically what you're concerned about, whether it's *I'm afraid I'll be laid off,* or *I'm afraid I'll be reassigned and my job won't be as interesting,* or *I'm worried because I don't know what will happen.* These are great Reminder Phrases to use while you're tapping.

Change is inevitable in life. When you feel excitement or anticipation about the change rather than fear, you're better able to avoid challenges and take advantage of opportunities.

EXERCISE: EMBRACE CHANGE WITH SOS TAPPING

Step 1: Think of a situation in your life that involves change that you are uncomfortable with. Identify the specific fear or discomfort that you have with the change; we will create an SOS Tapping routine around it. Write down your fears, and evaluate your SUDS level.

Step 2: If your SUDS level is an 8 or above, do Simple Tapping using your fears as your Reminder Phrases. (If it is below 8, skip to Step 3.) For example:

❖ *I'm afraid I'll be laid off.*

❖ *I'm afraid I'll be reassigned and my job won't be as interesting.*

Continue to tap several rounds if necessary, until the fear drops to a 7 or below. Be aware of different aspects, and try to focus on just one fear. If you have more than one fear about the change, you can repeat the exercise later with the other fear.

Step 3: If your SUDS level is 7 or below (or when it drops to 7 or below after using Simple Tapping), combine one of your Reminder Phrases with an Open Choice to create an Open Choice setup statement. (If your SUDS level is a 5 or below, skip this step and move to Step 4.) Tap the Karate Chop point as you say your setup statements three times, for example:

❖ *Even though I'm afraid I'll be laid off in the takeover, I'm open to the possibility that the situation might work out really well for me.*

❖ *Even though I'm afraid I'll be reassigned to boring work with the takeover, I'm open to seeing a new possibility in this situation.*

Tap one round using a negative Reminder Phrase, such as:

❖ *I'm afraid I'll be laid off in the takeover.*

Tap one round using a positive Reminder Phrase, such as:

❖ *I'm open to seeing a new possibility in this situation.*

Tap one round alternating negative and positive Reminder Phrases, remembering to end on a positive Reminder Phrase. (If you notice that your intensity drops very quickly, and you feel that it's a 5 or below at this point, you can skip doing this alternating round.)

Step 4: When your SUDS level is a 5 or below, you can use Specific Choice Statements. Possible Specific Choice setup statements you can use are:

❖ *Even though I'm still a bit worried that I'll be laid off, I choose to create an advantage for myself in this situation, even if I don't know what it is yet.*

❖ *Even though I'm still a bit worried because I don't know what will happen, I choose to create the best possible outcome for myself in this.*

Tap one round using a negative Reminder Phrase, such as:

❖ *I'm afraid I'll be laid off in the takeover.*

Tap one round using a positive Reminder Phrase, such as:

❖ *I choose to create the best possible outcome for myself in this.*

Tap one round alternating negative and positive Reminder Phrases, remembering to end on a positive Reminder Phrase. (If you notice that your intensity drops very quickly, and you feel that it's already a 0, you can skip doing this alternating round.)

Step 5: Reevaluate your SUDS level. Is it at a 0? If not, repeat Step 4.

Note if you have any other fears about this change. Those are different *aspects* of the challenge. If you find other aspects, repeat the exercise with your newly identified fear. After each tapping series, check in with how you feel. Does the intensity of the fear change, or does one fear disappear only to be replaced by another?

TELL THE TRUTH FASTER
(SUCCESS PRINCIPLE 50)

What stops us from telling the truth is fear. It may be concern that the other person will be hurt, or anxiety that we'll suffer consequences from sharing an unpleasant fact or opinion.

When you have fear, you're expending energy dealing with that emotion that might be spent doing other more productive and fulfilling things. When you have fear about telling the truth, it can be very tiring. Also, living a lie, withholding, or maintaining an act takes much more energy than living the truth does.

Removing the fear helps you approach the situation calmly and create the best emotional state for sharing the truth. Although you can certainly tell the truth in a state of fear, you'll be more capable of handling whatever arises if the fear has been removed.

Your fear comes from a belief about what will happen (or might happen) when you share the truth.

Take a moment to think about this: What is a situation in which you need to tell the truth, but are afraid to do so?

For example:

- *I'm afraid to tell my parents I'm marrying outside my faith.*

- *I'm afraid to tell my boss this new project is behind schedule.*

What is your belief about what will happen when you tell the truth?

- *I'm afraid that my parents won't speak to me again.*

- *I'm afraid that I'll be fired.*

Let's use SOS Tapping to clear that fear of telling the truth, and create an empowering reframe.

EXERCISE: TELL THE TRUTH FASTER WITH SOS TAPPING

Step 1: Write down a truth that you have been afraid to express to someone. (Avoid using this as an excuse to share negative judgments about others, such as *I think you eat too much sugar* or *You need to lose weight*.) Write down what you fear will happen. Remember to be specific.

Step 2: If you rate your fear at a level greater than a 7, do Simple Tapping on that fear. Tap around the points, and name the various thoughts. For example:

❖ *I can't tell my parents I'm marrying outside our faith.*

❖ *They'll be so angry.*

❖ *They'll never speak to me again.*

❖ *I don't see how they'll ever forgive me.*

❖ *I'm going to lose my parents.*

❖ *They'll be so angry.*

❖ *I don't know how to tell them.*

Continue tapping around the points with statements like this, until your fear level is at a 7 or below. Note that in a situation like this you may have several aspects, which you will need to treat separately. For example, you could fear that your parents will be angry at you marrying outside your faith, and you could simultaneously have a fear that it *is* wrong to do so. These are two separate aspects, so you'll want to go through this process twice, focusing on a different aspect each time.

Step 3: Once your fear is at a level 7 or below, create an Open Choice setup statement around this issue. (Remember to say your setup statement three times while tapping the Karate Chop point.) For example:

❖ *Even though I'm really afraid that my parents won't speak to me again, I'm open to a surprising new possibility.*

❖ *Even though I'm afraid I'll be fired when I tell my boss the truth, I'm open to finding a creative solution.*

Tap one round, using your negative Reminder Phrase, such as:

❖ *I'm really afraid my parents won't speak to me again.*

Tap one round, using your positive Open Choice Statement:

❖ *I'm open to a surprising new possibility.*

(If you feel that your SUDS level is already at 0, you can skip this next alternating round.) Tap an alternating round, switching between your negative Reminder Phrase and your positive Open Choice Statement. For example:

❖ **Top of the Head:** *I'm really afraid my parents won't speak to me again.*

❖ **Eyebrow:** *I'm open to a surprising new possibility.*

❖ **Outside of Eye:** *I'm really afraid my parents won't speak to me again.*

❖ **Under the Eye:** *I'm open to a surprising new possibility.*

❖ **Under the Nose:** *I'm really afraid my parents won't speak to me again.*

❖ **Chin:** *I'm open to a surprising new possibility.*

❖ **Collarbone:** *I'm really afraid my parents won't speak to me again.*

❖ **Under the Arm:** *I'm open to a surprising new possibility.*

Step 4: When your fear is at a 5 or below, create a positive Specific Choice Statement. Use the Specific Choice Statement to create the emotions you'd like to experience and how you'd like to express yourself. For example:

❖ *Even though I'm still somewhat afraid that my parents won't speak to me again, I choose to be loving and clear in my communication.*

❖ *Even though I'm still afraid I'll be fired when I tell my boss the truth, I choose to be calm and confident, and to act in complete integrity.*

Just as you did with the Open Choice Statement, tap a Choices Trio—one negative round, one positive round, and one alternating round. This will bring in your new empowering choice.

Step 5: Is your SUDS level for this fear now a 0? If not, repeat Step 4. How do you feel about telling the truth in this situation? Are there other aspects that you need to clear? If so, repeat the exercise until you feel no discomfort with telling the truth, and can take action to do so.

You may have several different fears that you believe, or your beliefs may change as you tap. Be aware of the different aspects of your fear, and be sure to work on each one until you have a "complete yes" about telling the truth.

TAPPING TIP: SKIPPING STEPS OR ROUNDS

As you become more experienced with tuning in to your emotions and evaluating your SUDS level, you may be able to skip steps or rounds and shorten the tapping process. For example, if you begin Simple Tapping on an issue, and your intensity drops from a 9 to a 5, you may not need to do an Open Choice series. Or, if you are in the middle of doing your Specific Choice series, and you've tapped your negative round and your positive round, then you feel as though your intensity is at a 0, you can skip the alternating round.

Of course, the reverse is true. You may need to do more than one series of Open Choice rounds, or more than one series of Specific Choice rounds, in order to lower the intensity of your fear to a 0.

As you're learning the techniques, it's a good idea to do all the steps. However, as you become more familiar, this fast technique can become even more efficient as you eliminate steps you don't need.

SUCCESS STORY

Janet was convinced that one of her subordinates, Tom, needed to be fired. Since she had recommended the hire, she feared that when she discussed the situation with her boss, Tisha, Tisha would become angry. This fear caused Janet to keep avoiding talking to Tisha.

Janet decided to use tapping to overcome her fear. She rated the level of her initial fear at a 7, with the statement *I'm afraid Tisha will be angry when I tell her we need to fire Tom.* After several rounds of Simple Tapping, the intensity of her fear dropped to a 4, and Janet considered what she would like to have happen in the conversation. (Note that she didn't use an Open Choice Statement, because her SUDS level had dropped enough that she was able to move directly into creating a Specific Choice.)

"Of course I'd like it if Tisha didn't become angry, but I may not be able to control that. What I can do is to take responsibility for hiring Tom. I can also state the case for his termination calmly and confidently, and prepare the facts ahead of time. I can choose to stay calm, regardless of Tisha's reaction."

Janet chose these setup statements:

❖ *Even though I'm still afraid that Tisha will get angry, I choose to take responsibility and remain calm during the conversation.*

❖ *Even though she might get angry, I choose to focus on my reactions and what I can do.*

❖ *Even though I'm still afraid, I choose to be a class act during this interaction.*

She tapped three more rounds. During the first round, she used Reminder Phrases about her fear as they occurred to her, such as:

- ❖ *I'm still afraid.*
- ❖ *She might get angry.*
- ❖ *She might yell at me.*
- ❖ *I'm still afraid.*

During the second round, she used positive Reminder Phrases based on her Choice Statements:

- ❖ *I choose to take responsibility for hiring Tom.*
- ❖ *I choose to stay calm during the conversation.*
- ❖ *I choose to be a class act.*

During the third round, she alternated the negative statements with the positive statements, ending with a positive statement:

- ❖ *I'm still afraid.*
- ❖ *I choose to take responsibility.*
- ❖ *She might get angry.*
- ❖ *I choose to remain calm.*
- ❖ *She might yell at me.*
- ❖ *I choose to be a class act.*

At the end of the third round, Janet reevaluated her fear. She was no longer afraid, but did feel a bit guilty for having hired Tom. She recognized this as a different aspect, and evaluated the intensity of her guilt as a 3.

Since the intensity was low, Janet immediately created a reframe of *Everyone makes mistakes, and I choose to learn and grow from mine.* She then created this setup statement:

- ❖ *Even though I feel guilty about having hired Tom, I choose to know everyone makes mistakes, and I learn and grow from mine.*

After tapping three more rounds—one negative, one positive, and one alternating—Janet removed the guilt, and she now felt prepared and eager to have the conversation with Tisha.

REVIEW AND SUMMARY OF TAPPING TECHNIQUES

FOR INTENSE EMOTIONS:

When you're in the grip of a strong emotion, use Simple Tapping to reduce the initial intensity. Don't worry about creating a setup statement; just tap a round and give voice to your intense emotion, including abusive or profane language if that's what feels true for you.

WHEN YOU FEEL GUILT OR FIND THAT YOU'RE JUDGING YOURSELF:

You may want to use a setup statement with the Original EFT Affirmation, or one of the variations described before. Repeat the setup statement three times while tapping the Karate Chop point. For example:

- ❖ *Even though I feel guilty that I ___, I deeply and completely accept myself.*

- ❖ *Even though I'm upset that I ____, I choose to accept myself anyway.*

- ❖ *Even though it was really stupid to ____, I'd like to find a way to accept myself.*

WHEN YOUR SUDS LEVEL HAS DROPPED TO A 7 OR BELOW:

You can add an Open Choice. Create an Open Choice setup statement, and repeat it three times while tapping the Karate Chop point. For example:

❖ *Even though I don't know how to resolve this, I'm open to finding a creative new solution.*

❖ *Even though I have this problem, I choose to be open to a way out.*

❖ *Even though I feel stuck with this, I'm open to a surprising new idea.*

After you say your setup statement, tap three rounds of all the points, using the Choices Trio Method (negative round, positive round with Open Choice Statement, alternating round).

WHEN YOUR SUDS LEVEL HAS DROPPED TO A 5 OR BELOW:

Add a Specific Choice Statement to install the empowering belief or positive emotion that you'd like to have. You can create a Specific Choice setup statement, such as:

❖ *Even though I'm afraid I'll be late to the meeting, I choose to be calm, confident, and effective in my presentation.*

❖ *Even though I'm afraid I'll want dessert tonight, I choose to focus on and feel great about my commitment to my health and well-being.*

Repeat your Specific Choice setup statement three times while tapping the Karate Chop point. Then tap three rounds of all the points, using the Choices Trio Method (negative round, positive round with Specific Choice Statement, alternating round).

You can continue to experiment with tapping and Choices to remove older or more constant fears, as well as any new ones that surface as you start expanding into a more empowered life.

CHAPTER CHECKLIST

I understand the difference between growth mindset and fixed mindset; and I have a growth mindset.

I know what the three types of beliefs are.

I know what a reframe is.

I know the difference between an Open Choice and a Specific Choice.

I know what SOS stands for, and I know the steps in SOS Tapping.

It's important to get specific in tapping because . . .

I'm now comfortable embracing change.

I've completed at least one SOS Tapping Exercise.

I now choose to tell the truth faster.

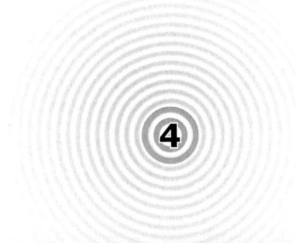

FOUNDATIONS FOR SUCCESS: RESPONSIBILITY AND FORGIVENESS

TAKE 100% RESPONSIBILITY FOR YOUR LIFE (SUCCESS PRINCIPLE 1)

One of the most challenging of the success principles for many people to fully embrace is the very first one: take 100% responsibility for your life. So let's begin by taking a look at the Limiting Beliefs and negative emotions that may come up for you.

Have you ever said, "I'm not responsible for *that* in my life!"? Perhaps *that* is the state of your marriage, your kids' school performance, your job, the success (or failure) of your business, your friends' behavior, your health, the economy, the political climate in Washington, the performance of your favorite sports team, eco-logical change, or the current head of state.

With some of these, it's pretty easy to see your connection to the situation. With others, it may be harder. However, if your goal is to create empowering beliefs in your life, the belief *I'm respon-sible* is always more empowering.

Usually the first emotion that comes up for people is anger. They say things like "I didn't create my husband cheating on me," "I'm not responsible for my disease," "I can't be held responsible for my children's behavior," or "It's not my fault that the business failed."

There could be two different barriers to your taking responsi-bility for your life:

1.   The thought of taking 100% responsibility seems scary, overwhelming, or just plain wrong.

2.   You don't object to the concept, but there is a particular incident or series of incidents for which you don't want to take responsibility.

We'll work first on the overall concept of taking responsibility, and then we'll discuss how to overcome single incidents that get in your way.

If any intense emotion has come up for you at the idea of tak-ing 100% responsibility for your life, or for some particular part of it, use Simple Tapping to reduce the intensity to a 5 or below. Then you can proceed, and you'll be able to appreciate and consider the following ideas.

(**Note:** If you had a particularly traumatic event in your life—such as a severe accident, illness, sexual abuse, or violent crime—and you have a very strong anger reaction to the idea of taking responsibility for it, you may want to seek the support of a tapping practitioner in reducing your reaction to that event. After the reac-tion is reduced, taking 100% responsibility is so much easier.)

We'll look at three different approaches to living this powerful principle more fully:

1. Just looking—claiming responsibility in order to learn

2. Inverse paranoia—claiming responsibility in order to empower yourself

3. Taking responsibility for your response

APPROACH 1: JUST LOOKING— CLAIMING RESPONSIBILITY IN ORDER TO LEARN

Using this approach, the most important question to ask is: *If I were to assume that I'm responsible for this, what could I learn from that?* However, you may have resistance to taking responsibility that would prevent you from considering that question. If so, the following exercise will be very helpful in overcoming it.

EXERCISE: TAKE RESPONSIBILITY IN ORDER TO LEARN

This exercise is a variation of the SOS Tapping we did earlier. Instead of a Specific Choice at the end, however, we'll use two different versions of an Open Choice.

Step 1: Identify your resistance to taking 100% responsibility. You may want to look at a particular event in your life that you don't want to take responsibility for, rather than the overall concept. How high is the intensity of the feeling (your SUDS level) for "*I'm not responsibility for <u>that</u>!*"?

Step 2: If your SUDS level is an 8 or more, do Simple Tapping to reduce the intensity to a 7 or below.

Step 3: Create an Open Choice setup statement that opens you to the possibility of what you could learn from this event. Repeat your Open Choice setup statement three times while tapping the Karate Chop (KC) point:

❖ *Even though I don't want to take responsibility for this, I'm open to the idea that I could learn from it if I did take responsibility.*

Reminder Phrases (negative round, repeat while tapping on each point):

❖ *I don't want to take responsibility for this.*

Open Choice Statement (positive round, repeat while tapping on each point):

❖ *I'm open to the idea that I could learn from it if I did take responsibility.*

Alternating round (repeat while tapping on each point):

❖ **Top of the Head:** *I don't want to take responsibility for this.*

❖ **Eyebrow:** *I'm open to the idea that I could learn from it if I did take responsibility.*

❖ **Outside of Eye:** *I don't want to take responsibility for this.*

❖ **Under the Eye:** *I'm open to the idea that I could learn from it if I did take responsibility.*

❖ **Under the Nose:** *I don't want to take responsibility for this.*

❖ **Chin:** *I'm open to the idea that I could learn from it if I did take responsibility.*

❖ **Collarbone:** *I don't want to take responsibility for this.*

❖ **Under the Arm:** *I'm open to the idea that I could learn from it if I did take responsibility.*

Step 4: Once your initial resistance to the idea of taking responsibility has decreased to a 5 or below, you can use tapping and a slightly different Open Choice Statement to trigger your creative thinking about *how* you might learn. For example, use this setup statement:

❖ *Even though I'm not sure I'm responsible for this, I'm open to accepting responsibility and learning from this experience.*

Reminder Phrases (negative round, repeat while tapping on each point):

❖ *I'm not sure I'm responsible for this.*

❖ *I'm not sure I want to accept responsibility for this.*

Open Choice Statement (positive round, repeat while tapping on each point):

❖ *What if I am responsible for this?*

❖ *I'm open to accepting responsibility for this.*

❖ *What can I learn from considering that I'm responsible?*

❖ *What does it mean that I accept responsibility for this?*

Alternating round (repeat while tapping on each point):

❖ **Top of the Head:** *I don't want to take responsibility for this.*

❖ **Eyebrow:** *What if I am responsible for this?*

❖ **Outside of Eye:** *I don't want to take responsibility for this.*

❖ **Under the Eye:** *I'm open to accepting responsibility for this.*

❖ **Under the Nose:** *I don't want to take responsibility for this.*

❖ **Chin:** *What can I learn from considering that I'm responsible?*

❖ **Collarbone:** *I don't want to take responsibility for this.*

❖ **Under the Arm:** *What does it mean that I accept responsibility for this?*

Remember, you can always make up your own phrases. That's a great way to make them more targeted, more meaningful, and more effective.

Step 5: How do you feel about the concept of taking responsibility for this event? Does it seem empowering or do you still feel resistance? Assess your new SUDS level. If you still feel resistance, ask yourself if it's the same resistance, or a different resistance. Repeat step 4 if needed.

When you feel empowered, congratulations!

◎

Many people equate responsibility with blame, shame, or guilt. They believe that if they're responsible for a negative event, or one they perceive as negative, then they should feel guilty and attach blame to themselves. Of course, adding on guilt and blame actually interferes with accepting responsibility!

Let's *reframe* this: Consider the possibility that guilt is actually a way to "let yourself off the hook" for what occurred, emotionally speaking. If you see yourself as someone who doesn't cause harm, and then harm occurs, feeling guilty about it is one way to say, "See, I'm really not such a bad person, because I feel so guilty."

By punishing yourself with guilt, you're trying to balance the scales emotionally. It's much more powerful to simply accept responsibility and not the guilt. The energy that you are expending beating yourself up could be spent taking action to balance or improve the situation, or at the very least spent in some other productive way.

If you find yourself unable or unwilling to accept responsibility because you don't want to feel guilty, try tapping on that. For example, you could try using tapping with the Original EFT Affirmation:

❖ *Even though I don't want to accept 100% responsibility for my life because I would feel too guilty about what I've done, I deeply and completely love and accept myself.*

Or using a Choice Statement:

❖ *Even though I don't want to accept 100% responsibility for my life because I would feel too guilty about what I've done, I choose to consider that there is another possibility.*

If you do take responsibility and then feel guilty, recognize that the guilt feeling is separate from the responsibility. It's a separate aspect that has now shown up. You can tap on the guilt using Simple Tapping, or use SOS Tapping to create a more empowering emotional choice.

APPROACH 2: INVERSE PARANOIA— CLAIMING RESPONSIBILITY TO EMPOWER YOURSELF

What if you could believe that the universe was conspiring in your favor? That's the concept in Become an Inverse Paranoid (Success Principle 6). Paranoia is believing that "they are out to get you," so inverse paranoia is living as though the universe is conspiring for your highest good. We can combine this concept with "Take 100% Responsibility" to create empowerment.

If you don't take responsibility, then you're acting as if you're a victim of fate, subject to the whims of chance. What happens to you may be good or bad, and you have no control over the events. This type of thinking can lead to resignation, fear, hopelessness, or anxiety.

Instead, if you combine the idea of taking responsibility for your life with the concept that the universe is working on your behalf, you're not a victim at all. You're in charge and the universe is supporting you, although it may not be evident how at all times. And this belief system empowers you in two ways.

First, it keeps you focused on solutions. If you're responsible, then you have the ability to be proactive in creating something different. You created the situation in the first place, and with the help of the universe, you can now create something different or better.

Second, there is a part of the brain called the Reticular Activating System (RAS). This part acts as the gatekeeper in your brain, allowing information to enter your conscious awareness. Since your subconscious mind takes in two million bits of data per second, and the conscious mind can process far less (only about 140 bits of data per second) something has to determine what the conscious mind gets to perceive, and what is left in the subconscious. The RAS is what controls this, and the RAS is programmed by your subconscious mind. It will only allow information into your conscious mind that matches its instructions. If you're not taking responsibility, and that causes you to feel like a victim, you literally will not be aware of opportunities that are available to you.

But I was the victim of a violent crime! Are you saying that I'm responsible for what happened to me?

The three approaches to living this success principle are designed to empower you, not diminish you. Violent crime often leaves people feeling helpless or powerless. Accepting responsibility can, if you choose, allow you to regain a measure of power. The third approach, taking responsibility for your response, may be the easiest to start with, but you can explore all of them.

The value of taking responsibility is that if you accept that you created something, you can *un*create it and create something different in the future.

SUCCESS STORY

Pamela writes: Several years ago, I was traveling a great deal for business, and very much wanted to stay in a non-smoking hotel room every night. Although I would book non-smoking hotel rooms, I would also call the hotel the morning of my arrival and ask if they would confirm it. I constantly worried that I would be booked into a smoking room.

One night I arrived somewhat late at a nice hotel that I had previously booked, only to learn that I had been given a smoking room, despite having called that morning to confirm the nonsmoking room. I was angry, but my options were to take the room or to pay for it anyway and leave to search for another hotel. I took the room and tried to sleep. Repeatedly during the night I awoke, was bothered by the smell, and got upset. I did some Simple Tapping, which enabled me to fall back to sleep, but I would wake up later and repeat the cycle. Finally, at 3 A.M. I asked, "Why did I create this?"

As I continued to tap and look for possible explanations, I realized that I had been living in constant fear that my needs would not be met. That explained why I would call the hotels the morning of my arrival to confirm what I had already booked. I saw this as an opportunity to create a new reality: *My needs are always provided for.*

I tapped:

❖ *Even though I don't like smoking rooms, the Universe always provides what I need.*

In this case, the Universe had provided me with a chance to remove my fear. I went back to sleep and slept the rest of the night with no more anger.

Shortly after this, the entire Marriott chain announced that all their hotels would be nonsmoking. In a whimsical way, I chose to take responsibility for this happening. Since then, no matter where I have stayed, I have never been afraid of having a smoking room, and I've never had another one.

APPROACH 3: TAKING RESPONSIBILITY FOR YOUR RESPONSE

If you can't find a blessing in the event, *create* a blessing with your response to the event. If you aren't yet able to take 100% responsibility for everything in your life, it's probably because a particular event or set of circumstances seems too far out of your control:

- *It's not my responsibility that I was abused by my parents.*

- *I'm not responsible for the fact that I was born with _____ condition.*

- *I'm not responsible for the global situation.*

One way to approach responsibility in challenging situations is to begin by taking 100% responsibility for your *response* to the event. Too often, if we refuse to take responsibility for an event, we pretend that our response is also outside our control.

- *I got angry, but it's a natural response—anyone would have!*

- *Of course I'm not loving. I was abused as a child.*

- *I'm only one person. What can I do about the situation in Africa?*

No matter what the event, you always have the ability to choose your reaction to the event. Viktor Frankl, author of *Man's Search for Meaning,* was tortured in Nazi concentration camps, but refused to hate his captors and torturers. He believed that when everything else had been taken from him, the one area where he still had control was his own reaction, and he chose to live in love and acceptance despite his circumstances. This is a powerful example of reframing.

Perhaps you feel that anger, blaming, complaining, or making an excuse is an appropriate response to a situation. You might have thoughts like:

- *He ruined me.*

- *It's Carol who created this problem, not me.*

- *I can't believe how bad the service is.*

- *It's not my fault that the shipment was late.*

If you feel this way, you're not taking responsibility. Here's why: If you feel *justified* in the way that you reacted—in blaming, complaining, or making excuses—you're saying that your response was rational, normal, or warranted. In other words, it was *right*.

Taking responsibility doesn't have anything to do with being right in that sense. It's a place to stand, a belief system that empowers and produces phenomenal results. When you "act as if" you are 100% responsible for what happens in your life, you can begin to look to see where maybe you *were* responsible—you ignored warning signs leading up to a problem because it would have been uncomfortable to act or to move, you didn't vote in the election, you didn't exercise or eat a healthy diet, you took some unwarranted shortcuts, you ignored feedback, and so on. Once you see and own these things, you can avoid making those same mistakes next time.

If you're upset enough about an event that you don't want to take responsibility for it, or even take responsibility for your response to it, you'll first need to clear the emotional charge from that event. You can clear the anger or upset using the techniques to clear strong emotions that you learned in the last chapter. When you're feeling calmer about an event, it's much easier to consider taking responsibility for it.

◎

Now that we've laid out all three possibilities for taking 100% responsibility for your life, you can work with whatever one appeals to you. Let's assume that you were involved in a traffic accident that was primarily the other driver's fault. In taking 100% responsibility, you could approach this situation as follows:

— You could ask, "If I assume responsibility for this, what can I learn from it?"

Your answer might be, "I can learn to keep a cool head when something like this occurs. I can learn not to drive during peak traffic hours if I don't have to. I can learn to make sure that all my automobile documentation is up to date."

— You could ask, "If I assume responsibility for this, how does this empower me?"

Your answer might be, "Since I somehow created this accident, I know that I can also create anything else I want."

— You could ask, "If I assume responsibility for my responses to this accident, what does that enable me to be, do, or have?"

Your answer might be, "I get to experience forgiveness for the other driver. Since I've let go of my anger, I get to feel the freedom from that release. I get to be grateful that it was not more serious. I get to learn that I am a survivor, and that what doesn't kill me makes me stronger."

EXERCISE: TAKE 100% RESPONSIBILITY FOR YOUR LIFE

Step 1: determine your resistance to the idea of taking 100% responsibility for your life. You've already tapped on "take responsibility in order to learn" in Approach 1. In this exercise, you'll look at other specific incidents or the entire concept of taking responsibility. Read the following statements; are any of these true for you?

I'm afraid to take 100% responsibility for my life, because . . .

- *I don't think I've done enough, and I feel guilty about that.*

- *What if I make mistakes and can't blame anyone else?*

- *It feels like too much pressure.*

- *It doesn't make sense to me.*

- *I don't believe I'm that powerful.*

- *I don't want to be that powerful.*

- *I don't want the responsibility that comes with that much power.*

- *I'll feel too guilty about things I've done.*

Choose one of these reasons above or identify your own situation. Say it aloud, and focus on what feelings arise. Measure your fear or discomfort. What is your SUDS level? If it's 7 or below, skip directly to Step 3. If your intensity is 8–10, however, go on to Step 2.

Step 2: Do at least two rounds of Simple Tapping, repeating your Reminder Phrases (your reasons or feelings from Step 1) as you tap each point. Reevaluate your fear. If it's still above a 7, do this round again. If it's 7 or below, go on to the next round.

(**Note:** If you find yourself tapping and tapping, but your emotions are still very intense, consider whether you are experiencing a change of *aspect*. So while the intensity of one feeling may be decreasing, you might not notice because it is being replaced with a different intense feeling. For example, you may feel angry, then embarrassed, and then sad. This is why it's important to note which emotion you're tapping on, so you can see your progress as you work through different aspects.)

Step 3: If your intensity is 7 or below, create an Open Choice to bring in possibility. Use your own Open Choice setup statement, or consider one of the following:

❖ *Even though I'm afraid to take 100% responsibility for my life because* [insert your reason here], *I'm open to a new, empowering perspective.*

❖ *Even though I can't take 100% responsibility for my life because* [insert your reason here], *I'm open to finding a new way to look at this.*

Tap one negative round with Reminder Phrases, such as:

❖ *I'm afraid to take 100% responsibility because* [insert your reason here].

❖ *I can't take 100% responsibility for my life because* [insert your reason here].

Tap one round with Open Choice Statements as Reminder Phrases, such as:

❖ *I'm open to finding a new way to look at this.*

❖ *I'm open to accepting responsibility for this.*

❖ *I'm open to a new, empowering perspective.*

Tap one alternating round. Remember to end on a positive phrase.

Reevaluate your fear or other emotional discomfort. If your SUDS level is still above a 5, do this round again. If it's 5 or below, go on to the next round.

Step 4: Create an empowering choice. Ask yourself what you could get out of taking 100% responsibility for your life. Perhaps you'd feel a sense of empowerment or autonomy. Perhaps you'd feel in charge, in command, or in service to a greater good. You'll use this to create a Specific Choice setup statement with the following format:

❖ *Even though I'm _still_ afraid to take 100% responsibility for my life, I choose to take responsibility and feel . . .*

  • *empowered.*

  • *that I create my life.*

  • *that the Universe is working for my ultimate good.*

Tap one negative round with Reminder Phrases, such as:

❖ *It's too much pressure to take responsibility.*

❖ *I'm afraid I'll take responsibility and fail.*

Tap one round with Specific Choice Statements as Reminder Phrases, such as:

❖ *I choose to take responsibility, and I feel [your choice here].*

Tap one alternating round. Remember to end on a positive phrase. For example:

- ❖ **Top of the Head:** *I don't want to take responsibility for this.*

- ❖ **Eyebrow:** *I choose to take responsibility, and I feel empowered.*

- ❖ **Outside of Eye:** *It's too much pressure to take responsibility.*

- ❖ **Under the Eye:** *I choose to take responsibility, and I feel that I create my life.*

- ❖ **Under the Nose:** *What if I take responsibility and fail?*

- ❖ **Chin:** *I choose to take responsibility, and I feel that the Universe is working for my ultimate good.*

- ❖ **Collarbone:** *I don't want to take responsibility for this.*

- ❖ **Under the Arm:** *I choose to take responsibility, and I feel empowered.*

Step 5: Evaluate your fear on the SUDS scale again. If there is any fear left, repeat Step 4.

You may be reluctant to take responsibility for your life for many diverse reasons. You may need to repeat this for several different fears. Clearing them and choosing to take 100% responsibility is so empowering, it's well worth the time and effort to do this.

SUCCESS STORY

Pamela writes: While I was writing this section of the book, I had an opportunity to look at taking 100% responsibility for my life. I thought I had been doing so for some years, but I realized instead that I was living with two core beliefs: (1) that everything that happens to me is a gift from the Universe/Divine/Spirit, and (2) that I am 100% responsible for my response to what happens to me.

As I thought about it, I decided that I felt completely empowered by these two beliefs, and it wasn't necessary for me to also believe that I actually created my own reality. The belief that I created everything in my awareness felt too hard to maintain.

The next day in meditation, I thought about these beliefs again—along with the idea of creating everything that happens to me—and it struck me that I was terrified of taking responsibility for creating everything in my life. I was willing to take responsibility for everything that I've done so far, but the thought of actually living in the belief that I create or allow everything in my world felt like an enormous responsibility, and very scary.

I knew immediately that I had to work on that, since I wasn't willing to let fear control my belief systems. I started with Simple Tapping, using phrases such as:

- ❖ *I'm afraid to take responsibility for my life.*
- ❖ *This is too big.*
- ❖ *I'm terrified of this.*
- ❖ *How can I be responsible for all of that?*
- ❖ *That's too big—what about my family, my clients, my community?*
- ❖ *I'm really scared of this.*

After just a few rounds, the fear subsided, and I was left in a confused state. I wasn't scared, but still not sure I wanted to take on this belief. So I used an Open Choice Statement to spur some creative thinking:

❖ *Even though I'm still not sure I want to take 100% responsibility for my life, I choose to be open to the empowerment this might bring me.*

For Reminder Phrases, I used:

❖ *I'm still not sure I want to do this.*

❖ *I wonder what this could bring to my life?*

❖ *I'm still not sure I want to do this.*

❖ *What if this could really empower me?*

❖ *I don't know if I want to do this.*

❖ *I'm open to the empowerment this could bring.*

❖ *What if this could give me all of my dreams?*

❖ *What if this is something that's a great idea?*

❖ *I'm open to a new way of being empowered.*

At the end of this round, I felt as though I could step into the belief of *I create or allow everything that happens to me—I take 100% responsibility for my life.* Because deciding to do this for the rest of my life still felt a bit big, I chose to take it on as a 30-day experiment, going all out. I put the thoughts, the emotions, and the language into all my daily rituals, including meditation, prayer, my gratitude journal, tapping, and so forth.

After 30 days, I had some big ideas, one resulting in $24,000! Everything seemed to be flowing more powerfully and effortlessly than ever before. I also felt more compassionate toward other people. I began to enjoy my new identity as someone who was 100% responsible. It felt good!

I chose to continue the experiment indefinitely.

RESISTANCE TO TAKING 100% RESPONSIBILITY

We'll now look at some of the most common patterns of resistance that occur when you begin taking 100% responsibility for your life.

Taking responsibility means consciously putting energy and intention toward everything in your life that you wish to create or allow. There are many ways to refuse responsibility, but they all ultimately create the same situation: you put energy or intention toward something you claim that you don't want, rather than something that you do want.

RESISTANCE #1: BUT IT'S *HIS* FAULT!

When you feel that you are suffering as a result of someone else's action, your first inclination may be to start blaming. Rather than empowering you by removing you from responsibility, blaming actually disempowers you. You become the victim of someone else's action or inaction.

Once you get into the habit of taking 100% responsibility for your life, your desire to blame others will fall away. If you're just beginning to work with this success principle, it can be challenging to step into taking responsibility when you're very angry or upset about an event. Therefore, we'll want to reduce or eliminate the anger as a first step in taking 100% responsibility.

SUCCESS STORY

Randy was very angry at his co-worker Sam. Randy and Sam had been working on a project together, but Sam did not do his part, and Randy realized that it would be difficult or impossible to complete the work on time. Randy didn't feel that he could ask his manager for an extension, and was worried about repercussions if the work was late. He knew that he needed to take a solution-based approach to working with Sam, rather than stewing in anger, but felt very strongly that this situation wasn't his fault.

Randy knew that he first needed to reduce his anger in order to constructively look at options, and get out of the "blame game." He rated his anger at a 9 on the SUDS scale.

He first used Simple Tapping, with the Reminder Phrases:

❖ *I am so angry at Sam.*

❖ *Why couldn't he have done his work?*

❖ *He had no right to do this!*

❖ *I'm so angry!*

❖ *He should have done his work.*

After tapping for some minutes, Randy found himself thinking *I'm afraid of what the boss is going to say.* This fear was a different aspect from the anger.

Remember aspects? These are the different thoughts and different emotions that comprise an upset. It's important to be aware of a new aspect appearing, so you can focus your tapping, and so you're aware of the progress you're making.

Randy's shift from anger to fear was an indicator that his anger had dropped enough that another emotion became more prominent. He then rated the intensity of his fear at a 7.

Again, he used Simple Tapping, with the Reminder Phrases:

❖ *I'm afraid of what the boss will say.*

❖ *What if we get penalized?*

❖ *What if we get fired?*

❖ *I'm afraid we're in real trouble.*

His fear dropped to a 4. Randy now described it more as "concern" than "fear." He was still angry at Sam, and rated his anger also at a 4. He chose to work on the concern first.

Because his emotion (concern) was less than a 5, he added a Choice Statement:

❖ *Even though I'm concerned about what the boss will say, I choose to find an effective way to handle this.*

He tapped three rounds using the Choices Trio Method. During the first round, he focused on his concern:

❖ *I'm concerned about what the boss will say.*

❖ *He'll be upset at us.*

❖ *What happens if this project is late?*

❖ *I'm concerned about how the boss will handle this.*

During the second round, he focused on the solution:

❖ *I choose to find an effective way to handle this.*

❖ *I know I can find that way.*

❖ *I choose to believe I can turn this around.*

During the third round, he alternated these ideas, ending on a positive statement.

Randy's concern was now at a 0, and his anger toward Sam had dropped to a 2. Randy was now ready to take responsibility for this event:

❖ *Even though I'm still a little angry at Sam, I choose to accept responsibility for this event.*

❖ *Even though I don't know how I could have prevented this, what if I could be empowered by accepting responsibility?*

❖ *Even though I'm still a little angry at Sam, I choose to focus on the solution to our situation.*

Again, Randy tapped three rounds, using the negative statements in the first round, then the positive statement in the second round, then alternating them.

At the end, Randy no longer felt angry at Sam. He was actively seeking solutions to the situation, and made the following choice:

I choose to take 100% responsibility for this situation.

When I look at it, I learn that I could have checked in with Sam earlier and more often, and I would have noticed the problem in the earlier stages when it would have been easier to handle.

Since I created it, I can also create a positive solution that moves my life and my work forward.

I choose to respond in a powerful way, looking at solutions rather than assigning blame. Also, by taking responsibility, I feel more empowered and more creative, and these feelings will help me handle any conversations with my boss more effectively.

RESISTANCE #2: I WANT TO COMPLAIN!

The urge to complain, to share our misery with others, is very common. You can look at this desire to complain as a craving, just like food cravings or other addictive cravings. It's a clear denial of taking 100% responsibility.

There is a difference between complaining to someone who can do something about your issue, and complaining to someone who can't. Let's look first at complaining to those people who can't change the situation. This comes from a false sense of helplessness.

Helplessness is perhaps the most disempowering feeling you can experience. In contrast, anger feels much more powerful—it is a "step up" on the emotional scale because it feels more empowering than helplessness. When we complain, we often feel anger, and so feel less disempowered than we did when the event occurred.

You may also complain out of a desire to feel connected with others, to feel heard, or to feel justified. When we complain to our family and friends, we're usually looking for sympathy for our problems, for agreement that we were wronged, or for validation of our values.

Although anger feels more powerful than helplessness, neither one serves you in the long term. Anger can be a motivator for action, and it's not wrong to feel it—but it still contains the energy of being a victim. It's just less empowering than a calm resolve to take action.

The urge to complain responds very well to tapping, as in the following exercise.

EXERCISE: ELIMINATING COMPLAINING WITH SOS TAPPING

Step 1: Identify your personal challenge. How strong is your desire to complain? Do you want to complain to a friend, a co-worker, or your spouse? You may feel helpless or angry at your situation now, and either one can spur the desire to complain. Whatever situation you want to complain about will be your Reminder Phrase for this exercise. However, you won't tap on the desire to complain. Instead, you'll tap on the upset, and remove that.

Step 2: Evaluate your SUDS level. If it is 8 or above, use Simple Tapping first to reduce the intensity. Note that there may be a part of you that is reluctant to use tapping, because you may fear losing your anger and returning to a feeling of helplessness. If you're willing to tap, you can remove both the anger *and* the helplessness.

If you're not sure how to tap on the anger, imagine that you're complaining to a friend. You can tap while you complain; you just don't need the other person there to listen. This is actually a great way to get in touch with the emotions that are upsetting you. Just remember—no complaining without tapping, and do it alone. Don't subject someone else to your complaining language!

Step 3: When your SUDS level is at a 7 or below, create an Open Choice setup statement to create more empowering interpretations. For example:

❖ *Even though I'm still angry, and I don't feel that I can do anything about this situation, I'm open to an empowering idea.*

Tap one negative round with Reminder Phrases from Step 1. Then tap one round with your Open Choice statement. Tap one more round alternating between the ngative Reminder Phrase and your Open Choice statement.

Step 4: When your SUDS level is at a 5 or below, create a Specific Choice setup statement about taking responsibility.

❖ *Even though I'm still angry, and I don't feel that I can do anything about this situation, I choose to find a way to take responsibility.*

Tap one negative round with Reminder Phrases from Step 1.

Tap one round with Specific Choice Statements in question form. These will allow you to create new, empowering interpretations. Some examples are:

❖ *What if I took responsibility for this situation?*

❖ *Would that help me feel less helpless?*

❖ *How could that empower me?*

❖ *How could I take responsibility in this?*

❖ *I'm open to the benefits of doing that.*

Step 5: Evaluate your SUDS level. If it is at 2 or lower, review the different ways of taking 100% responsibility for your life and choose one or more of them for this situation. How do you feel empowered to take responsibility for the situation that you want to complain about? Tap one round with your new empowering thought. Here are some examples:

❖ *I choose to take responsibility for this.*

❖ *I created this, and I can create a solution.*

❖ *I choose to acknowledge what I learned from this.*

❖ *I'm grateful for the lessons from this.*

❖ *I love how I'm choosing to respond to this event!*

If you can address your complaint to someone who can do something about it, you'll still want to go through the process above. It will put you in an empowered frame of mind, which can lead to:

- Asking for what you want

- Expecting the best—that someone takes action on your complaint

- Standing firm about what you'd like to see happen

RESISTANCE #3: I FEEL *SO* GUILTY!

Although most people assume that accepting responsibility will lead to feelings of guilt, we mentioned earlier that guilt can actually be used as an avoidance of responsibility.

Blaming yourself is one of the ways of refusing to take responsibility, although it doesn't appear that way on the surface. Many people equate "blaming yourself" with "taking responsibility," but the energy behind them is totally different, because blaming yourself leads to guilt.

Responsible means "being accountable, or being the cause of an action."

Guilty means "having done wrong or committed an offense."

Blaming yourself means making yourself wrong, criticizing and condemning yourself. When you blame yourself, you alternate between stern judgment (the critical voice) and accepting blame (the guilty voice). Neither of these voices empowers you.

Yet the "guilty voice" of our conscience is there for a reason. How can we honor the need for a conscience while not being disempowered by guilt?

Let's use an analogy. Physical pain is a signal to avoid certain behaviors—if you put your hand on a hot stove, the pain will cause you to remove your hand before more damage is done to your body. Similarly, our negative emotions point to something that needs attention. Fear, anger, or upset are all indicators that we have an old trigger or a limiting belief. Therefore, when we feel a negative emotion, it's not an invitation to stay stuck, become a victim, complain, blame, or any other method of avoiding responsibility. It's simply an indicator to us that something isn't working—something is off in our energy system, caused by our beliefs, fears, or way of relating to the world. So instead of thinking of a negative emotion as a state of being that we can't change, we can begin to see it as a "system error" signal, announcing that "You need to do some work here."

Our conscience works the same way. When it twinges, saying, "You shouldn't do that" or "You shouldn't have done that," it's an indicator that we have work to do. In doing the work, the guilty feelings should also be handled, like turning off a "system error" light. If our conscience never twinges, that's also a problem—it means our system error light isn't functioning. However, if we're continually feeling guilt, it's like a system error light that's on all the time. It's not helpful, and we have work to do to clear the situation.

Releasing guilt can be done in two ways: using a Choice Statement, or forgiving yourself.

1. You can use a Choice Statement to install a more empowering interpretation of events. This often works well for mild feelings of guilt:

❖ *Even though I feel guilty about having been rude to that salesclerk, I choose to be grateful for what I've learned. I'll do things differently next time.*

❖ *Even though I feel guilty for having forgotten Mike's birthday, I choose to use this as an opportunity to declare myself a considerate person, and begin living that reality.*

2. Releasing more powerful feelings of guilt is based on forgiving yourself. In the next section, we'll use tapping to make forgiveness easier, and at the end, we'll discuss forgiving yourself.

ACTION STEP: OVERCOMING MILD GUILT

Create a Specific Choice setup statement around a situation in which you feel mild guilt (SUDS level 5 or less). You can use the examples above to help you craft your own. Then use the Choices Trio Method (one negative, one positive, and one alternating round) to remove the guilt and install an empowering Choice.

Evaluate your feelings, and create a negative Reminder Phrase:

❖ *I'm feeling a little guilty that* . . .

Create an empowering Specific Choice Statement:

❖ *I choose to* . . .

Combine these two for a Specific Choice setup statement, which you will repeat three times while tapping the Karate Chop (KC) point:

❖ *Even though I'm feeling a little guilty because* [your reason], *I choose to* [your Specific Choice Statement].

Tap one negative round using the Reminder Phrases. Then tap one round using your Specific Choice Statements. Then, if necessary, do an alternating round, remembering to end on a positive statement.

Reassess your SUDS level of guilt for this incident. If the level is above a 0, repeat the exercise. See how many new empowering interpretations you can create.

COMPLETE THE PAST TO EMBRACE THE FUTURE (SUCCESS PRINCIPLE 29)

If you're carrying around anger, hurt, or resentment toward another person, the person you're truly hurting is yourself. Think of all those emotions as "kinks" in your energy system that are keeping your energy from flowing into great relationships, good physical health, and financial success in business. It's easy to see how holding on to a state of unforgiveness can impact your success! You have less energy to devote to moving ahead, and anything you want to receive can get stopped by the blocks in your system.

When you're constantly feeling angry, hurt, or resentful, even if it's under the surface, you tend to evaluate new situations in terms of those emotions. You meet new people with suspicion; tend to be short or unpleasant to family, friends, and colleagues;

and damage your physical health with stress. When you clear the energy blocks causing the negative emotions, you are more present in the moment and able to interact positively with others, you feel better about yourself, and you attract more of what you want into your life.

In *The Success Principles,* there are six steps to forgiveness: (1) acknowledge your anger and resentment; (2) acknowledge the hurt and pain it created; (3) acknowledge the fears and self-doubts that it created; (4) own any part you may have played in letting it occur or letting it continue; (5) acknowledge what you were wanting that you didn't get, and then put yourself in the other person's shoes and attempt to understand where he or she was coming from at that time, and what needs the person was trying to meet— however inelegantly—by his or her behavior; and (6) let go and forgive the person. You can use tapping to acknowledge, release, and move through each of the steps more easily and effortlessly.

Because tapping works with the subconscious, you may find that you take these steps out of order, as you respond to the emotions that emerge during tapping. That's okay. However, it's important to inquire into each step to make sure that it is cleared in order for the forgiveness process to be complete.

TAPPING TECHNIQUE: ACCEPTANCE CHOICE

As you work through the various emotions associated with the forgiveness process, you may want to push aside some of them. Anger can be uncomfortable because many people were taught that it's wrong, and hurt can feel too painful to acknowledge. This leads us to a powerful new statement that we can use in our tapping for dealing with emotions.

We've looked at setup statements with the Original EFT Affirmation:

❖ *Even though I have* [this problem], *I deeply and completely love and accept myself.*

We've also looked at Choice setup statements:

❖ *Even though I have* [this problem], *I choose* [a new em-powering belief or action].

Now we'll combine these in an Acceptance Choice, an accep-tance statement about emotions:

❖ *Even though I feel* [emotion], *I choose to accept myself and my feelings.*

This Acceptance Choice is particularly powerful with anger, fear, and other strong emotions. It allows you to acknowl-edge your feelings and accept them, which are the first steps in releasing them.

SUCCESS STORY

Cheryl, an author and speaker, needed to make calls to ex-pand her speaking opportunities. She was very uncomfortable with this, because she feared that she would do a poor job of "selling herself."

She rated the fear at a 7, and started with an Acceptance Choice:

❖ *Even though I'm afraid I'll do a poor job on these calls, I choose to accept myself and my feelings.*

Reminder Phrases included:

❖ *I'll do a poor job.*

❖ *They won't want to hire me.*

❖ *I'm afraid I won't sell myself.*

❖ *I hate selling myself, so I'm going to do a poor job of it.*

❖ *Why would I want to make those calls?*

❖ *They aren't going to hire me anyway.*

❖ *But I am a great speaker.*

❖ *I wonder if I could learn to be a great salesperson.*

- ❖ *Or at least an adequate one.*
- ❖ *I wonder if I could learn.*
- ❖ *There are lots of things I've learned to do.*
- ❖ *I do have a product I believe in.*
- ❖ *Even though I can't sell right now . . .*
- ❖ *I'm open to the possibility I could learn.*

Cheryl said that the fear was down considerably, but she was now mostly afraid of being on the phone with a stranger, and trying to make a great first impression. She acknowledged that this was a different aspect. She said that she had the knowledge of how to make a good first impression, having taken classes on this, but she just hadn't done it. She rated her fear of this new aspect at a 3 or 4.

In identifying positive Specific Choices that she would like to use, Cheryl picked:

- ❖ *Even though I still have some of this fear, I choose to remember that I'm good with people.*
- ❖ *Even though I still have some of this fear, it's just another human being on the phone.*
- ❖ *Even though I still have some of this fear, I might make their day, they might need me.*
- ❖ *Even though I still have some of this fear, there's always another phone number to call.*

Reminder Phrases (note that this is an alternating round) included:

- ❖ *I still have some of this fear when I think about making those phone calls.*
- ❖ *It's just another human being on the phone.*
- ❖ *I only have 6.2 seconds to make a good impression.*
- ❖ *I am good with people.*
- ❖ *I still have some of this fear.*

❖ *But it's just another human being on the line.*

❖ *I'm going to make someone's day; someone will need me.*

❖ *I may still have some of this fear.*

❖ *If I do flub up, there's another number to call.*

Cheryl reported the fear was gone, and she was ready to call people.

EXERCISE: TAPPING FORGIVENESS PROCESS

The seven steps to the Tapping Forgiveness Process are:

1. Releasing anger and resentment

2. Releasing hurt, sadness, and pain

3. Releasing fears and self-doubt

4. Releasing any other negative emotions

5. Accepting responsibility

6. Acknowledging your wants and desires

7. Offering love, compassion, and forgiveness

This is a very powerful process that works best on specific incidents. If you have a long pattern of repeated incidents that you're angry about—for instance, a long period of abuse from a parent—you'll get better results if you pull several incidents out and work on them one at a time.

Fortunately, there does seem to be a cumulative "domino" effect in tapping. If you have 100 incidents with a single person that you need to forgive, once you go through this process with some small number (perhaps 5–15), the rest will usually "collapse," and you'll be in a state of forgiveness about all of them.

Step 1: Releasing Anger and Resentment. Measure your anger or resentment about the event. Remember, your SUDS level evaluates how you feel *now,* not how you felt at the time. If your SUDS level is 8 or higher, do Simple Tapping until it is 7 or below. Then create an Acceptance Choice setup statement, such as:

❖ *Even though I'm really angry that* [this person did that], *I choose to accept myself and my feelings.*

Tap several rounds with negative Reminder Phrases, focusing on your anger and speaking it at each point. You can either speak about the event or your anger about it. Use the words that allow you to "tune in" as much as possible to the feeling of the anger. For example, you can use Reminder Phrases such as:

❖ *He betrayed me.*

❖ *He embezzled that money.*

❖ *He lied to me.*

❖ *I'm so angry.*

❖ *I'm furious at him.*

Evaluate your anger after several rounds, and see if it has diminished. If not, you'll want to do additional rounds. (You won't be doing any rounds at this point with positive Reminder Phrases.)

If you're still not getting results, look to see whether you're thinking about a single event or if you're thinking about a pattern of events, which is too broad to produce immediately evident results with tapping. It's common, especially with people you are close to, to be angry for several different events. For this exercise, focus on just one.

You might also experience a change of aspect. As your anger diminishes, you may become aware of another emotion in the incident, such as hurt, sadness, or regret. If you feel yourself going directly into compassion or forgiveness for the other person, that's also fine. As soon as the SUDS level of your anger has diminished to a 0, or another emotion has taken its place, move to the next step.

Step 2: Releasing Hurt, Sadness, and Pain. Measure your hurt, sadness, and pain regarding the situation. (If you don't feel any of these emotions, move on to the next step.) Measure your SUDS level, then tap one series, starting with the following Acceptance Choice setup statement:

❖ *Even though I feel this* [hurt, pain, or sadness], *I choose to accept myself and my feelings.*

Tap several rounds using these Reminder Phrases or make up your own:

❖ *I'm hurt when I think about this.*

❖ *I have all this sadness.*

❖ *It's painful to think about this.*

After several rounds, stop and reevaluate your hurt, sadness, or pain. If it's above a 0, repeat this step. If another emotion has come forward, move on to the next step.

Keep in mind that you may tap away all of your anger, then move on to hurt, only to feel anger again. The most likely reason for this is that there is another aspect of the situation that needs to be cleared. For example, if your partner had an affair, you may be very angry thinking about the betrayal. After tapping on the anger, you may feel hurt, and tap that away. Then when you think about the situation, you might become angry again, this time thinking about the pain that this affair caused your child. That's a different aspect, and you'll need to tap away that anger as well. If, however, you find yourself also angry at your partner's lover, you'll want to complete tapping on your anger with your partner, then go tap through it again for your anger toward the lover.

Step 3: Releasing Fears and Self-Doubts. Measure your level of fear and self-doubt about the event. (If you don't feel any fear or self-doubt, move on to the next step.) Measure your SUDS level, then tap one series, starting with the following Acceptance Choice setup statement:

❖ *Even though I feel this* [fear or self-doubt], *I choose to accept myself and my feelings.*

Tap several rounds using these Reminder Phrases as prompts or make up your own:

❖ *I'm afraid when I think about . . .*

❖ *I doubt myself when I think . . .*

❖ *I am afraid of you when . . .*

❖ *I am afraid I might never . . .*

After several rounds, stop and reevaluate your fear or self-doubt. If it's above a 0, repeat this step. If another emotion has come forward, move on to the next step.

Step 4: Releasing Any Other Negative Emotions. Assess whether you feel any other negative emotions that may keep you from moving into forgiveness on this issue. (If you don't feel any other negative emotions, move on to the next step.) If you do feel any other negative emotions, measure the intensity of that emotion, then tap one series with the following Acceptance Choice setup statement:

❖ *Even though I feel this* [negative emotion], *I choose to accept myself and my feelings.*

Tap several rounds focusing on the negative emotion, making up appropriate Reminder Phrases. After several rounds, stop and reevaluate your negative emotion. If it's above a 0, repeat this step. If not, move on to the next step.

TESTING YOUR WORK

Don't try to rush to forgiveness. After you think you've released all your negative emotions about a situation, check in with yourself to see if there are any additional emotions from other aspects. Ignoring unfinished emotions will eventually sabotage you, and you'll need to clean them up later anyway. Here are two ways to check that you've cleared all your emotions:

1. Tell the story. Talk through the specific incident that you're focused on for this exercise. If you feel *any* intensity—anything other than calm neutrality and a SUDS level of 0—stop immediately and tap on that emotion and that specific aspect. Then begin telling yourself the story again.

Each time you tell it, the story will be a bit different. You'll remember different aspects and details. That's good! You're pulling up all the elements that need to be cleared.

Continue the process of telling the story, stopping to tap at any sign of intensity (even a 1 or 2), until you can tell the whole story all the way through with no negative emotions.

2. Visualize the event. Visualize what happened in great detail. Start at the beginning, before you feel any negative emotion. What were the sights, sounds, smells, tastes, and feelings of the incident? (**Note:** do *not* do this until you've completed the first four steps of the Tapping Forgiveness Process to reduce the intensity of your reactions, so you don't cause yourself unnecessary distress.)

If you feel your emotions getting intense, stop and tap on that part of the event. You can tap silently while you visualize, or you can create a tapping series with a negative Reminder Phrase and the Acceptance Choice setup statement that we've been using in this section. When that part of the event feels clear, run the visualization again and look for any additional negative reactions. Continue this process until you feel calmly neutral (SUDS level of 0).

Step 5: Accepting Responsibility. Once your negative emotions have been eliminated with tapping, you will be more easily able to take responsibility for this event as part of your taking 100% responsibility for your life.

This tapping series is not meant to clear emotions as much as it is meant to integrate the tapping you have just done with the empowering position of taking responsibility.

Start with the Choice setup statement:

❖ *Even though I had all these negative emotions about this situation, I choose to take responsibility for it in my life.*

Tap one round with a Reminder Phrase such as:

❖ *I choose to take responsibility for this situation.*

Say it firmly as you tap each point, and see what comes up for you. If you find any resistant thoughts, such as, *Well, it wasn't really my responsibility,* go back to "Success Principle 1: Take 100% Responsibility for Your Life" and work through those thoughts. If it feels true and empowering, move on to the next step.

Step 6: Acknowledging Your Wants and Desires. At this point, you can begin to examine your expectations in this situation, and you'll probably have some objectivity about them that wasn't available to you before you started the process. Although you may not have received or achieved what you wanted, ask yourself what feeling you wanted from that situation. The answer will usually be, "I wanted to feel special/loved/safe/happy." These are things that you can give yourself! You don't need to rely on someone else to provide those for you.

If someone broke a promise, you may realize that the promise made you feel special, loved, or appreciated—and breaking it removed that feeling. You can re-create that yourself.

If someone didn't honor a contract, this may trigger the thought that people can't be trusted. In other words, you wanted to trust but lost that opportunity in this situation. However, it's up to you whether to trust other people or not. You can get that feeling back yourself. It's simply a decision whether to trust or not.

We'll use a Specific Choice setup statement for this:

❖ *Even though I wanted ___, I choose to consider that I can create that in my life.*

Tap one round, using Reminder Phrases such as:

❖ *I wanted . . .*

❖ *I wanted to feel* [special, loved, etc.] *and I thought this situation would give me that.*

❖ *I wanted to feel* [special, loved, etc.].

Tap another round, using Reminder Phrases such as:

❖ *What if I could create that feeling myself?*

❖ *How could I create that feeling myself?*

❖ *Is there a way that I could provide that?*

❖ *I'm open to providing that for myself.*

Tap an alternating round, with Reminder Phrases such as:

❖ *I wanted . . .*

❖ *What if I could create that feeling myself?*

❖ *I don't know if I could do that.*

❖ *Is there a way that I could provide that for myself?*

❖ *I really wanted it from . . .*

❖ *How could I create that feeling myself?*

❖ *I wanted it that particular way.*

❖ *I'm open to providing that for myself.*

Visualize the situation again. Repeat this step if you still find yourself wanting that feeling from the situation.

Step 7: Offering Love, Compassion, and Forgiveness. At this point, the negative emotions should all be eliminated; after all, you've acknowledged your feelings and taken responsibility for the situation. The final step is to offer love, compassion, and forgiveness.

This step can be done with Simple Tapping. Picture the person you've been working with, and tap at least one round. Your Reminder Phrases might start with:

- ❖ *I understand . . .*
- ❖ *I appreciate . . .*
- ❖ *I am thankful for . . .*
- ❖ *I forgive you for . . .*
- ❖ *I love you for . . .*

If it still feels challenging to say these, put the words *I choose to* or *I'm open to* in front of these affirmations as you tap.

- ❖ *I choose to understand . . .*
- ❖ *I choose to appreciate . . .*
- ❖ *I'm open to being thankful for . . .*
- ❖ *I'm open to forgiving you for . . .*
- ❖ *I choose to love you for . . .*

You may tap as many rounds as you like in order to generate these feelings. In the absence of the negative emotions, feeling these feelings becomes much easier!

RESISTANCE TO FORGIVENESS

One common resistance to forgiveness is that the other person doesn't deserve it. But remember the quote, "Holding on to anger and resentment is like drinking poison and expecting the other person to die." You may find as you tap through the Tapping Forgiveness Process that you get stuck, and your intensity won't diminish. In that case, ask yourself, *What would it mean if I let this* [emotion] *go?*

You may get answers such as "it would mean it didn't matter" or "it would mean that the person got away with it." You might feel that it invalidates your suffering, or worry that it would allow the situation to happen again. Remember, forgiveness is all about *your* relief. Forgiving someone doesn't mean that what they did was ethically or legally acceptable. Forgiveness is a gift that you give to yourself. If you want to forgive someone at the deepest level, including yourself, you must eliminate your resistance to forgiveness.

There are reframes for each of these beliefs. Most of these beliefs are based on some concept of unfairness or injustice, with an underlying belief that if forgiveness occurs then somehow justice has not been served. Once you begin tapping away your fear, anger, or frustration, reframes will probably occur to you naturally. Although we'll suggest some new empowering thoughts, the best reframes always come from you.

Just doing some Simple Tapping on these beliefs may reduce the intensity of your upset about these ideas.

EXERCISE: OVERCOMING RESISTANCE TO FORGIVENESS WITH SOS TAPPING

Step 1: Look at how you feel about forgiving someone for some incident. Do you have a belief that prevents you from forgiving? What exactly is your belief? Identify your resistance.

Possible negative Reminder Phrases:

❖ *I can't justify what she did.*

❖ *If I forgive him, it means I suffered for nothing.*

❖ *I can't forgive him and let him get away with it.*

Complete the following statements:

• *I can't forgive because . . .*

• *The emotion I feel when I think this is . . .*

Step 2: Assess your SUDS level. If the SUDS level is 8 or more, do Simple Tapping to reduce the intensity before attempting any reframes.

Step 3: When your SUDS level is at a 7 or below, introduce an Open Choice. Create your Open Choice setup statement in the following format, and repeat it three times while tapping the Karate Chop point.

❖ *Even though I can't forgive because* [your reason here], *I'm open to . . .*

Tap one round with your negative Reminder Phrase, such as:

❖ *I can't let him get away with it.*

Tap one round with your Open Choice Statement, such as:

❖ *I'm open to a new perspective in this.*

Tap one alternating round:

❖ **Top of the Head:** *I can't let him get away with it.*

❖ **Eyebrow:** *I'm open to a new perspective in this.*

❖ **Outside of Eye:** *I can't let him get away with it.*

❖ **Under the Eye:** *I'm open to a new perspective in this.*

❖ **Under the Nose:** *I can't let him get away with it.*

❖ **Chin:** *I'm open to a new perspective in this.*

❖ **Collarbone:** *I can't let him get away with it.*

❖ **Under the Arm:** *I'm open to a new perspective in this.*

Step 4: Reassess your SUDS level. When the intensity is a 5 or below, you can begin tapping using a Specific Choice.

First, create your Specific Choice. What would you like to believe, or how would you like to feel about forgiving? Has anything new opened up for you? Then use your Specific Choice to create a Specific Choice setup statement. Remember the format is:

❖ *Even though I still can't forgive because* [your reason here], *I choose . . .*

Examples of Specific Choice setup statements are:

❖ *Even though I don't want to let this* [emotion] *go because it would mean* [your worry], *I choose to give myself the gift of releasing this.*

❖ *Even though I'm afraid if I release my* [emotion] *that this situation will happen again, I choose to consider that there are other ways to protect myself.*

❖ *Even though I can't release this* [emotion] *because I've had it for so long, I choose to consider that it's time to give myself this gift.*

Tap one round with your negative Reminder Phrase, then one with your Specific Choice Statement.

Assess your SUDS level. If at this point, your SUDS level is a 0, you're done! Otherwise, do one alternating round, and reassess your SUDS level again. If your intensity is a 0, congratulations! If it's still not yet a 0, repeat this step.

FORGIVING YOURSELF

The most effective way to forgive yourself is to go through this process while looking at yourself as the "other person." Particularly if you're working on forgiving yourself for something that happened long ago, you may see that younger version of yourself as a different person than you are today.

You can even refer to yourself in the third person, saying your name instead of saying "me" or "myself." When you do this, do the last step twice. The first time, look at yourself as separate, the same way you did the rest of the exercise. The second time, refer to "myself," such as *I choose to love myself for . . .*

◎

If forgiveness is a gift you give yourself, what happens if you believe that you don't deserve it?

This belief that you don't deserve it could keep you from tapping in the first place. However, if you start the process, you'll almost certainly make some progress in clearing your emotions. Remember this reframe: if you're hanging on to guilt, you're punishing yourself in order to make yourself feel better, in a backward way.

Also, since we know that we tend to behave in a way that is consistent with how we see ourselves, when we see ourselves as not deserving, as guilty, as just wrong, we're actually less likely to take better actions in the future!

It's important to remove any blocks to your feeling worthy and deserving of success. Forgiving yourself is just as important to your success as forgiving others.

Try to create your own SOS Tapping exercise to overcome resistance to forgiving yourself. Here are some examples to get you started.

Examples of negative Reminder Phrases:

❖ *I feel so guilty.*

❖ *I shouldn't have done that.*

❖ *I wish I had done something else.*

❖ *I feel so ashamed.*

Examples of positive Reminder Phrases that support your Open Choice:

❖ *How can I take responsibility instead of blame?*

❖ *How could I create myself as someone new?*

❖ *How could I step into a new possibility?*

❖ *Who do I want to be in this type of situation in the future?*

Example of an Open Choice setup statement:

❖ *Even though I don't believe that I deserve it, and I want to carry this guilt around as punishment, I'm open to a new idea about this.*

Examples of Specific Choice setup statements:

❖ *Even though I think I ought to be punished for what I did so I'll just carry around this guilt, I choose to use my energy in more productive ways.*

❖ *Even though I want to hold on to this, I'm open to a new possibility: that as long as I see myself this way, I'm more likely to do things I don't want to do.*

SUCCESS STORY

Elaine, an experienced tapper, sent in this story about using the Tapping Forgiveness Process:

> *I had been robbed of $1,000 in a scam, at a time when that was a great deal of money for me. Rationally, I knew that I was very lucky, and that many people lose their life savings in situations like this. I had done some work on it, and pretty much thought that it was behind me. However, when I thought carefully about the people involved, I realized I was still quite angry and was struggling with forgiving both the scam artists and myself.*
>
> *I decided to use the Tapping Forgiveness Process to work on the issue.*
>
> *I was very angry about the incident, even eight years after it had happened, so I tapped for Step 1.*
>
> *Setup statement:*

❖ <u>*Even though I'm very angry, I choose to accept myself and my feelings.*</u>

Reminder Phrases included:

❖ *I'm very angry.*

❖ *They didn't care about me at all.*

❖ *They didn't care how much they hurt me.*

❖ *I'm so mad at them!*

❖ *People like that shouldn't be allowed to live. [I know this is very extreme, and I was surprised at the extent of my anger when I focused on it. Since I like to consider myself a caring person, I had been pushing the anger away. I could see that wasn't serving me, so I just let myself experience it and it faded very quickly after that.]*

❖ *I'm so mad at them.*

❖ *They just didn't care.*

❖ *They are just human beings.*

❖ *Not very nice human beings.*

❖ *But they're just not very aware.*

❖ *Maybe they shut themselves down so they won't feel the hurt they're causing.*

At this point, I was actually feeling a bit sorry for the scam artists, and for the unfulfilled life I believed they were living. I no longer felt angry, and went on to Step 2.

I felt sadness for the pain that I had gone through as a result of this incident, and the pain I believed the scam artists were in. My sadness was at about a 6.

I tapped:

❖ *Even though I'm sad that I've struggled with this for years, I choose to accept myself and my feelings.*

Reminder Phrases:

❖ *I'm sad about all this struggle.*

❖ *Apparently, this has been affecting me even when I thought it was over.*

❖ *I'm sad about those people, too.*

❖ *They can't be happy the way that they are living.*

I continued tapping several rounds in this way, until I felt completely neutral and was not experiencing any sadness or hurt. I decided to continue to Step 3.

I felt some real fear that I could be taken advantage of again in the future, and had doubts about my ability to prevent it. My fear was at a 5.

I tapped:

❖ *Even though I'm afraid I'll be taken advantage of again, I choose to accept myself and my feelings.*

Reminder Phrases:

❖ *I'm afraid I'll be taken advantage of.*

❖ *What if someone else tries to rip me off?*

❖ *I don't think I'll be smart enough to stop it.*

❖ *I just don't recognize that kind of thing.*

❖ *Actually, my intuition was talking to me. I just ignored it.*

❖ *I won't do that again.*

❖ *I'm still afraid I'll be taken advantage of.*

❖ *I know that if I fear it, I'll attract it.*

❖ *I could make a more positive choice.*

I considered the choice I choose to attract only good people in my life, but I didn't feel comfortable with that choice. Instead, I chose, The Universe always conspires for my good. I used the setup statement:

❖ *Even though I'm still a bit afraid I might be taken advantage of again, I choose to know that the Universe always conspires for my good.*

Negative Reminder Phrases:

❖ *I'm still a little afraid.*

❖ *It could happen again.*

❖ *I will be listening to my intuition more now.*

❖ *It still might happen.*

Positive Reminder Phrases:

❖ *I choose to know that the Universe conspires for my good.*

❖ *The Universe brings me only people who serve my highest good.*

After tapping a Choices Trio using this Choice, I no longer felt afraid of being taken advantage of. Instead, I felt like my life was filled with blessings.

I was not aware of any other negative emotions, so I moved on to Step 5.

Before I started this process, I had felt both upset and sad about the amount of time I had spent being angry, having sleepless nights, and feeling stressed. I also felt guilty for having had thoughts of revenge. After coming through the Tapping Forgiveness Process so far, I could see that my "drama" was created by me. My suffering and pain was created by me. Now it was easy to take responsibility.

I tapped:

❖ *Even though I had all this drama, suffering, and pain, I know that I created it; I choose to take responsibility for it and create something totally different!*

Negative round:

❖ *I created all this drama.*
❖ *This suffering and pain was my creation.*

Positive round:

❖ *I choose to take responsibility for it.*
❖ *I know I can create something different!*

I did only two rounds, a negative and a positive round, and felt clear on this. I didn't feel I needed the alternating round this time.

When I looked at Step 6, I felt like I had wanted to feel like a special person when the incident had happened, and that the other people (I didn't want to call them "scam artists" anymore) didn't treat me that way. The intensity was only a 4, so I went right into a Choice.

So I tapped:

❖ *Even though I wanted to feel special and valued, and I didn't feel treated that way, I choose to know that I am, no matter how things may appear.*

Negative round:

❖ *They didn't treat me like a human being.*
❖ *I wasn't valued.*

Positive round:

❖ *I am always valuable.*

❖ *I am an expression of the divine, and infinitely valuable.*

Again, I felt complete without the alternating round.

I then tried Step 7, saying, "I am grateful for this event" and "I forgive you" to the other people. I tapped a round with each phrase.

At the end I felt warm and loving, and felt like my memories of the event, which had been clear before, were now very hard to recall.*

I had thought that I would have to tap on forgiving myself, but after all this other work, I felt at peace with everything that I had done and the way I had acted. It's just what I did, and I can make different choices as I move forward.

What a powerful process!

(***Note:** This is fairly common when overcoming a traumatic memory. When you remove the emotional charge of the memory, there is no longer a reason for the brain to store it in the "important—remember this" section.)

CHAPTER CHECKLIST

I know the three different approaches to taking responsibility.

I know why feeling guilty is sometimes a way of avoiding responsibility.

I've done at least one tapping exercise for taking responsibility for my life.

I've done the Tapping Forgiveness Process for at least one person.

I know how to create an Acceptance Choice setup statement.

◎   ◎   ◎

5

ACCELERATING SUCCESS: TAPPING FOR ACTION AND RESULTS

RELEASE THE BRAKES (SUCCESS PRINCIPLE 10)

If you're driving a car and suddenly realize that you've left the emergency brake on, you won't just give it more gas to go faster. You'll simply release the brake, and then with no extra effort, move forward much more quickly and easily.

In life, if your self-talk and actions aren't set for success, they can function in the same way as that emergency brake, slowing your forward progress.

Whenever you attempt to move outside your comfort zone, your mind and body react with danger signals. The danger is to your identity, the concept that you have about yourself. It's natural for your mind to react to threats to your identity, even if you're the person threatening it. For example:

— If you have an identity as someone who only makes $30,000 a year, it can be threatening to your sense of self to become someone who makes $100,000 a year.

— If you have an identity as a single person, it can be threatening to think of becoming married.

— If you have an identity as an overweight person, it can be threatening to think of becoming a healthier weight.

It may not seem like there is a threat to tripling your income, but if you have wanted to do it and have not yet succeeded, it's very possible that something inside you is protecting you from a perceived threat. However, you may not be aware of feeling threatened, especially if another part of you really desires the identity change.

To clarify this, one of the best questions to ask yourself is:

What would be the downside of this change?

Or:

What negative consequences or events might occur as a result of this change?

Perhaps you believe that if you begin to make more money, you'll have to work too hard and not have enough time for your family. Perhaps you believe that your friends will abandon you if you're suddenly wealthy. Or perhaps you believe that wealthy people are unethical or always unhappy.

Similarly, becoming slender and attractive can feel dangerous for some overweight people. You may begin to attract the attention of the opposite sex, which may not be comfortable. Or if you're already in a relationship, changing your appearance may put pressure on the relationship.

These beliefs will sabotage your ability to change, no matter how many affirmations you say. Saying affirmations—just the words—does not create change. It's feeling the emotions associated with the affirmations coming true that creates the change. If emotionally you are feeling *I'd rather just stay the same; it's too uncomfortable or dangerous to change,* then that's exactly what will happen.

It's vital to discover the emotions that are behind your affirmations, and make sure that they are in alignment with the affirmation coming true. You can use tapping to achieve this.

TAPPING TECHNIQUE: CONTINUOUS TAPPING

Up to this point, you've always tapped in "rounds," beginning at the top of the head and going down to under the arm. Usually, you've tapped the Karate Chop (KC) point while doing a setup statement prior to tapping the rounds.

Now we'll use a new technique, Continuous Tapping. With Continuous Tapping, you'll simply tap all the points in sequence, just as if you were doing multiple rounds. However, you won't be using the KC point, because you won't be using a setup statement. Also, you won't necessarily be speaking as you tap each point. You may continue tapping on one point as long as you like before moving on to the next point, and you may skip points as well. The objective is to tap continuously until the exercise is over.

Simple Tapping and Continuous Tapping can look very similar. The difference is that Simple Tapping usually involves tapping on one point for only a few seconds, or as long as it takes to say one phrase, then moving to the next point. With Continuous Tapping, you may stay on a point for a minute or more, perhaps while you have part of a conversation, visualize an event, or explore a physical sensation in your body.

Continuous Tapping is not a stand-alone technique. Instead, we'll incorporate it into many other techniques in the upcoming sections.

TAPPING TIP: THE TRUTH METER (TM) LEVEL

Up to this point, we've used the SUDS level to identify the level of distress or upset caused by a given emotion. As we proceed, you'll want to measure how true a belief *feels* to you.

We will use the concept of a *truth meter,* and the phrase *TM level*, to distinguish the intensity of a belief from the intensity of an emotion (which will still use the SUDS scale).

As with the SUDS scale, we will use a 0–10 scale; 0 will mean *not true at all for me* and 10 will mean *the belief feels totally true to me.*

The belief might be a limiting belief, in which case your goal would be to get the number to a 0; or the belief might be a positive affirmation, in which case your goal would be to get the number to a 10.

SUPERCHARGING YOUR AFFIRMATIONS

In *The Success Principles,* there are excellent guidelines for creating powerful affirmations. Affirmations can be terrific tools for mental, emotional, and vibrational change. However, if you have a "Yeah, but . . ." reaction associated with your affirmations, they will often backfire, and leave you no better off than before (and possibly worse!).

A "Yeah, but . . ." is the little voice in your head that will disagree with an affirmation when you're preparing to step into a new, more powerful reality.

For example, if your affirmation is *I am easily and consistently earning $100,000 a year,* the little voice in your head may say something like, *Yeah, right—in your dreams! Not in this economy!* or *Who do you think you're kidding? You've never made more than $50,000 a year at anything.*

The words of your little voice are your *actual* affirmation. You can see how that could keep you stuck! Depending on the strength of that little voice, you could repeat your affirmation for months or years without it having any positive effect, since it always ends with a negative disclaimer that cancels out the chosen affirmation.

TRANSFORM YOUR INNER CRITIC INTO AN INNER COACH (SUCCESS PRINCIPLE 32)

The inner critic is that little voice. While you may think that speaking harshly to yourself can motivate you to more success, usually that kind of self-criticism is damaging and ineffective. One of the best ways to address this inner critic, and turn it into a powerful force to support your success, is the following tapping process.

We can use tapping to transform the "little voice" so that your affirmation sounds and *feels* true to you. This means that your mind, emotions, and energy will be in alignment with the affirmation, and that you'll accelerate the achievement of your results!

TAPPING TECHNIQUE: LITTLE VOICE TAPPING

(**Note:** Watch the DVD section on Little Voice Tapping for more information and examples.)

1. Close your eyes, and begin Continuous Tapping. Continue tapping through all eight points without stopping; you will keep tapping throughout the exercise. Focus on a single tapping point for each step; once you complete a step, move on to the next tapping point.

If you need to open your eyes to check these steps, that's fine. You can also have a friend read them to you one at a time.

2. Speak your affirmation aloud. Listen for that little voice in your head, and let it speak loudly—don't silence it. If you've

121

been trying to silence it for some time, this may take some quiet time and thought before you clearly hear it.

3. Identify what the voice is saying when you speak your affirmation. What are the words that it's using to disagree with your affirmation?

4. Then imagine—if those words were coming from a face, what would it look like? These are just some possibilities:

- Someone you know
- Someone you don't know
- A monster or other unpleasant fantasy image
- An animal
- An object, a shape, or a form

5. Visualize the face in front of you so that you can have a conversation with it. Don't worry if you can't see it clearly. Many people don't "see" visualizations; they just imagine them vaguely. That's fine. If you're more comfortable with the auditory modality, then you can work with the voice itself, without a face.

6. Tell the little voice (LV) that although you've not been listening in the past, you're now available to listen to what it has to say. Often just this step will change the tone and the words of that voice, since up until now it has been ignored for so long!

7. Ask it, "Why are you telling me this?" and then listen carefully to its response. Usually what the voice says is some variation on the theme of *I don't think that you can do this, and I don't want you to fail.* It may take some questioning to get to this point, and some dialogue back and forth with the little voice.

8. Consider what the voice is saying, and see if there is any way that it can be interpreted as either "I want you to be happy" or "I want to keep you safe." (Even voices of critical parents almost always have one of these messages behind them.) You may want to keep asking questions of the voice until you clarify one of these two messages, or something similar.

9. When you have one of these messages that indicates that the voice is actually trying to act in your best interest (although misguidedly), the next step is to *thank the voice* for its concern and caring. You don't have to thank it for its actions, only for the motivation behind them. This is a very important step. The voice represents a part of you that has been ignored and disempowered. By expressing gratitude, you're actually practicing self-acceptance, which is the first step to change.

Think of the voice as an employee who cannot be fired. Rather than ignoring this employee who has been sabotaging the operation, you can retrain him to work for you. Expressing gratitude improves employee morale so that the employee will listen to you and be willing to be retrained. Take particular notice of what happens when you thank the voice; the reaction is usually profound.

10. After expressing your gratitude, tell the voice that what you're looking for now is different, and ask if it might be willing to support you in a new way. This is very important. These voices usually won't go away, but they can be retrained. They are very powerful parts of you, and this step turns them from a liability into a serious asset!

11. You now want to explain to the voice that working with the new affirmation will lead to your happiness or to your safety. As you explain it, the reality of your new affirmation will become stronger for you as well! (See the following sample conversation for help with this.)

12. You may need to negotiate with the voice to come to an agreement on how it will support you. Requests work very well. For example, "Instead of what you've been saying, I'd like you to support me from now on by being a cheerleader whenever I say my affirmation. That way, I would never worry about failure, because I would always have you cheering me on. Would you be willing to take on this new role?"

13. When you have agreement from the voice, again offer your gratitude for its support. Ask if there is anything else it needs to tell you or hear from you at this point, and listen carefully until the conversation is complete.

14. Repeat your affirmation aloud, and listen for any new "Yeah, but . . ." You should hear only the positive support that your newly trained "assistant" is offering.

15. Some people find at the end of this exercise that the appearance of the face has changed. It may have changed from one person into another (such as from a monster into an angel), or changed color or form in some other way. You may even want to sketch this new face as a reminder of your "cheerleading squad."

16. When you say good-bye to your new friend, stop tapping and take a deep breath.

LITTLE VOICE TAPPING—SAMPLE CONVERSATION

You: I am enjoying the spectacular view from my beautiful 5,000-square-foot new home in the Rocky Mountains.

Little Voice: That's never going to happen!

You: Okay, I'm listening to you. Could we have a conversation about this?

[Listening to the voice, in your imagination it looks like your grandmother.]

LV: It's about time you listened to me.

You: You've been talking to me for quite a while, and I haven't listened. But today I'm listening—why do you say that my home in the Rockies will never happen?

LV: You don't have the money for something like that! And besides, you'd have to move and what would happen to your friends? If you say it and it doesn't happen, you'll just be disappointed.

You: I really appreciate that you don't want me to be disappointed. Why is that?

LV: If you get your hopes up and something doesn't happen, you'll feel terrible.

[You realize that your grandmother often said, "Don't get too excited in case it doesn't happen."]

You: So you're trying to keep me from feeling terrible?

LV: Yes, but you're not making it easy.

You: Thank you for that. I mean it. I'm grateful that you've been trying to keep me from feeling terrible all these years.

LV: Thank goodness you finally noticed.

You: I like to feel great, and it sounds like you're wanting me to feel that way, too.

LV: I don't know about great, but I don't want you disappointed.

You: I appreciate that. And one of the ways that I feel great now is by creating things in my life that I want very much. I do this by affirming and visualizing them, and feeling as though they actually are happening now. The thing is, when I do this, many of them start coming true! So I wonder: would you be willing to help me in a new way? You've been working so hard to help me before, and I have this important job that I need help with now—would you be open to helping me with that?

LV: What new way?

You: Sometimes things happen that seem as though my visualizations aren't coming true, or I get impatient with how long it's taking. Then, I admit, I'm tempted to get disappointed. What I really need is a cheerleader who will say to me, "Let's look at a way this could be a blessing. If you assume that the universe is conspiring in your favor, how could what is happening be a part of that?" That would be a huge help in keeping me from disappointment. So what do you think? Would you be willing to be a cheerleader, and help me look out for blessings to keep me from being disappointed?

LV: I think I could do that.

You: That would be great! I'm so grateful that you're willing to help me in this way. Is there anything else you want to tell me right now?

LV: No, but if I think of something, you can be sure I'll say it.

You: And since you're my cheerleader and blessing finder, I'll be very happy to hear it! Thank you for working with me in this way. I am enjoying the spectacular view from my beautiful 5,000-square-foot new home in the Rocky Mountains.

LV: That view looks good. Let's get going and figure out how to get there.

SEE WHAT YOU WANT, GET WHAT YOU SEE (SUCCESS PRINCIPLE 11)

Visualization is a success tool that is almost always under-utilized, considering its powerful effect on the subconscious. You can improve the effectiveness of your visualizations by using tapping to overcome resistance and doubts.

If you have some doubts about your ability to visualize, you can use a Specific Choice Statement to make yourself more comfortable with the process. Of course, if you don't believe you can visualize at all, that's a limiting belief and you may want to create a complete SOS Tapping exercise to transform it. If your intensity about the belief is moderate, try creating an exercise based on the suggestions below. If you feel comfortable visualizing, skip straight to the Visualization Tapping.

Here are some possible Specific Choice setup statements and some Reminder Phrases that you might use to create a tapping routine.

Specific Choice setup statements:

❖ *Even though I don't think I visualize well, I choose to allow myself to explore this process.*

❖ *Even though I don't know that I'm visualizing correctly, I choose to do my best and know that it will be fine.*

Reminder Phrases (negative round):

❖ *I don't think I visualize well.*

Reminder Phrases (positive round, Specific Choice Statement):

❖ *I choose to do my best and know that it will be fine.*

Alternating round:

❖ **Top of the Head:** *I don't think I visualize well.*

❖ **Eyebrow:** *I choose to do my best and know that it will be fine.*

❖ **Outside of Eye:** *I don't think I visualize well.*

❖ *Under the Eye:* I choose to do my best and know that it will be fine.

❖ *Under the Nose:* I don't think I visualize well.

❖ *Chin:* I choose to do my best and know that it will be fine.

❖ *Collarbone:* I don't think I visualize well.

❖ *Under the Arm:* I choose to do my best and know that it will be fine.

Repeat until you feel comfortable enough to try visualizing.

ACTION STEP: OVERCOMING LIMITING BELIEFS TO VISUALIZATION

If you don't believe that you can visualize, create a tapping exercise to overcome that limiting belief. Create Reminder Phrases based on your belief. Assess your TM level—how true does it feel on the truth meter? Create Open Choice and Specific Choice setup statements, and do as many rounds of tapping as necessary. Then assess your new TM level.

TAPPING TECHNIQUE: VISUALIZATION TAPPING

1. Close your eyes, and begin Continuous Tapping. Continue tapping through all eight points without stopping; you will keep tapping throughout the exercise. If you need to open your eyes to check these steps, that's fine.

2. Visualize the object, event, or goal that you intend to attract. Create every detail of it in your mind. What does it look like? What sounds will you hear? What will you feel physically? Are there tastes and smells associated with this?

3. As you visualize, you may find limiting beliefs coming up, such as *I could never have something like this* or *This is impossible.*

Keep tapping as you visualize, and let the thoughts go through your mind. Don't try to silence them. As you tap, you're actually working on clearing those limiting beliefs.

4. Add feelings to your visualization. This is the most important part of your visualization, which is one reason that it's okay to just "think" your visualizations if you can't "see" them. How will you feel when you acquire that object or achieve that goal? Will you feel calm, excited, or proud? Will you feel happy, joyful, or grateful? Allow yourself to feel those positive feelings through at least one entire tapping round.

5. When you end the visualization, take a moment to see if there are any remaining limiting beliefs about the visualization. You can just continue visualizing every day while you tap. After a few days, the limiting beliefs will often vanish. If they are still there, you can work on these limiting beliefs using any of the different tapping methods that we've explored so far.

For an example of a great use of Visualization Tapping, read the following success story about Tom.

SUCCESS STORY

Tom, an amateur musician, was going to play his first public performance at a retirement home. He was very nervous about doing this, so he decided to use Visualization Tapping. He began tapping and imagined what would happen during that evening.

First he saw himself arriving at the location, which he was already familiar with. He saw himself getting his guitar out, tuning it, and preparing to play. Up to this point, he hadn't felt very nervous. Once he imagined beginning to play, he saw himself making mistakes and getting flustered. He continued to tap for a few minutes on the upsetting image of himself getting flustered, until he felt calm.

Tom then backed up the visualization, and saw himself making mistakes but handling them with ease so no one else listening knew that they had occurred. He saw the audience being attentive and appreciative. He imagined completing his set, and being complimented by the activities director on the music he had provided. He imagined that his two adult daughters attended the performance and were proud of him.

Tom repeated the Visualization Tapping about 20 times before the actual event. Sometimes he visualized himself playing perfectly, and sometimes he visualized himself making mistakes but handling them in a professional manner, until he was equally comfortable with either visualization.

Tom reported that he was quite calm and relaxed at his first public performance, and that he played as well as he did at home—quite a feat for an amateur musician! His daughters did attend, and were proud and impressed with their father's skills.

ACTION STEP: VISUALIZATION TAPPING

Think of an upcoming event that you have concerns or a fear about. What is your SUDS level for the event? Go through the Visualization Tapping Technique, and reassess your SUDS level after. Were you able to get to a SUDS level of 0? How many different times did you visualize while tapping? Did anything unexpected happen?

BE WILLING TO PAY THE PRICE (SUCCESS PRINCIPLE 16)

To become a master at a sport, art, or business takes time and dedication. Too many adults have a dream of mastering a sport or musical instrument, or of turning their passion into a business, but give up because the path seems too hard, takes too long, or they simply don't feel capable enough.

You can make your own choices about what's important to you. If you don't choose to pursue a dream because the price is not one you're willing to pay, that's a choice. Since you take 100% responsibility for your life, you can make those choices.

Yet what if you'd like to pursue a dream, but simply have fears and limiting beliefs about whether or not you're capable? That's where tapping can come in.

In the book *Mastery* by George Leonard, he sets forth expectations and steps to take to achieve mastery in any endeavor. One of the characteristics of the path to mastery, according to Leonard, is that you experience plateaus, which are long periods of seemingly no improvement. Then you have a brief burst of improvement, followed by another plateau. During a plateau, Leonard advises that you enjoy the process and the constant practice of your craft, knowing that another burst of improvement will eventually happen.

You could just try living with the frustration of making seemingly slow progress. However, that frustration can keep you from progressing if you fall into beliefs such as *It's taking too long, This is too hard,* or *I'll never learn this.* You may not take the actions you need to take, or sabotage yourself so that it becomes easier to quit. These beliefs and frustrations may even have you give up on your goal altogether!

Tapping can enable you to "pay the price" with far more patience and enjoyment. After all, why not enjoy the journey to your goals and dreams?

You can use George Leonard's concepts to create powerful reframes and positive Specific Choice setup statements. Do any of the following resonate with you?

- ❖ *Even though I'm frustrated by how I'm progressing, I choose to enjoy the process of learning.*

- ❖ *Even though I'm afraid I'll never be good enough at this, I choose to consider that mastery does come with consistent practice.*

❖ *Even though I feel embarrassed that I'm not better at this, I choose to accept myself where I am right now, and know that I'm always improving, even if I can't see it yet.*

EXERCISE: ENJOYING THE JOURNEY

Identify an area in life in which you're pursuing mastery, whether it's the practice of a sport, study of a musical instrument, or the creation of a business. Complete the following statement: *I completely enjoy the journey of . . .*

What is your truth meter (TM) level after saying this affirmation? Note that there may be things that you enjoy on this journey as well as parts that you do not enjoy as much. You may need to create separate statements to carefully identify what it is that you don't enjoy.

Complete the following statement: *While pursuing my goal of _____, one frustration* [or substitute another emotion] *I have is . . .*

What is your SUDS level after completing the above statement? Now you can begin SOS Tapping.

For a SUDS level of 8 or above, create a Reminder Phrase and do a round of Simple Tapping. Once your emotion has reduced in intensity, move on to the next step. For a SUDS level of 6 or 7, create an Open Choice setup statement, and use the Choices Trio Method: tap one negative round with your Reminder Phrase, tap a positive round with your Open Choice Statement, then tap an alternating round. Then reassess your SUDS level. If it has reduced to 5 or less, move on to the next step.

For a SUDS level of 5 or less, create a Specific Choice setup statement. Then use the Choices Trio Method. Then reassess your SUDS level.

Finally, repeat your affirmation: *I completely enjoy the journey of . . .*

What is your TM level now?

ACTION STEP: REFLECTING ON YOUR JOURNEY

Write down any notes you have after doing the SOS Tapping exercise "Enjoying the Journey." Mark a date 30 days from now on your calendar. On that date, consider the following questions:

- *In what way has my enjoyment of this pursuit increased?*

- *Am I getting better results as a result of my new enjoyment? What are they?*

- *Is there something else that I need to do in order to get even better results?*

TAKE ACTION (SUCCESS PRINCIPLE 13)

One big difference between successful and unsuccessful people is that successful people consistently take action. Interestingly, successful people usually have more failure than unsuccessful people . . . but they also have more success. This is because they take action—even if they are afraid, unsure, and don't have all the information they'd like.

You can use tapping to decrease fear and increase your confidence, so taking action becomes much easier. What actions do you want or need to take that you haven't yet taken? Perhaps you've wanted to . . .

- Start a new hobby
- Find a new job
- Finish (or start) a book
- Date a new person
- Create or expand your business

What is keeping you from taking action? Consider the following examples:

- *It's not perfect.*

- *I don't know enough.*

- *I'm not good enough yet.*

- *It's too risky.*

- *No one has asked me to.*

- *I have to take care of something else first.*

Make a list of the actions you need to take to achieve your dreams. Then fill in the blanks in the following sentence:

I haven't taken action because [the reason], *and that means that if I took action now what would happen is* [what you fear].

What you have put in the second blank is your Reminder Phrase. The intensity of the fear that you feel is your SUDS level.

Now you can begin crafting your own tapping exercises to specifically target your challenges! Here are examples of how you might begin:

- *I haven't taken action on creating a website because I'm afraid it won't be good enough, and that means that if I took action now, what would happen is people would criticize me.*

- *I haven't taken action on starting a business because I don't have time, and that means that if I took action now, what would happen is my children would suffer.*

- *I haven't taken action on finding a new job because I'm afraid I'll find one, and that means that if I took action now, what would happen is I might have to relocate, and that would be hard.*

Your Reminder Phrases would be:

- ❖ *People would criticize me.*

- ❖ *My children would suffer.*

- ❖ *I might have to relocate, and that would be hard.*

You could use Simple Tapping immediately to start working on those fears. The real power comes, though, when you create a new belief or interpretation. Let's create empowering reframes for these examples that we can use in Choices Statements.

CREATING EMPOWERING REFRAMES

Since we introduced the concept of reframes in this work, we've been creating new reframes for each challenge. These are empowering new beliefs to counteract the limiting beliefs and negative emotions that keep you from achieving success.

If you can create empowering reframes, you'll have one of the most powerful tools available to help you overcome both internal and external obstacles. And you can use the reframes to craft your tapping phrases, so that they have maximum effectiveness.

How do you create a reframe? Here are just a few ways that we'll explore how to:

1. Turn a neutral belief from negative to positive by changing the underlying assumptions

2. Challenge a limiting belief

3. Be open to the opposite

4. Ask powerful questions, such as "What if I . . ." and "How could I . . ."

5. Create a different scenario

6. Use humor and exaggeration

Whenever you encounter a belief you have that doesn't serve you, you have the chance to create a reframe. Tapping simply helps the reframes stick, making it easier for you to believe them by removing fears and other negative emotions around those beliefs, and by opening your subconscious to new ideas.

You can get reframes from many sources. Reading books, magazines, and articles about self-improvement can often give you powerful reframes. However, you may read these and think *It would be nice to feel that way—if only I could believe it!* Tapping can help you incorporate reframes into your belief system.

As we continue to examine resistance to implementing the success principles, you'll get the opportunity to create your own reframes for overcoming your resistance. In fact, the ability to create your own reframes is a crucial component to being able to tap effectively. Fortunately, not only does tapping help reframes take hold, it also helps you create them.

Let's start by looking at the first couple of options.

Option 1—turn a neutral belief from a negative interpretation to a positive one. Let's examine the first example, *People will criticize me.* This is a neutral belief, depending on whether or not you fear criticism. If you didn't fear criticism, how else might you interpret this statement? What supporting beliefs could you put underneath it?

- *People will criticize me, and it will be good to have feedback so I can improve.*

- *People will criticize me, and I can't please everyone.*

We can use these to create Choice Statements:

- ❖ *Even though I'm afraid people will criticize me, I choose to be grateful for any feedback.*

- ❖ *Even though I'm afraid people will criticize me, I choose to know that I can't please everyone.*

Option 2—challenge a limiting belief. But what about the second example? *My children will suffer* is not a neutral belief, it's a limiting belief. Let's start by questioning the belief itself. One question to ask is from The Work of Byron Katie[8]: *Can you be absolutely sure that is true?*

Perhaps, when you start a business, you may become busier and have less time for your children. However, this doesn't necessarily mean that they will suffer. Other possibilities include:

- Your children benefit, since although you spend less time with them, it is of higher quality.

- Your children get to spend time with your spouse or other caregivers, and this enhances their social skills and adaptability.

- Your children learn the value of passionately pursuing one's dream.

You can create Specific Choice or Open Choice setup statements using these ideas, such as:

❖ *Even though I'm worried my children will suffer if I start a business, I'm open to the idea that this might actually benefit them.*

❖ *Even though I'm afraid my children will suffer if I start a business, I choose to consider that it will benefit them when I model how to pursue your dreams.*

Remember, it can be challenging when you're in the grip of a strong fear to see any reframes at all. That's why we use Simple Tapping and Open Choices to reduce emotional intensity; then you can begin the work to come up with new ideas.

UNLEASH THE POWER OF GOAL SETTING (SUCCESS PRINCIPLE 7)

Most people on a path to success know the power of setting goals. Yet we resist setting them. Or we keep them vague and undefined, which means that they aren't really goals, just good ideas.

Resistance to setting goals usually comes from one of two concerns: (1) *I'm afraid to set a goal that I can't reach; if I don't reach it, I'll feel like a failure* or (2) *I'm afraid if I set a goal I'll feel trapped. What if it's in conflict with my inner guidance?*

We've already discussed fear of failure, but let's revisit it in this new discussion.

To do this, we first need to establish *why* you want to set goals. Setting goals gives you the following:

- A focus for what you do, and a way to measure your success.

- A strong message to your subconscious mind of what you want it to work on.

- A strong message to the Universe about what you intend, so you can receive support.

Most important, in working toward your goals, you become the person who can achieve those things, even if you don't completely reach your goal.

Instead of looking at a goal as an indicator of your worthiness, look at it as a game—then play that game full-out, with everything you've got. When you believe that your worthiness is determined by whether you achieve your goal or not, you'll be too fearful to work effectively. And besides, it's not true!

Which of these ideas (which double as setup statements) would make the most powerful reframe for *you?*

- ❖ *Even though I'm afraid of setting this goal, I choose to let the Universe know my clear intention.*

- ❖ *Even though I'm afraid of setting this goal, I choose to enjoy who I'll become as I pursue it.*

- ❖ *Even though I'm afraid of setting this goal, I choose to accept myself whether or not I complete my goal.*

Option 3—be open to the opposite. What if you're afraid of being trapped by your goals, or afraid that your inner guidance will conflict with your goal? Let's take the first idea—being trapped by your goals—and turn it around completely. If you feel trapped, the opposite would be feeling more freedom. This is a great technique to use with an Open Choice Statement.

Consider the following statement:

❖ *Even though I'm afraid of being trapped by my goal, I'm open to the idea that it could actually create more freedom.*

You don't have to know how this could be true to use this tapping statement. You could just tap and see what occurs to you. Often, as you tap with an Open Choice, new ideas will occur to you that you weren't aware of before.

What if, instead of being trapped, your goals actually created greater freedom for you? How could that be possible? Perhaps, when you set your goals, you'll realize some things that you need to let go of in order to achieve those goals. Perhaps you'll be able to focus better than you did before, and eliminate distractions from your life. Both situations could create greater freedom for you.

Option 4—ask powerful questions. In addition to the Open Choice that creates the opposite of the belief that is stopping you, there are two other questions that you can use in tapping that can transform you from stuck to successful: *What if I . . . ?* and *How could I . . . ?*

For example:

• *What if I could create more freedom by setting goals?*

• *How could I create more freedom by setting goals?*

As soon as you ask these questions, your subconscious mind goes to work to answer them. New ideas and possibilities occur to you. You can use these as part of a Choice setup statement, or you can use them as part of your Reminder Phrases. For example:

❖ *Even though I feel trapped by setting this goal, what if I could create more freedom by setting goals?*

❖ *Even though I feel trapped by setting this goal, how could I create more freedom by setting goals?*

Then tap one round using negative Reminder Phrases such as:

❖ *I feel trapped by setting this goal.*

For the second round, use one or more of the following Choice Statements as positive Reminder Phrases:

❖ *I'm open to creating more freedom.*

❖ *What if I could create more freedom by setting this goal?*

❖ *How could I create more freedom?*

For the third round, alternate negative and positive phrases, remembering to end on a positive one. For example:

❖ *I feel trapped by setting this goal.*

❖ *What if I could create more freedom by setting this goal?*

❖ *I feel trapped by setting this goal.*

❖ *I'm open to creating more freedom.*

❖ *I feel trapped by setting this goal.*

❖ *How could I create more freedom?*

❖ *I feel trapped by setting this goal.*

❖ *What if I could create more freedom by setting this goal?*

Option 5—create a different scenario. Another way to overcome this fear of being trapped is to dig down underneath it, and bring up the more powerful fear that's driving it. Ask yourself, "What would it mean that I was trapped by my goals?"

Perhaps you believe that it would mean *I'd be doing something I hated for months or years* or *I'd pursue my goals to the detriment of my health.*

Now that those deeper fears are illuminated, you can tap to decrease the fear, and create completely different scenarios for the future. Some people at this point will ask, "Why do you need tapping? It's ridiculous that someone would pursue their goals to the detriment of their health. That's a silly fear, and you don't need tapping to undo it."

However, everyone is different. Some people have pursued goals to the detriment of their health (or they've seen someone close to them do this). Thus, for them, that is a real possibility and so a real fear. That fear might keep someone like that from setting any goal in the future.

When you remove the fear, you can envision and create a new scenario. You can also use this idea to remove the fear that your inner guidance will conflict with your goal. What new scenario can you create that doesn't have your inner guidance conflict with your goals? We'll use these concepts for creating empowering reframes in upcoming sections, as you begin to craft more and more of your own tapping exercises.

ASK, ASK, ASK
(SUCCESS PRINCIPLE 17)

One of the most challenging things for some people on the path to success is to ask for what they need. In *The Success Principles,* it states: "Take the risk to ask for what you need and want. If they say no, you are no worse off than when you started." However, if you're fearful, you won't believe that statement.

If you get a no, you may believe that you will feel humiliated, embarrassed, rejected, or depressed. So not only do you have the no, you have these negative emotions also. It makes sense that you might be unwilling to take the risk unless you can get rid of the fear by changing your belief about the outcome.

Also, some people are afraid to ask, because as long as they haven't asked, there is still some hope that it might be a yes. These people would rather not ask, and live in uncertainty and hope, than ask and get an answer. Unfortunately, there are negative consequences to this approach. Because you want or need something that you're not getting, you aren't moving as fast as you could be toward your goals. There is also energy that is wasted in wondering about the answer, and fearing a no.

Now let's discuss the final option we mentioned earlier for creating a reframe.

Option 6—use humor and exaggeration. Feeling humiliated, embarrassed, or rejected is a choice. You can make a different one.

Ask yourself this question: *What's the worst that could happen if I asked for what I wanted?*

Jot down your answers. Some of them may be reasonable, and some may be fearful exaggerations, such as *I'll be so embarrassed I'll have to go live in a cave,* or *She'll never speak to me again.* We can use the exaggerations to have some fun with tapping.

TAPPING TIP: USING HUMOR AND EXAGGERATION IN TAPPING

As with our previous exercises, if the intensity of your fear is above a 5 use Simple Tapping and Open Choices to decrease the intensity before proceeding. Humor doesn't work very well when you're terrified!

When your fear is at a 5 or below, create some exaggerations about what you fear will happen in the situation, such as:

- *The entire town will give me the silent treatment.*

- *I'll have to go live in a cave.*

- *My asking will endanger civilization as we know it.*

- *I'll break out in a rash and turn bright red.*

Then create a setup statement using the exaggeration with the Original EFT Affirmation or a Specific Choice Statement. For example:

- ❖ *Even though if I ask for this it will endanger civilization as we know it, I deeply and completely love and accept myself anyway.*

- ❖ *Even though I know if I make this request I'll break out in a rash and turn bright red, I choose to accept myself anyway.*

Tap through the points, using your exaggeration as a Reminder Phrase. Exaggerating your voice and facial expressions will help this sink in as well. Your fear will disappear or become amusing to you, and won't stop you anymore.

One of the elements of "Ask, Ask, Ask" is that you often have to ask more than once. This can be very uncomfortable for some people, who believe that "No means no," and there is no point in asking a second time. However, circumstances change and people change their minds—so asking at a different time, on a different day, with different information, can change the outcome.

An Open Choice can be very useful in this situation to build confidence:

❖ *Even though I got a no before, and I'm afraid I will again, I'm open to a compelling new way to make my request.*

❖ *Even though I'm afraid she'll say no again, I'm open to a surprisingly creative way to have this conversation.*

❖ *Even though I'm afraid of getting a no, I'm open to this conversation being powerful and beneficial for both of us.*

Removing your fears of asking over and over for what you want will make a profound difference in your success. Although it is possible to ask for what you want even when you're afraid, if you ask from a place of fear, you're more likely to get turned down. Remember, you tend to attract what you expect. You're also more likely to create excuses that result in putting off asking, and sabotage yourself. You may also ask in a subtly hostile or resentful way, or a way that otherwise lacks power. If you feel scared and powerless while you're asking, it makes it less likely that you'll get a yes.

The techniques for this success principle will also work with resistance to Success Principle 44: Find a Wing to Climb Under; and Success Principle 46: Mastermind Your Way to Success. Most of the fear and limiting beliefs about these success principles have to do with asking and rejection.

The following story is an example of using a powerful reframe and humor in tapping.

SUCCESS STORY

Edie, a fairly successful consultant, wanted to increase her business and income. However, she was very uncomfortable with the idea of earning more money because she believed she would have to work very hard to reach her goal of $500,000. She wasn't even sure she was capable of working that hard.

Her belief that she would have to work very hard was at a 10 on the truth meter (TM) scale, so we began with an Open Choice. Notice that we can introduce an Open Choice even with a level 10 intensity because it's a *belief*, not a fear. We're using the TM, not the SUDS, level.

Setup statement:

❖ *Even though I don't know that I can work hard enough to earn $500,000, I'm open to a new way to look at this.*

Negative Reminder Phrases:

❖ *I'll have to work too hard.*

❖ *I don't even know that it's possible to make that much money.*

❖ *That's so much more than I make now.*

❖ *How much harder can I actually work?*

❖ *I don't think I can work that hard.*

Positive Reminder Phrases:

❖ *I'm open to a new idea.*

❖ *I'm ready for a new possibility.*

❖ *What if I didn't have to work that hard?*

❖ *What if I could figure out a way to make more money with less work?*

We then transitioned into Specific Choice Statements without an additional setup statement:

- ❖ *I could probably make that much money if I structured things differently.*
- ❖ *I choose to make $500,000 this year.*

Edie said that she now felt it might be possible to make that much money, but that it would be morally wrong to make that much money for consulting, because it was so easy for her. Again we started with an Open Choice setup statement:

- ❖ *Even though it's not right for me to be so well paid for what is so easy for me, I'm open to a new idea.*
- ❖ *Even though it's wrong for me to take so much money for what I love to do, I'm ready for a new perspective.*

Her negative and positive Reminder Phrases were:

- ❖ *I can't take that much for consulting.*
- ❖ *I love to do it.*
- ❖ *It's so easy for me.*
- ❖ *Isn't it wrong to get paid so much for what I'm so good at?*
- ❖ *Actually, it would definitely be wrong to be paid well for something I'm not good at.*
- ❖ *So is it okay for me to be paid well for what I'm good at?*
- ❖ *My abilities are a gift from God.*
- ❖ *But I shouldn't profit from God's gifts to me.*
- ❖ *I know I should use God's gifts, I just shouldn't profit from them.*
- ❖ *I do believe that God wants me to be wealthy.*

(Note the use of slightly sarcastic humor coming up.)

❖ *I'll just have to get my wealth in some other way than my gifts.*

❖ *It's okay for me to win the lottery or receive some other windfall.*

❖ *The only way it's not okay for me to receive money is for my gifts.*

❖ *Sorry, God, You'll have to find some other way to shower me with abundance.*

❖ *I don't want to receive abundance through my gifts.*

❖ *Why would I make it that hard for the Universe to give me abundance?*

❖ *Why couldn't I take it through my gifts?*

❖ *I'm open to receiving abundance and money for the expression of my gifts and talents.*

❖ *I choose to be well paid for what I do well.*

❖ *In fact, I'm open to the possibility that I should be paid best for what is my genius.*

❖ *What if I should be paid the best for what is the easiest for me?*

❖ *This is what I'm the best at.*

❖ *That's totally different.*

❖ *I like the idea of using my gifts.*

❖ *I like the idea of being showered with abundance through my gifts.*

❖ *I choose to be well paid for my best gifts.*

❖ *I choose to receive $500,000 this year for my gifts.*

After this tapping routine, Edie was very enthusiastic about implementing her new business plan, and had no qualms about receiving that much income without working much harder.

EXERCISE: ASKING FOR WHAT YOU WANT

Try this SOS Tapping exercise for asking for what you want: What's one thing that you need to ask for that would significantly improve your life? What do you fear will happen if you ask for it? There may be more than one of these fears. (These are your Reminder Phrases.)

Assess your SUDS level for each fear. If the SUDS level is 8 or more, do Simple Tapping to reduce the intensity before attempting any reframes.

When your SUDS level is at a 7 or below, introduce an Open Choice and create your setup statement: *Even though I ____, I'm open to . . .*

Tap a Choices Trio (negative round, positive round, alternating round). Then reassess your SUDS level. Repeat as necessary.

When your intensity is a 5 or below, you can create your Specific Choice setup statement. What humorous situation could you come up with regarding asking for what you want? Remember the format is: *Even though I'm still a little afraid of asking because* [your humorous exaggeration], *I choose . . .*

Tap a Choices Trio (negative round, positive round, alternating round). Then reassess your SUDS level.

If your intensity is a 0, congratulations! (If it's not yet a 0, continue tapping with Specific Choices until it is.)

REJECT REJECTION (SUCCESS PRINCIPLE 18)

The reason that people fear rejection isn't being told no as much as what they make it mean. If you ask for, apply to, or submit something and get rejected, what does that mean to you? Some common answers are:

- *I wasn't good enough.*

- *I'm not a good* [writer, actress, student, employee, etc.].

- *My* [book, idea, project, looks, mind] *isn't good enough.*

- *They didn't want me.*

- *I'm not worthy, lovable, capable, etc.*

Getting new information is one aid to creating reframes. In *The Success Principles,* there are many stories about famous people whose work was rejected many times before it sold, was published, or became well known. Many inventions that we now take for granted, such as telephones and personal computers, were initially rejected by others as having no value.

Given that information, what reframes could you create to counteract the rejection?

- ❖ *Even though they didn't want me, I'm still a good ___.*

- ❖ *Even though that person rejected me, there are still many more I can ask.*

- ❖ *Even though I was rejected, I choose to say "Next!"*

- ❖ *Even though I feel hurt, I choose to learn from this experience in a way that empowers me.*

Some people take rejection as an indicator that they are no good at something, or not good enough. Remember the fixed and the growth mindsets? The problem with this belief of "no good" comes when you don't believe that you have the ability to get any better. For example, *I know I'm not a good cook, and I don't believe that I can get better with practice.*

If you don't believe that you can get better than you currently are, the thing to work on is developing a growth mindset. Before you can deal with problems around rejection, you'll need to believe that you can always improve, always grow in whatever skill or area you desire. For example, *I know I'm not a good cook, and I believe that I can get better with practice.*

The reframes are literally limitless. Have fun creating your own reframes to counter rejection. How many can you create?

EXCEED EXPECTATIONS
(SUCCESS PRINCIPLE 24)

When you exceed people's expectations, they notice. When you go the extra mile, you stand out as extraordinary. So why wouldn't you do this?

One way to see what's beneath a reluctance to exceed expectations is to ask yourself, *What would happen if I exceeded expectations?*

Your answer might be:

- *I'd have to work too hard.*

- *I wouldn't be appreciated.*

- *I'd be taken advantage of.*

You'll then want to look beneath those beliefs for the emotion, and the story, that accompanies them.

For example, *I'd have to work too hard* is usually accompanied by the emotion of fear, and a belief that you would lose too much free time or time with your family. Do you remember that one way to craft a reframe is to claim the complete opposite? This is a great time to use that idea:

❖ *Even though I don't want to exceed expectations because I'm afraid I'll have to work too hard and lose free time, I choose to consider that I could have as much or more free time.*

The thought *I'd be taken advantage of* usually has a belief behind it, such as *People will always take advantage of you if you let them,* or *People always take advantage of me.* Once you work to change those beliefs, the fear of being taken advantage of will fade. Also, you will no longer attract people to you who do that!

If you have these limiting beliefs, they will keep you doing the minimum for your boss, your co-workers, your spouse and family, your employees, your customers and clients . . . and it will cost you money, relationships, career advancement, and success.

Once you've worked on these fears and limiting beliefs, one of the ways to implement this success principle is to create an identity for yourself as someone who always exceeds people's expectations. You can create this identity with an affirmation such as *I always exceed expectations* or *I am committed to exceeding expectations.*

TAPPING TECHNIQUE: FIRM STAND TAPPING

This tapping technique uses a positive affirmation, such as *I choose to exceed expectations,* combined with the fears or limiting beliefs that keep you from believing and living that affirmation. (**Note:** Watch the DVD section with Firm Stand Tapping for more information.)

So far in tapping we have not used positive Specific Choice Statements until the SUDS level has decreased to a level 5 or below. In Firm Stand Tapping, however, we'll state a positive affirmation as a way to trigger disagreement, similar to the way we triggered disagreement in Little Voice Tapping.

Begin with Simple Tapping or Continuous Tapping:

- ❖ **Top of the Head:** *State your positive affirmation. It will probably feel unreal and uncomfortable, and like a lie.*

- ❖ **Eyebrow:** *State your fear or limiting belief.*

- ❖ **Outside of Eye:** *State your positive affirmation.*

- ❖ **Under the Eye:** *State your fear or limiting belief again. (You can change this statement each time, or use the same one. Over time, the statement that you use will shift as your emotions shift.)*

- ❖ **Under the Nose:** *State your positive affirmation. (This never changes.)*

- ❖ **Chin:** *State your fear or limiting belief.*

- ❖ **Collarbone:.** *State your positive affirmation.*

- ❖ **Under the Arm:** *State your fear or limiting belief.*

Keep repeating this until the unreal and uncomfortable feeling disappears from your affirmation. This can take a number of rounds. The affirmation should slowly begin to feel more believable and more likely to be realized. You want to keep tapping until you believe the affirmation 100%.

Firm Stand Tapping can be used as a stand-alone technique, but it's also great for getting out all the aspects of an issue. In other words, as you keep affirming what you want to believe, the rest of your fears and limiting beliefs will all come up. You can take note of them while you're tapping, then continue Firm Stand Tapping on *those* fears and beliefs, or use a different technique such as SOS Tapping or Little Voice Tapping to finish clearing them.

Here's an example of a Firm Stand Tapping sequence:

- ❖ *I choose to exceed expectations.*
- ❖ *It's too much work.*
- ❖ *I choose to exceed expectations.*
- ❖ *I don't have enough time as it is.*
- ❖ *I choose to exceed expectations.*
- ❖ *People won't appreciate it if I do.*
- ❖ *I choose to exceed expectations.*
- ❖ *No one notices when I go the extra mile.*
- ❖ *I choose to exceed expectations.*
- ❖ *Well, some people do.*
- ❖ *I choose to exceed expectations.*
- ❖ *But some people don't.*
- ❖ *I choose to exceed expectations.*
- ❖ *Why should I exceed expectations?*
- ❖ *I choose to exceed expectations.*
- ❖ *I'd like to be appreciated for my work.*
- ❖ *I choose to exceed expectations.*
- ❖ *No one's going to appreciate me if I <u>don't</u> exceed expectations.*
- ❖ *I choose to exceed expectations.*

❖ *I suppose I could try it.*

❖ *I choose to exceed expectations.*

❖ *I'm still not sure it will work out.*

❖ *I choose to exceed expectations.*

❖ *It would be nice to be appreciated.*

❖ *I choose to exceed expectations.*

❖ *What if I could be appreciated?*

❖ *I choose to exceed expectations.*

❖ *What if my hard work paid off?*

❖ *I choose to exceed expectations.*

❖ *That would be nice.*

❖ *I choose to exceed expectations.*

❖ *I'm open to my hard work paying off.*

❖ *I choose to exceed expectations.*

❖ *Okay, I'm ready to step into this.*

❖ *I choose to exceed expectations.*

CHAPTER CHECKLIST:

I know what a reframe is.

I know six different ways to create empowering reframes.

I understand how to do Continuous Tapping.

I know what the truth meter and TM level are.

I've done a Little Voice Tapping Exercise.

I've done a Visualization Tapping Exercise.

I've completed the SOS Tapping exercises "Enjoying the Journey" and "Asking for What You Want."

I know how humor and exaggeration can be used in tapping.

◎   ◎   ◎

6

HEALING THE PAST: REMOVING THE TRIGGERS THAT SLOW YOUR SUCCESS

TRANSCEND YOUR LIMITING BELIEFS (SUCCESS PRINCIPLE 33)

We've been discussing how to use tapping to overcome limiting beliefs throughout this section of the book. In *The Success Principles,* it was suggested that to turn around a limiting belief, you use a four-step process: (1) identify a belief that limits you; (2) describe how it limits you; (3) decide how you would like to be instead; and then (4) create a statement that affirms that new belief, repeating it for 30 days to install it.

We can use tapping to speed up the process of transcending our limiting beliefs. Rather than taking 30 days to continuously affirm the new belief, hoping that we don't forget a day or two, we can speed up the process by using tapping to first reduce the emotions that are causing the limitation.

We all believe what we believe for a number of reasons. It's usually a combination of the following:

- We were programmed to do so at a young age.

- We've had experiences that provide evidence for the belief.

- We've been continually told what to believe.

- We have subconscious reasons to hold our belief, such as *It will keep me safe* or *It will help me be loved.*

Consider what limiting beliefs you might have. For example:

- *I am stupid, incapable, or a failure.*

- *No one wants to help me.*

- *It's not okay to focus on my needs.*

- *What I think is not important.*

In order to change a belief such as these, it's usually not effective to tap something with a Reminder Phrase like:

❖ *Even though I am stupid and incapable . . .*

This belief is made up of many supporting beliefs, and events that give us "evidence" that it's true. When that belief has been triggered or reinforced, it continues to grow. To turn it around, you'll need to dismantle the events that have convinced you of this belief.

Ask yourself the question: *What recent event had me feeling stupid and incapable?*

Is there another interpretation that you can make for the event? If so, tap to remove that belief for that particular event. You can use this setup statement, for example:

❖ *Even though I feel stupid and incapable because I botched the task at work, I choose to consider that everyone makes mistakes.*

However, even if you clear any guilt or shame about that event, you may still be left with that belief. Further questions you can ask are: *When did I make the decision that I was stupid and incapable?* and *When do I remember feeling stupid and incapable early in my life?*

Beliefs like this don't come out of nowhere. They are usually the result of childhood situations that caused you to make decisions about yourself and about the world. These childhood experiences got stuck in your subconscious, and now your subconscious is feeding you these beliefs as though they were reality. You can change the messages from your subconscious, but first you have to become aware of them.

SUCCESS STORY

This is a great example of clearing the emotional charge around a limiting belief that was created from a specific event. Gwen was working on taking 100% responsibility for her life, and trying to clear her limiting beliefs with tapping. This is her story.

After several sessions of tapping I realized that the message I was getting was, Tapping isn't going to work. I'm stuck and I'm a victim of these messages. They are so deeply programmed I'll never get past them. Whoa! That was a big "Aha!" that I wasn't taking 100% responsibility for myself. This stuff never ceases to surprise and amaze me!
So I began tapping:

❖ *Even though I feel stuck and I know that tapping won't work on this one, I'm open to seeing a new way of looking at it.*

❖ *Even though I know I'm stuck—and no matter what I do with tapping I'll stay stuck in this*

155

one—I'm willing to see it from a brand new perspective.

❖ *Even though I don't know how I could possibly see the messages "I don't know" and "I have no idea" from a different perspective I'm open to the idea that it is possible.*

I did an extra setup statement just for good measure:

❖ *Even though I feel like I'm a victim of these messages and I can't see how I can take 100% responsibility for them, I'm open to accepting responsibility and learning from the experience.*

Presto! That triggered something, and I was in tears . . .

I continued with the Reminder Phrases:

❖ *I'm not responsible for this.*

❖ *What if I am responsible for this?*

❖ *I'm open to accepting responsibility for this.*

❖ *What can I learn from considering that I am responsible?*

❖ *What does it mean that I accept responsibility for this?*

❖ *I feel stuck in this one and the tapping won't get me out of it.*

❖ *I need help, but I can't ask for help because I'm a bother.*

Then I asked, If I could wave a magic wand over myself, what would I love to create in this situation?

Instantly I recalled a memory of my mom spanking me with a wooden paddle that had a picture of a deer and a bear on it with the words, <u>A cute little dear with a bare be-hind.</u> When I asked her what I did wrong, she would reply, "I'm not going to tell you! If you don't know, you'd better figure it out!"

Well, I'm 52, and guess what I've been doing most of my life? Trying to "figure it out"! Reading, taking classes, listening to CDs in the car . . . searching and searching. The problem is that I don't know what "it" is. This is a very old wound I've attended to hundreds of times via counseling and the like; but I've never seen it in this way before.

My message was that if I don't "figure it out" or have the answer, then I'm "stupid"! Again I found myself in tears. So I did a reframe: "I'm smart, strong, and capable; and I know about a lot of things. And the answers to the things I don't know, I know how to find."

I put the reframe into Reminder Phrases, then tapped on the fear that I'm stupid, along with the positive choice that I'm smart, strong, and capable.

I feel like a completely <u>new</u> woman this morning.

HOW CHILDHOOD TRAUMA SABOTAGES US AS ADULTS

Although we tend to think of dramatic and newsworthy events such as car accidents, natural disasters, or violent crime as traumatic events, ordinary day-to-day events can create the same trauma symptoms in our bodies and minds. For children, these "everyday traumas" might include being spoken to harshly by a teacher, being teased or laughed at on the playground, or being carelessly told by a relative that they are stupid, lazy, or worthless. For adults, these can include finding out about a partner's infidelity or experiencing a sudden financial loss.

Cutting-edge neuroscience is discovering new information about the way we handle trauma, including these everyday traumas. According to Robert Scaer, M.D., author of *The Body Bears the Burden,* when an event is perceived by the brain as traumatic, all the sensory data is immediately downloaded into our subconscious mind. In a sense, the information is "frozen" there, while the body goes into flight, fight, or freeze mode. In animals, there is a "discharge response" that allows the frozen data to be removed from the system. In humans, we don't usually experience or allow the discharge response.

One way that humans may discharge the freeze response is by shivering or shaking. Since this is usually seen as a bad thing, the response may be suppressed or discouraged, and the frozen traumatic response remains. Some cultures have movement rituals that allow traumatic responses to be discharged, but Western culture has no such rituals. While we may feel numb and dissociated from the trauma on one level, on another level it is being constantly replayed within us.

When our subconscious perceives something that reminds us of the trauma, we say that the trauma is "retriggered." There are two problems with this retriggering response:

1. The situation that is triggering us may not actually have any relation to the original trauma. For example, if you were verbally abused as a child, hearing someone yelling angrily may retrigger you, even if that person isn't yelling *at* you.

2. Studies show that when we are retriggered, we respond with the same capabilities, resources, and coping mechanisms that we had at the time of the original trauma. This means that if you were traumatized at age five, when you are retriggered you respond to that trigger with the intelligence, resources, and coping abilities of a five-year-old!

The implications for our success, or our struggle with it, are staggering. Each time you encounter something that reminds you of a trauma you experienced at a young age, you respond in the way you would have responded at that age.

This means that a 12-year-old might be running your romantic relationships, an 8-year-old could be handling your conflict management, and a 10-year-old might be running your business. Clearing out these old triggers is essential to being able to use all the skills and tools you have developed for your personal growth, and for your pursuit of success.

Fortunately, tapping is very helpful in removing these old traumas; the following is a specific technique designed for this.

TAPPING TECHNIQUE: MATRIX REIMPRINTING

Matrix Reimprinting was designed by EFT Master Karl Dawson and Sasha Allenby to clear the "frozen moment" of trauma. You can work with this brief description for now, but for more complete information, you can visit **www.matrixreimprinting.com**.

STEP 1: IDENTIFY THE SCENE

Begin Continuous Tapping. You'll maintain this through the entire exercise. Visualize the younger version of yourself, which Matrix Reimprinting calls the **ECHO** (for Energy Consciousness Hologram), near the moment when the trauma occurred. Imagine the scene as though it were a movie, and watch the movie up until a point at which there is emotional intensity.

STEP 2: FREEZE THE SCENE, AND STEP IN AS YOUR CURRENT SELF

It's very important for this technique that you are interacting from the position of your current self engaging with your ECHO, rather than seeing the event from inside the body of your younger self.

STEP 3: INTRODUCE YOURSELF TO YOUR ECHO, AND EXPLAIN THAT YOU'RE HERE TO HELP

Most ECHOs are very grateful to have help show up.

STEP 4: ASK THE ECHO IF YOU CAN TAP ON HER, OR YOU CAN INVITE HER TO TAP ON HERSELF

Sometimes when you arrive in a scene, your ECHO may immediately want a hug, or may be unwilling to be touched. Be willing to be flexible with whatever presents itself.

STEP 5: IMAGINE TAPPING ON THE ECHO AS YOU TAP ON YOURSELF

Ask the ECHO what she (we'll assume it's a she for this example) is feeling. Allow the ECHO to share her fears, anger, upsets, or anything else that she is experiencing. Keep tapping with her (Simple Tapping is fine) to allow those feelings to begin to diminish.

STEP 6: ASK YOUR ECHO IF THERE IS ANYTHING SHE WOULD LIKE TO DO TO RESOLVE THIS SITUATION

For example, she can:

* Bring in new resources, such as a magic wand

* Change what happened

* Invite somebody or something else in for help and guidance, such as a nurturing adult, a teacher, a grandparent, a policeman, or a spiritual figure such as Jesus or a guardian angel

* Do what she didn't do or what she wishes she had done in that situation, such as speak up, say no, or ask directly for what she wanted

This is a step at which some people get stopped, saying *But it didn't happen that way! No one showed up to help me.* You can heal this trauma if you use the power of your imagination and your subconscious mind to create a new experience.

One technique is to pull a magic wand out of your pocket and use it to create new people or new resources. Especially when the ECHO is a child, this is usually well received.

Depending on the situation, here are just a few of the possibilities:

— You, the adult, will stand up to an adult figure in the scenario such as a parent or teacher, and get him to behave differently. He could treat the ECHO with respect, apologize to her, or give her love and affection. (If you resist the idea that the other figures in the scenario can change, it is possible for you or the ECHO to tap on the resistance. Once the ECHO is no longer feeling scared or angry, she will often start feeling compassion for the person who caused the trauma, and wish to help him. You don't want to force this, but it is always a possibility.)

— You can take the ECHO to another location entirely, out of the building or the country! Sometimes ECHOs wish to get away from the scene, and sometimes they prefer to stay and have the scene turn out differently than it originally did. Either is fine. It's up to the ECHO.

— If the ECHO resists changing the original people in the scene (for example, a scary parent), you could bring in another relative or authority figure to take care of and protect the ECHO. These can include fictional characters, religious figures, neighbors, teachers, angels, or whatever the ECHO chooses.

The objective is to have the ECHO feeling good and safe, wherever she is and whomever she is with. Sometimes ECHOs will want to play with you, and you can choose to do that. Child ECHOs will often go off and play with friends after the negative emotions have been eliminated.

STEP 7: PUT THIS IMAGE OF GOOD FEELINGS AND SAFETY IN YOUR MIND, AND IMAGINE IT EXPANDING INTO EVERY CELL OF YOUR BODY

STEP 8: SEND THIS PICTURE OUT THROUGH YOUR HEART INTO THE "MATRIX," THE FIELD OF UNIVERSAL ENERGY

STEP 9: RETURN TO THE PRESENT, AND LOOK BACK AT THE MEMORY AGAIN

If there are still some negative emotions, you can go back in and clear that. However, it is not unusual to have the memory changed, or for the memory to be fuzzy and hard to hold onto. Some people can remember the original memory but with no emotion, and also remember a "new" memory that they just created with much better feelings associated with it.

With Matrix Reimprinting, you can actually rewrite your past (or at least the way that you remember it!).

(**Please note:** This is a very powerful technique. If you are working with "big T" Traumas such as severe abuse, please consult a Matrix Reimprinting practitioner for assistance. Refer to the Next Steps section in the back of the book.)

SUCCESS STORY

Sylvia shares this empowering story:

I'm 43 years old and married to a very sporting outdoor man who loves mountain biking. We have two vital young sons together. I had a continuing horrible vision of getting old, feeling stiff, and one day just sitting on a bench and watching my husband and my boys cycling around me on their bikes. I couldn't join them because I was unable to ride a bike.

My overprotective mother forbade my father to teach me how to ride a bike when I was very young, and later I was too embarrassed to ask for help. It was a situation that overshadowed my school years because I lived in a German city where most people went on bike rides along the beautiful riverside after school or work and on weekends. It was "the" family thing to do.

I went to a therapist who worked with kinesiology, and worked with an NLP master. Both gave me powerful sessions in which I believed I would go home and ride a bike, but I never did. Once I was back home, the thought of touching a bike was just too stressful and overwhelming.

When I was in my late 20s, I spent some days in the Netherlands at the sea with some friends where it was popular to take long bike rides through the dunes. Maria, a good friend, convinced me to give it a try. After a few minutes on a bike, I remember her horrified scream: "Sylvia, breathe!" I had such a strong panic attack on that bike that I literally stopped breathing. That was the last time that I touched a bike, and I made the decision that "this is just not meant to be for me."

Through Pamela Bruner, I was introduced to the EFT technique Matrix Reimprinting. I listened to one of her demonstrations on a teleclass and just "got it." I thought, <u>I have to put this technique to the test,</u> and used it on my phobia of bikes right after the call. It took me around seven minutes with lots of crying.

Here's the description of what I did:

While tapping, I tried to concentrate on the core feeling, which I knew was embarrassment. Feeling it strongly, I asked myself while still tapping, <u>Where did this come from?</u>

I suddenly remembered a school scene when I was 11 years old. I saw myself in the classroom. We were discussing with the teacher the plans for our class outing. He asked, "Is there anyone who, for whatever reason, can't come with us next Wednesday to our bike ride along the Rhine?" An-other girl and I raised our hands and answered in one voice, "I never learned how to ride a bike." The whole class burst into loud hysterical laughter.

While still tapping I froze this memory in my mind and stepped into the picture. I walked up to my 11-year-old self and introduced myself. I asked her how she felt. My younger self was crying and said that she felt embarrassed and deeply ashamed: "Something is wrong with me. I'm not like the others. I don't belong with the hip kids."

I asked her if I was allowed to touch her and to tap on her body. She agreed. I told her that this tapping would soothe her and help her. Using the words she used as well as her beliefs, I tapped on her Karate Chop point with a setup statement and then did several tapping rounds on her in my imagination while also doing the same on myself physically. It was very intense for me. I sobbed quite a lot, and I don't remember all the details of our exchange. But there was a deep trust from her side and a deep love from my side in this encounter. That on its own was a gift for me: to meet my younger self with these qualities of relating to each other.

After several rounds of tapping, I asked her how she felt. She said, "Okay. Safe." I asked her if she needed anything else, and she said, "A hug." So I gave her a hug and we said good-bye to each other. I came back into the present moment still tapping silently on myself, and finished this amazingly deep session with this belief pouring out of me: <u>I'm able to change in deeper and more meaningful ways than I've ever imagined.</u>

After that I left my house and visited three bike shops in my hometown. I not only touched bikes, I was able to sit on them and play with them in the stores under the eyes of the salespeople!

Back home that same evening, I ordered a bike online, which arrived two days later. I just needed a bit of tapping for maybe two minutes to calm my excitement while my husband put it together. Then I pushed it into our backyard park with its safe, small walkways, and off I went! For 15 minutes I rode my new bike feeling happy, proud, relieved, and so vital. After three days of 10- to 20-minute training rides and just a bit of tapping on my collarbone when I felt excitement rising (mostly when the bike got very fast or I went down a hill), I felt safe enough to leave our driveway and started up and down the main road.

On day six I was able to ride with my husband and sons through the whole subdivision while cars, dog walkers, and other bikers passed us . . . and I felt <u>free</u>! Can you really grasp what that means for me? To be free from such an old trauma that I had given up on myself to change?

The unexpected best part of this is my new strong belief: <u>I'm able to change in deeper and more meaningful ways than I've ever imagined.</u> As someone who works professionally as an executive coach and seeks to grow into her highest potential, that's just the best belief to have.

You can use Matrix Reimprinting to change the memories that have been supporting your limiting beliefs. You can do a Matrix Reimprinting tapping session on any memory, whether it's from childhood or just earlier in your adult life.

EXERCISE: CLEARING THE PAST WITH MATRIX REPRINTING

Identify a limiting belief that you'd like to change, and rate how true that belief feels to you using the truth meter scale.

Identify the earliest memory from your past that supports that belief, or the event that you believe caused you to create that belief.

While doing Continuous Tapping, walk through the steps of the Matrix Reimprinting process. Tap through the entire process, until you "return to the present."

Look back at the memory now. How does it feel to you? Here are some of the things people report: "I don't see the old memory anymore, I see the new memory that I changed it into," "It just feels like I can't find the memory, like it's hidden in a fog," and "The events still seem the same, but now I feel peaceful and happy when I think about the memory." You may have a different reaction, but be open to surprising results.

Examine your limiting belief again. Has your TM level changed? If it's not yet a 0, what is still holding it in place? If you have other memories holding the belief in place, repeat this exercise with another memory. If your TM level is lessened but not yet 0, you can use SOS Tapping to further reduce it.

◎

In addition to Matrix Reimprinting, you can do Simple or Choice Tapping to remove the negative emotions around an event that supports your limiting beliefs. When you no longer have a "charge" around an event, it's much easier to reinterpret the event with an empowering reframe.

Continuing our example, let's suppose you have the limiting belief of *I am stupid and incapable.* You've used Matrix Reimprinting to clear a memory of a teacher telling you that you were stupid, which was when you decided the belief was true.

It's possible that you've already shifted the limiting belief just by clearing the early memory, but if not, there may be other memories that have triggered and reinforced that limiting belief. You could use Matrix Reimprinting on those memories, or you could use Simple or Choice Tapping to clear the negative emotions around them.

For example, perhaps you didn't do as well in school as you thought you should, didn't get into the college you wanted, or failed at a large project at work.

Treat them as independent events at first. Examine your feelings about them. Are you resentful about not being accepted to the college of your choice, or embarrassed about a school or work failure? If your SUDS level is 8 or above, use Simple Tapping on those emotions to reduce them until you are at a 7 or below. Then work on the belief, beginning with an Open Choice:

❖ *Even though I still believe I'm stupid because I_____, I'm open to a new interpretation.*

When your SUDS level is 5 or below, you can use an Acceptance Choice or Specific Choice:

❖ *Even though I still believe I'm stupid because I_____, I'd like to accept myself anyway.*

❖ *Even though part of me still believes that I'm stupid because I_____, I choose to consider that there could be another explanation.*

This other interpretation doesn't mean that you don't take responsibility for the event! But you can take responsibility in many ways that are more empowering, such as:

❖ *I choose to consider that I failed because I mistakenly believed I was stupid. I'm willing to release that belief now.*

Only you can determine which reframe will be empowering for you. Keep tapping on the "evidence" that supports your limiting belief until you can step 100% into a new, empowering belief about yourself!

KEEP YOUR AGREEMENTS (SUCCESS PRINCIPLE 54)

The busier we get, the less we seem to keep our agreements. We may casually make and then break them, feeling that breaking the agreement is justified if we have a "good reason." Yet a broken agreement plus an excuse is *not* the same as an agreement that is kept.

When you make agreements and then break them, other people will begin to doubt your word. Worse yet, *you* will begin to doubt your word. You will know yourself as someone who doesn't keep agreements, and this will undermine your self-confidence and self-worth.

Some people try to resolve this by refusing to make agreements at all. If this describes you, know that this is a fear issue, so you'll want to look at the underlying fear and do some tapping on that.

But what if you tend to make agreements and break them?

Unlike the other success principles, this may be one that you just don't feel is very important. Or you may feel that you only break agreements when it's "not your fault." Or you may feel that keeping your agreements most of the time is good enough.

First, ask yourself, *What is my commitment around agreements? How strongly do I feel that it's important to keep them?*

What identity do you want to create for yourself? How is keeping agreements part of that identity?

You may find the concept of keeping your agreements empowering but challenging. Perhaps you think you'll be too overwhelmed by too many tasks if you keep all your agreements. In this case, you've said yes to too many agreements!

You may have some resistance to the idea of saying no to some of the requests in your life. Perhaps you're afraid of offending people, or afraid of their anger or disapproval. Let's approach the situation like this:

Identify the belief that's running this resistance. For example, *People will be mad at me if I say no to them.*

This is a great example of a neutral belief. The truth is some people may be mad at you, and some may not. So what? However, if that thought causes you fear, you can tap on that. First, use Simple Tapping if the fear is intense. When it begins to diminish, try a Choice like one of the following:

❖ *Even though I'm afraid _____ will be mad at me for saying no, I choose to only make agreements that I intend to keep.*

❖ *Even though I'm afraid _____ will be mad at me for say-ing no, I choose to say yes to myself and my needs.*

❖ *Even though I'm afraid _____ will be mad at me for say-ing no, I choose to make agreements because I want to, not because I'm afraid.*

Sometimes you will need to break an agreement. In that case, you want to communicate that as soon as possible and accept re-sponsibility for cleaning up any consequences. If you are resistant to doing that, look at some of the reframes and choices in Chapter 4, under Success Principle 1: Take 100% Responsibility for Your Life. Many of those will apply in this situation.

If the idea of keeping your agreements still feels onerous, you can create a Choice Statement to affirm the opposite. You can use this in a Choices Trio, or use it with Firm Stand Tapping:

❖ *I choose to make only agreements I intend to keep.*

❖ *I choose to easily and consistently keep my agreements.*

❖ *I choose to communicate with the affected party as soon as I know I will need to break an agreement.*

If you find that you sabotage yourself by not writing down your agreements, which makes it more likely that you won't keep them, using these affirmations can help train the subconscious to look for ways to make keeping agreements easier. This includes writing them down, carefully considering which agreements you'd like to make, and saying no more often.

Keeping your agreements is an important part of the mindset of success, and doing so will change both your outer and inner worlds. When you keep your agreements, you will begin to see yourself as a person of integrity. This increases your self-esteem and self-confidence, which impacts all areas of your life. When the rest of the world knows you as someone who keeps your agree-ments, you will be more respected and sought after as a friend, romantic partner, and potential business associate.

ACTION STEP: TAPPING TO KEEP YOUR AGREEMENTS

Evaluate how true the following statement is for you: "I commit 100% to keeping my agreements." What is your TM level?

When you say that, what comes up for you? Are there fears, doubts, or arguments? What are your challenges to committing to keeping your agreements?

Choose the technique that seems most appropriate to you for this obstacle: SOS Tapping, Little Voice Tapping, or Matrix Reimprinting. Do the work to clear the challenge.

Repeat the statement, "I commit 100% to keeping my agreements." What is your new TM level?

USE FEEDBACK TO YOUR ADVANTAGE (SUCCESS PRINCIPLE 19)

Are you afraid of receiving feedback? You're not alone. Most people are uncomfortable with feedback, and look for ways to avoid it. They certainly don't ask for it!

If you're afraid to ask for feedback, you're cutting yourself off from information that could make you a better spouse, parent, employee, business owner, friend, and human being. Even if you don't ask for feedback, you probably receive it anyway, so let's look at how you handle the feedback that you get.

If you're taking 100% responsibility for your life, then you understand that feedback is part of what you've created. You can interpret that you've created feedback to make your life unpleasant, but it's far more empowering to act as if you've manifested the feedback, positive or negative, for the purpose of improving your life.

Still, sometimes you receive feedback that's upsetting and may make you want to cry, fall apart, get angry, or ignore it. What input have you received lately that you rejected, and couldn't possibly imagine being grateful for?

Sometimes we reject feedback because it seems critical or unhelpful. In that case, something that can help you use it wisely is to take a proactive role in getting constructive suggestions. For example, if your spouse says "You're not a good partner," that's feedback. Getting angry, ignoring it, or falling apart is unlikely to improve the situation. However, if you ask, "Specifically, what would you like to see me do differently?" then you're asking for feedback in a way that you can learn and benefit from.

Not everyone is skilled in giving feedback, so you may have experienced feeling hurt in the past by unskillful criticism, even when the content was useful. This is a great opportunity to use tapping to clear your past pain, so you can be receptive and open to feedback in the future, regardless of the skill level with which it is delivered.

For many people, criticism that they received as children caused so much distress that they are unable to effectively handle critical comments today. If you have difficulty accepting input, then using Matrix Reimprinting to clear the hurtful memories can make it easier for you to receive feedback gracefully and effectively. The following story is an example of how this happened for one person.

SUCCESS STORY

Marta, an active senior, was working part-time for a small firm, handling their filing and bookkeeping. Although she knew intellectually she was competent, any slightly critical comment from her employer tended to cause her eyes to fill with tears of embarrassment. She had this reaction even with comments that were only intended to direct her to do work differently, but weren't overtly critical. She knew that her reaction was hurting her work experience, but felt she couldn't control it.

Marta began by examining her feelings and memories, looking for the first time she had that "tearing up" reaction. Since it was accompanied by feelings of shame, embarrassment, and incompetence, she looked for an early occasion during which she'd felt those. She remembered a time when she was seven years old and had had a similar reaction.

Marta had been given the responsibility of planting the family garden even though it was far too big a job for her. Although she worked all day on it, she couldn't get the holes dug well enough, the dirt fertilized, and so on. At the end of the day, she reported that her father was dismissive, and her mother criticized her for doing such a poor job.

We used Matrix Reimprinting to work on this memory. Marta began Continuous Tapping.

Marta could "see" her younger self going up to her room and crying because she felt like a failure. In her imagination, she stepped into the room with her younger self:

> *Marta:* I'm here to help you. I know you're feeling bad, and I want to help. Can I tap on you? *[She starts tapping on Little Marta, who is crying.]*

> *Little Marta:* I couldn't do it right!

> *Marta:* What are you feeling?

> *Little Marta:* I feel bad that I let Mom and Dad down. I should have done better. I just couldn't do it all. I'm not very good.

> *Marta:* I know you feel that way, but you did a great job out there on your own, working on that garden.

> *Little Marta:* Then how come Mom and Dad said it wasn't good?

> *Marta:* I don't know. Maybe they were just wanting a garden, but weren't thinking it would take so much work. That was really a mistake on their part.

> *Little Marta:* I should have done better.

> *Marta:* [while continuing to tap on Little Marta] You did the best you could, didn't you?

> *Little Marta:* Yes.

Marta: That's really important, to do the best you can. That's the most important thing you can do. I think you're great and really smart.

Little Marta: Really?

Marta: Yes. You're a smart girl, and you do great work. If you keep doing your best, you'll do many wonderful things. *[Little Marta is smiling now.]* If you could have anything you wanted right now, what would you like? I have a magic wand right here, and you can get anything you want.

Little Marta: I want the garden full of flowers and vegetables and Mom and Dad to be so happy.

Marta: [gives Little Marta the magic wand] Go ahead, make that happen. Now, is there anything else you want?

Little Marta: A hug.

Marta gave Little Marta a hug, and reported that Little Marta was dancing around her garden while Mom and Dad looked on with pride and approval. After leaving Little Marta, Marta imagined taking that image of the little girl and the garden into every cell of her (Marta's) body, and breathing it out through her heart into the world around.

After this session, her perception of criticism when she was at work changed considerably. She no longer felt shame or had tears, but could listen to the message and respond appropriately. She reported a *much* improved work experience!

FACE WHAT ISN'T WORKING (SUCCESS PRINCIPLE 30)

Implementing Success Principle 30: Face What Isn't Working, can bring up much of the same resistance as Success Principle 19: Use Feedback to Your Advantage. Whether it's coming directly from others or you're getting other signals about what isn't working in your life, it's all feedback. Learning to listen to and appreciate it can make it more likely that you will be able to face what isn't working.

SUCCESS STORY

Sandra really wanted to find a life partner. Since it wasn't working for her not to have one, she chose an affirmation and used Little Voice Tapping. She then picked an affirmation that she knew would get a response: *I am joyfully married to my perfect partner.* Here's the exchange that went on between her and her Little Voice:

LV: Are you nuts? You don't deserve that!

Sandra: Why don't I deserve that?

LV: Because all you have ever done is create anger, unhappiness, and tension wherever you are.

Sandra: Would you let me see you, please?

LV: [stepping out of the shadow, as a very small child] Here I am.

Sandra: Thank you for letting me see you. Would you please let me know how I created so much anger and unhappiness?

LV: It started from the time you were born . . . there was tension because your mother went to live with Grum and Pop [Sandra's father's parents] when she was pregnant with you, and that caused friction. Then when you were born, Grum took over your care. Pop was jealous and didn't like you. Your mother just left you and went to work. And remember when your dad came back from overseas? He didn't spend much time with you either. All you have ever done is cause trouble and unhappiness wherever you are.

Sandra: I was pretty small to have really caused all that, don't you think? I learned eventually that Grum and Pop were pretty much that way for years. It didn't just happen because I arrived. I also learned that both Mom and Dad were doing the best they were capable of at that time. You must remember. What do you think?

LV: Well, maybe. But your mother did put you in day care as soon as you moved to Miami. What about that?!

Sandra: You're right, she did. Remember, Dad was going to college, and Mom needed to work so we would all survive. She didn't do that to get rid of me.

LV: Maybe. But you still caused a lot of friction in your family.

Sandra: How did I cause a lot of friction?

LV: Well, sometimes you made your parents angry.

Sandra: That's true, but not on purpose. I don't think I am a bad person, do you?

LV: No, not really.

Sandra: Have you sabotaged so many of my hopes and dreams because you thought I didn't deserve them?

LV: Yes, you caused unhappiness, so you didn't deserve any.

Sandra: Wow, you are very powerful. Did you really believe that I didn't deserve any happiness?

LV: I didn't want to see you left alone and hurt anymore.

Sandra: So, you were protecting me?

LV: Yes.

Sandra: When I really wanted something, you made sure it didn't fully happen for me, in all areas of my life.

LV: Yes. Dad always told you not to rely on others, and to take care of yourself. Others will only let you down.

Sandra: I want to thank you for all your hard work over the years.

LV: I was just protecting you.

Sandra: And you have done an excellent job. Thank you! Now I want to ask you for your help. [**Note from authors:**

this is a great use of gratitude in order to gain the partnership of the Little Voice.]

LV: [smiling] You do?

Sandra: Yes. You know, I have learned a lot over the years, and value every experience. I have set some pretty fantastic goals for myself and need your help in attaining them.

LV: What do you mean?

Sandra: I am asking you to partner with me in creating a new life. I realize that I cannot do anything to the degree that I want to without your help. And I promise, this will be fun.

LV: It will?

Sandra: And sometimes a little scary, because we will be delving into new areas, changing old limiting beliefs, and developing new ones. What do you say?

LV: Okay. Sounds like fun. What do I have to do?

Sandra: Just support me. And trust me.

LV: Okay.

Sandra: I would like to see you smile.

LV: [big smile] Is this going to be fun?

Sandra: Yes, it will. A new adventure for us both. And thank you for all you have done.

As Sandra concluded, "This tapping took several minutes . . . with some tears, but the most amazing relief when it was over. Since then, whenever I have felt the beginning of doubt or hesitation, I go right back in and talk it over.

"I can honestly say that my overall energy level has been higher since starting this process. And I don't feel the heaviness in my heart that always seemed to linger there."

JUST SAY NO!
(SUCCESS PRINCIPLE 42)

How much of your to-do list comes from other people's requests?

Most of us get more requests from others than we can possibly honor. These people include family members, friends, neighbors, co-workers, acquaintances, and associates. While some of those requests may be in alignment with your long-term goals, many of them won't be. How you handle those requests can greatly affect your level of success.

Difficulty in saying no to other people's requests can come from two general areas. One is a fear of how the other person will respond. You may be afraid that he or she will be upset or offended at your no. The other area is that you may feel that saying no says something about you, such as, *I'm not a nice person if I say no.* Or perhaps you've always said yes to a particular request, so you feel it would be inconsistent to say no now.

First, we'll deal with the concern about other people's reactions. By this time, you're probably aware that we're looking for a reframe that will allow you to take an empowering stance in saying no.

One reframe would be to question the validity of the assumption that *He will be upset if I say no.* However, if it's appropriate for you to say no, whether or not the other person gets upset can't be the determining factor in taking action. Otherwise, you're the victim of the other person's moods and emotions.

So let's dig a little deeper. What are you afraid will happen if you say no?

- *He won't like me anymore.*

- *She'll refuse to speak to me.*

- *We'll have an argument, and I'll have to spend time cleaning up the hurt feelings, and then I'll have to do what I said no to anyway!*

All of these thoughts keep you in the mindset of a victim. It is possible instead for you to create an opening for this situation to occur differently. We'll use SOS Tapping to do this.

First, if your SUDS level is 8–10, do Simple Tapping to bring the level of fear down to a 7 or below. Then, invite in new possibilities by using an Open Choice setup statement:

❖ *Even though I'm still afraid that she'll refuse to speak to me if I say no, I'm open to a creative solution to this situation.*

❖ *Even though I'm still afraid we'll argue if I say no, I'm open to the idea that I can communicate my needs and wants effectively.*

❖ *Even though I don't know what will happen if I say no, and I'm afraid of the worst, I'm open to how I could handle this in a way that honors my needs.*

Tap a Choices Trio on one of these, or one that you create, and rate your fear or upset again. This is a great opportunity to throw in some *What if I . . .* statements while you're tapping.

❖ *What if it could be easy to say no?*

❖ *What if I could find the perfect way to do this?*

❖ *What if this turns out even better than I hope?*

When your intensity is at a 5 or below, consider the possibilities you might create in this situation. Before we look at some examples, let's look at a habit that will make it far easier to say no.

Recently a couple we know told us they were in a 90-day "no zone." Having overcommitted themselves for months to the point of illness, they set a new policy: "If it's not already on the schedule in the next 90 days, we're saying no to it, including all invitations for social events, charitable events, additional work appointments, and so forth." This gave them time to relax and recover, and to examine how all of their activities supported (or didn't support) their long-term goals.

If you have difficulty saying no to requests, this idea might seem very foreign and uncomfortable to you. In reality, it's very freeing.

Establishing policies makes it much easier to say no to requests. Having policies means that you don't have to evaluate all of the requests that you receive on individual merit. Some of those requests will fall under a policy, and you can invoke that policy to make the decision easier.

Also, knowing what your short- and long-term goals are makes it easier to see how responding to a request can impact them. When you write down your goals and then write down the daily actions that you're taking to support those goals, you can make clear decisions about whether you have the time and energy to take on other projects or tasks that may not be in alignment with those goals.

This helps us create reframes. There are a number of empowering choices you could make in the Specific Choice portion of your tapping routine, such as:

❖ *Even though I'm still a bit afraid to say no, I choose to be proud of myself for doing what's right for me.*

❖ *Even though I'm still somewhat afraid to say no, I choose to support my goals and priorities with my no.*

You can also use this process for Success Principle 43: Say No to the Good So You Can Say Yes to the Great.

Sometimes we are presented with opportunities that require us to take risks. We have to leave the comfort of what is known, familiar, and safe—and sometimes what is working for us pretty well—in order to step into situations that could fulfill our wildest dreams. Saying no can support you in doing that.

EXERCISE: SAYING NO TO CREATE FREEDOM

Make a list of all your obligations for a certain period of time (it can be the next month or the next three months—it doesn't matter). Identify those obligations that you need to let go of in order to give attention and energy to the rest of your life. You can also include activities that you are routinely asked to do, to which you usually say yes.

This step can be very challenging. What usually comes up are statements like:

- *I can't possibly let go of that obligation; I'll be a bad person if I do.*

- *They'll hate me, or be angry at me, if I tell them, "No, I can't do that."*

- *If I let go of that activity, I'd lose . . .*

- *But I've always been the person who can do it all!*

Write down your fears and beliefs about saying no and removing obligations from your list. Then use one of the processes that you have learned, such as SOS Tapping or Little Voice Tapping, to transform that belief or remove the fear.

Note your SUDS level at the beginning of the exercise and compare it to your SUDS level at the end of the exercise. Write down a statement that is your new commitment to yourself. Begin it like this: *I now choose to say no to all invitations and obligations that _____.*

SPEAK WITH IMPECCABILITY (SUCCESS PRINCIPLE 51)

On the surface, this success principle looks like an easy one to implement. Of course we want to speak with impeccability! However, when we are presented with the opportunity to gossip, to speak poorly or criticize another person or ourselves, we often take it.

One of the common reasons for resistance to this principle is the fear that we'll lose our connections with people if we can't gossip with them, or if we can't agree with them when they complain about a person. You can dispel this fear using the techniques we covered with Success Principle 42.

But what if you don't like someone? What if you're angry at someone or feel that they've done something wrong? Are you required not to speak about that in order to be impeccable in your speech?

This is where tapping comes in. Using tapping to reduce the anger you feel in a situation can make you less likely to feel the need to share it. Interestingly, the technique that you use to reduce the anger looks very much like the way that you might vent to another person—just without the other person there.

EXERCISE: SPEAKING IMPECCABLY TO CREATE POWER

If you're angry or upset enough that you feel it's important to vent to another person, why not try this simple technique first?

Step 1: Imagine that you are talking to another person, and begin Simple Tapping while you do so. Whether you imagine that you're talking *to* the person you're upset with or *about* that person to another, just say whatever you want to say while you tap. Notice how your feelings shift and change. Continue Simple Tapping until your SUDS level is 5 or below.

Step 2: Create two statements about the situation that you want to gossip about. Create one statement that maligns the other person, insults him, or makes him wrong. Create a second statement in which you take responsibility for the interaction, express gratitude, or find something that you can appreciate about the other person.

Step 3: Say the first statement aloud. Notice how your body feels. It will probably feel constricted and weak.

Step 4: Say the second statement aloud. Do you notice your body feeling stronger, calmer, or more at peace? Does your energy feel more expansive?

(You may want to incorporate the second statement into a Choic-es Trio, and keep tapping until your anger is at a SUDS level of 0.)

Step 5: Create a Specific Choice setup statement using the first statement as your negative Reminder Phrase, and the second state-ment as your Choice Statement. For example:

❖ *Even though I'm still a little angry with her for insulting me like that at the meeting, I choose to be proud that I reacted calmly, and grateful for the opportunity to show my composure.*

Step 6: Use these two statements to tap a Choices Trio.

Step 7: Evaluate both your upset and your desire to gossip about it with someone else. If they aren't yet 0, continue tapping until they are.

Negative comments not only can poison people against us and keep us focused on what we don't want, they literally weaken us physically. Tapping to both eliminate the upset, and the desire to share that upset, will greatly strengthen your personal power.

But aren't there things in the world that are just wrong and that we should speak out about? I understand about not gossiping, but what if a company, an organization, or a nation is doing something wrong. Do I lack impeccability if I talk about that?

Here's a simple test to discover whether you're speaking from a place of power or not. Ask yourself: *Am I calm about this issue? Am I speaking to someone who can do something about it?*

If you're raging, you're not in a position to be effective to create change, no matter how worthy the cause. This is the time to use Simple Tapping to reduce the intensity of your anger. You can then use Open Choices to find a more pow-erful alternative to venting, and explore options for actually transforming the situation.

If you're speaking to someone who can't do anything about the situation, you're venting or gossiping. Go talk or write to someone who can change things!

THE CYCLE OF ANGER

If it's true that negative comments weaken us, why does anger feel so powerful?

When we look at emotions on a scale, "despair" and "hopelessness" would be at the bottom of the scale, and "ecstasy" and "bliss" would be at the top. In between those emotions are a number of different levels of emotions that give us varying degrees of power.

One of the reasons that anger feels powerful is that it *is* more powerful than despair or hopelessness. It's a step up the "vibrational scale." Unfortunately, what often happens is that people will feel helpless to change a situation, and experience despair. They will lift themselves out of despair by getting angry, but then they want to release the anger, either because "it's not good to be angry" or they simply get tired of it. This often leads to falling back into despair, feeling horrible and powerless, and climbing out into anger, thus repeating the cycle.

The Cycle of Anger

helplessness & despair

releasing anger without healing
the underlying/limiting belief

struggling to leave helplessness -
moving up the vibrational scale

believing or being told that
anger is not a good emotion

anger, rage

The way to break this cycle is to leave anger for an emotion that's more empowering, such as calmness or compassion. You can make Choices to experience these emotions, once your anger is reduced to the point where you feel capable of making an empowering choice (usually a 5 or below).

Lift yourself out of anger by claiming your power. Take 100% responsibility, believe it's possible, and take action.

WHEN IN DOUBT, CHECK IT OUT (SUCCESS PRINCIPLE 52)

When you make assumptions about what a person is thinking or feeling, you risk missing opportunities and damaging your relationships. Yet so often people won't ask because of fear of what the answer might be.

Because so many people carry around underlying beliefs such as *I'm not good enough* or *I'm not lovable,* they tend to interpret situations in light of these beliefs. If someone cancels a date or an appointment with you, you may be inclined to interpret that action as *He really doesn't want to be with me,* or *She has no interest in doing business with me.*

Asking for the reasons behind others' words and actions means that you can operate with clarity and confidence. Usually we don't ask because we anticipate an answer that will confirm our worst fears, such as *I'm not loved* or *I'm not valued.*

Even if you believe that you'd rather not know, think about what that is costing you:

- The fear is a constant drain on your energy.

- You may damage a relationship by making an assumption about the other person's thoughts or feelings, since you will constantly be acting on that assumption.

- If it is time for a relationship to end, you may lose new opportunities by staying.

To take action on this success principle, first acknowledge your fear.

What do you believe will happen, or what do you believe you will hear, when you "check it out"? For example, you might think:

- *I'm afraid he'll tell me this is over.*

- *I'm afraid that she doesn't want to spend time with me.*

- *I'm worried that I'm really just an inconvenience to her.*

- *What if he says that my work isn't any good?*

Letting yourself be controlled by fear will keep you from success in many aspects of your life. However, as we've noted before, fear is not a rational emotion. It's controlled by a different part of the brain, so you can't just tell it to go away. Tapping, however, can interrupt the fear so you can make rational, empowering choices.

Now it's time to develop your own tapping exercise. Here are some sample Open Choice setup statements, and some tips on creating empowering Specific Choice Statements.

Sample Open Choice setup statements:

- ❖ *Even though I'm still afraid that he'll tell me this is over, I'm open to having this turn out in a powerful way for me.*

- ❖ *Even though I'm still afraid that she'll confirm she doesn't really like me, I'm open to a new level of honesty in this relationship.*

- ❖ *Even though I'm afraid I'll get feedback that I don't want to hear, I'm open to the possibility that "checking it out" could help me learn and move forward.*

You want to create the most empowering Specific Choices that you can. Making a choice that attempts to control or predict another person's behavior is not as empowering a choice as claiming your own emotions and actions. Here is an example of how you can turn a disempowering choice (one that depends on another person) to an empowering one.

Don't say:

❖ *Even though I still have some of this fear, I choose to know that John really admires my work.*

Do say:

❖ *Even though I still have some of this fear, I choose to welcome feedback to make my work even more admirable.*

❖ *Even though I still have some of this fear, I choose to admire myself for having the courage to ask for John's feedback on my work.*

How you choose to feel about "checking it out" is up to you. What empowering choice can you make?

SUCCESS STORY

This is a very interesting tapping success story. This is not actually Matrix Reimprinting, since Gina never taps on a younger self. Instead, she sees herself as her younger self but knows that the memory is not real. What this wonderful story shows us is that we can clear issues even if we aren't aware of the originating event. All of the setup statements use the Original EFT Affirmation. At the end, we used Visualization Tapping, but could also have used Choices.

Gina came to me due to her discomfort with networking events. Although she felt that she was a competent businessperson, even an excellent one, whenever she went to a networking event she would feel very emotional and often cry when they were over. She felt that this was hurting her career, and she wanted to enjoy networking events.

Gina related that her fear didn't seem to be connected to a fear of public speaking, since she had many times addressed groups both smaller and larger than the networking events she had been to. I asked her what, specifically, she had experienced at the events.

She reported that while she sat there waiting for her turn to speak, she felt like she wanted to bolt from the room, and felt like she wanted to cry. She felt very disliked by the group, almost hated.

I asked if, consciously or rationally, she felt that the group disliked her, if she had any evidence of this. She said no, this was just a feeling. She knew it was irrational, but it was overpoweringly strong.

I then asked her to close her eyes and think back in her past to see if she had had those feelings prior to the networking event. She immediately said, "I see myself on a playground, but that's funny—I've never seen that playground before. That's not a real memory. It's just a flash of imagination." She then attempted to find a "real" memory with those feelings but was unable to.

I told her that since the important thing was to clear the emotions and the energy disruption, we could work equally well with an invented memory as we could with a real one. I asked if she could tune in to the playground again, and feel those uncomfortable feelings that were similar to the ones from the networking event. She was immediately in touch with the feelings.

I asked her to describe what was going on in the playground. Gina related that she seemed to be about eight years old. There were lots of children around, and they were going to do something together, like build a clubhouse. She reported feeling excited about this. She reiterated that although she could clearly see this scene, she was quite certain it hadn't really happened.

Then, she said, a little dark-haired boy appeared, and all the children started looking to him for leadership. This created some emotional intensity (a 6 on the SUDS scale), so we stopped here and tapped.

Setup statement:

❖ *Even though they are all looking at and listening to him, and they hate me, I love and accept myself.*

Reminder Phrases:

❖ *They're all looking at him.*

❖ *They're all listening to him.*

❖ *They hate me.*

We tapped one complete round, all points, and she reported that the focus had now changed slightly. She now felt, *I want them to listen to me; they aren't listening to me! I just want to hate them for this.* Intensity had changed to a 10, she felt angry and frustrated, and she began to cry.

Her new setup statement:

❖ *Even though they won't listen to me, I love and accept myself.*

❖ *Even though it's so frustrating that they won't listen to me, I love and accept myself.*

❖ *Even though I want to hate them for ignoring me, I love and accept myself.*

Reminder Phrases:

❖ *Listen to me!*

❖ *Why won't you listen to me?*

❖ *I'm so angry!*

❖ *I want to hate them all.*

❖ *I'm so frustrated!*

❖ *Why won't they listen to me?*

One complete round brought the intensity down to a 6. She reported that the *I want to hate them* feeling was gone. We did another round with slightly modified wording.

Her new setup statement:

❖ *Even though I think that they should be listening to me—why aren't they listening to me?—I have good ideas for the clubhouse, too. I love and accept myself now.*

Reminder Phrases:

❖ *They should listen to me.*

❖ *I have good ideas, too.*

❖ *I want them to listen to me.*

This complete round of tapping brought the intensity down to a 2. I asked her what she would like to have happen on the playground—what would be the best outcome for her?

She said that she didn't care if the other children took her ideas for the clubhouse or not. She was okay with going with someone else's ideas; she just wanted to make sure that her ideas were heard.

I asked her to begin Continuous Tapping on all the points, and asked her to visualize the other children listening to her ideas. I asked her to imagine that she was heard, and that her ideas were carefully listened to. Gina reported that she no longer felt anger at the little dark-haired boy, and she felt appreciated by the other children.

I asked her to visualize attending a networking event, and see if she felt any intensity. She reported that she felt the same appreciation in visualizing the networking event that she had felt visualizing the playground. After checking for any other events that might have contributed to or resembled these feelings, and not finding them, the session was over.

When I followed up with her two months later, Gina reported that she had attended three different networking events with no recurrence of the discomfort. She had enjoyed the events and acquired several new clients from them.

CLEAN UP YOUR MESSES AND INCOMPLETES (SUCCESS PRINCIPLE 28)

According to research, the average American spends an hour a day looking for things because of clutter or misplacement. Can you imagine how much more you could do if you had that extra hour to spend productively?

Messes and incompletes can be in the form of physical clutter—too much stuff in our homes, cars, garages, and offices. But they can also be in the realm of personal relationships—people we need to forgive, acknowledge, say no to, appreciate, pay, or collect from. Each one of these messes and incompletes occupies part of our mental or psychic space, as well as the physical space, and can slow us down and drain our energy.

So why do people have so many incompletes?

In terms of physical clutter, the answer is usually emotional. We hold on to things because of an anxiety or fear that we'll someday need what we're keeping. In some cases, the onset of collecting too much stuff corresponds with a trauma, such as the loss of a loved one. If we merely removed all the things, it wouldn't help clear the underlying anxiety. This anxiety must be addressed, or else the clutter will simply return. In severe cases, just the thought of clearing the clutter can cause a panic attack. More commonly, it will trigger discomfort and thoughts such as:

- *What if I need some of this someday?*
- *I don't know what to do with all this.*
- *I can't possibly clean all this up, it's too overwhelming.*
- *If I clean it up, it'll just come back.*

Because tapping is such an excellent technique for reducing anxiety, it's great to use on clutter. Use the thought of taking action to bring forward your specific fears and limiting beliefs.

When visualizing taking action, assess your SUDS level of distress. Next, do rounds of tapping until you reduce that number to

0 for all aspects. Once you are at a SUDS level of 0 for an event, then there is no barrier to your taking action.

Cleaning up incompletes with people will often raise the type of fears we saw with Tell the Truth Faster (Success Principle 50). You may need to share uncomfortable truths, own up to something, or apologize. You may need to take action to make something right.

EXERCISE: CLEANING UP THE INCOMPLETES

Now we'll use Little Voice Tapping in order to clean up some of the incompletes we just discussed.

Step 1: First make a list of incompletes in your life. You may want to separate the list into physical incompletes, such as *Fix the broken screen door* or *Empty the overflowing junk drawer,* from relationship incompletes, such as *I need to apologize to Sue.*

Step 2: Work on only one item on the list at a time. As you read the list, say to yourself *I could do that* and listen for the Little Voice to disagree. With some items, the Little Voice may enthusiastically agree, and with some, it may say *No, you can't, because* . . . Pick one item you'd like to work on that the Little Voice says you can't or shouldn't do.

Step 3: Go through the Little Voice Tapping Routine to discover why the Little Voice believes that this incomplete should not be addressed. Remember to offer gratitude to the Little Voice for trying to keep you safe and happy. Retrain the Little Voice to support you in cleaning up your messes and incompletes. Think of how you can let the Little Voice know that doing this is something that you both want.

Step 4: Once you and your Little Voice are in agreement about cleaning up the incomplete, commit to a date and time by which that will occur.

SUCCESS STORY

Joe, a businessman, asked for help with his fear of flying. He reported that he thought he knew where it came from; he had been accidentally locked in a bathroom on a bus as a young child. This was a perfect time to use Matrix Reimprinting. Since Joe and I were together in person, I tapped on him rather than have him tap on himself. I believe the results would have been the same had he been tapping on himself.

I asked Joe if he could see his younger self in his mind, locked in the bathroom, and he said that the memory was very clear. I asked if he could put himself in the bathroom with the young boy, and he said yes.

I instructed him to immediately tell "Joey" he was here to help, and to ask if he, Joe, could tap on little Joey. Joey said yes. Joe was now mentally tapping on little Joey.

Here is a transcript from our session:

Pamela: Ask him what he's feeling now.

Joe: He's scared because he can hear his mother yelling, wanting to get him out. There's noise, they're working on the door.

Pamela: Can you quiet the noise so you and he can talk?

Joe: Yes.

Pamela: As you're tapping, is he still scared?

Joe: He's wondering what he did wrong to be locked in.

Pamela: What do you think you can tell him?

Joe: You didn't do anything wrong, Joey. It just happened. You're a good boy. He's feeling a little better now.

Pamela: In your mind, Joe, reach in your back pocket and pull out a magic wand. Show it to Joey, and tell him that he can do anything he wants with it. He can make the bathroom gigantic so you two can play, or bring in friends or even a pony.

Joe: He likes the magic wand. *[Smiling]* He made the sink a waterfall!

Pamela: Great. What else would he like to do?

Joe: He made the bathroom bigger so there is lots of room.

Pamela: Great. Anything else? Anyone he wants in here?

Joe: No, he's happy in here with me.

Pamela: How's the door coming?

Joe: It's just opening now. Joey's going out and he's being hugged by his mother.

Pamela: Ask him how he's feeling.

Joe: He's so glad that he's out of the bathroom now. He doesn't ever want to go back in.

Pamela: Is he scared of the bathroom?

Joe: A little.

Pamela: Is there anything you could do so that he wouldn't be scared of it?

Joe: Hey, Joey, come over here. See, we can open the bathroom now anytime we want to. Do you want to see? Would you come in here with me? He's willing to come in, and I'm opening and closing the door. He's happy that he doesn't have to be scared of the closed door anymore.

Pamela: What's he feeling now?

Joe: He just wants to go and play. But he wants to know that I'll stay with him. He wants to know if he can keep the magic wand.

Pamela: That's good. Wanting to play is usually a sign that kids are done with the hard stuff. Are you willing to tell him that you'll always be here for him?

Joe: Yes. Joey, I will always be there for you, all you have to do is ask. I gave him a hug, told him he could keep the wand, and he's gone off to play now.

Pamela: I want you to start coming back to the present, but don't come back all the way. Come partway, into the in-between space where everything is energy, and you're outside of time. Energy is not bounded by time. So imagine who you would be now if someone had come into that bathroom when you were a little boy and given you a magic wand, and helped you to not be afraid. Take that image, and imagine it coming in through your head, and percolating down through every cell of your body, suffusing each cell. Then breathe in, and exhale that image out through your heart, into the world around you. When you're ready, taking all the time you need, come back to the present.

Joe: I'm back.

Pamela: When you look back at the incident in the bus bathroom, how do you feel now? Does that memory feel different?

Joe: Yes, it does. It feels light. All I can remember is playing with the wand.

Pamela: When you think about getting on an airplane, how does that seem to you?

Joe: It doesn't seem scary at all. It feels easy.

Pamela: Keep imagining you're on the airplane. Look around, and notice a really lively 80-year-old man grinning at you. Remember you told Joey you'd always be there for him? That's you, in the future, still fulfilling that promise. He'll be there to help you if you need it.

Joe: [with tears in his eyes] I see him. That's so amazing. And I still have the wand.

Pamela: Yes, it's great. You can open your eyes when you're ready. Unfortunately, we can't give this work the real test here. You'd need to get on an airplane.

Joe: But we could try an elevator. I've had trouble with those all my life, too. I try to avoid them. It's a real struggle to get into them.

Joe and I went to the elevator and got on, pushing the button for the top (19th) floor. Joe was grinning. "This feels easy," he said. We rode up and down several times, then I got off the elevator and Joe rode up and down by himself. He was grinning broadly and reported no challenge or troubling emotions at all. Although Joe's success can't be fully measured until his next plane ride, he has considerable confidence about it; and he has the tools he needs, including the wand and the image of his future self there to help him.

This session took only 25 minutes.

CHAPTER CHECKLIST

I understand the reasons that trauma sabotages us as adults.
I understand the Cycle of Anger.
I've done all the tapping exercises in this chapter.

CREATING THE NEW YOU: TAPPING FOR EMPOWERMENT AND TRANSFORMATION

HOW DO I TAP ON . . .

One of the most common questions that new tappers often ask us starts with the phrase: "How do I tap on . . . ?" For instance: "How do I tap on abundance?" "How do I tap on success?" "How do I tap on a headache?" "How do I tap on procrastination?" and "How do I tap on fear of failure?"

These questions have no answer. You can't "tap on abundance" any more than you can get "directions to somewhere." However, if what you want is more abundance in your life, there may be ways in which tapping can support you in achieving that goal.

Here is the process for determining how to use tapping to achieve your goals.

STEP 1: DETERMINE WHAT YOU WANT

I want abundance isn't a clear goal. Examples of clear goals would be:

- *I want an income of $150,000 a year by December 1st of next year.*

- *I want a 4,000-square-foot home on the ocean within 30 miles of San Diego, California.*

- *I want three days a week off to enjoy my hobbies while maintaining my income of $100,000 a year.*

STEP 2: DETERMINE WHAT IT WILL TAKE TO GET THERE

Take a large sheet of paper, and draw a line down the center. On the left side of the page, write down the actions you will need to take to achieve your goal.

When you begin listing your actions, you may have thoughts come up such as, *That will never happen,* or *I could never do that.* Write those down on the right side of the paper.

You may also have the reaction *I don't know what it would take to get there.* Not knowing how to get to a goal is not, by itself, a limiting belief; it's a neutral belief. Ask yourself, if you have that belief, what's underneath it. Do you believe that you could learn what it takes to get there? Can you find someone who does know, and get the information from him or her? Or do you feel that you're incapable of learning what it takes to get there? If that feels true for you, add that to the right side of the paper.

STEP 3: TAP ON THE LIMITING BELIEFS
THAT APPEARED IN STEP 2

Create a setup statement using your limiting beliefs in an Open Choice or a Specific Choice.

- ❖ *Even though I don't believe that I could ever be paid that much . . .*

- ❖ *Even though someone like me doesn't deserve a home like that . . .*

- ❖ *Even though it's not possible to earn that much and take three days off a week . . .*

Little Voice Tapping is also a great technique for working on these limiting beliefs. The Little Voice is probably trying to keep you from wanting something it doesn't think you can have, so that you won't be disappointed. Can you tap with the Little Voice to enroll it in helping you work toward this goal, and get it to keep you from being disappointed whenever you face challenges in your pursuit?

BE CLEAR WHY YOU'RE HERE
(SUCCESS PRINCIPLE 2)

Perhaps you've already clarified your life purpose. If so, great! If not, you'll want to do so. (There is an excellent exercise for identifying your life purpose on page 23 of *The Success Principles.*) Regardless of how you go about doing this, it's very important to have some statement of life purpose.

Your life purpose can act as a litmus test for all of your other goals. Asking yourself, "Does this goal support and further my living my life purpose?" will keep you focused.

Your life purpose can also help you accomplish more. Without an overriding purpose and vision, it's easy to drift, accomplishing very little.

Living in alignment with your life purpose will also bring you maximum satisfaction and happiness. As the saying goes, "You don't want to get to the top of the ladder of success only to find it's leaning against the wrong wall."

Despite all the good reasons for doing so, some people still shy away from getting clear on, and living from, their life purpose. This could be caused by beliefs such as:

- *I don't know how to determine my life purpose.*

- *I can't be sure it's right, and I don't want to live from the wrong one.*

- *My life purpose isn't good enough (or big enough).*

- *If I have a life purpose, I'll have to take on more responsibility.*

Most of these, in a broad sense, center around the fear of committing to a course of action. However, consider what would happen if you do identify a life purpose, then five years from now decide that it has changed. Are you worse off than if you hadn't lived from that purpose? No! You can use this notion to create a powerful reframe to support you in claiming your life purpose. For example:

- ❖ *Even though I'm afraid I'll identify the wrong life purpose, I choose to consider that whatever I claim might be right for now.*

- ❖ *Even though I don't want to live from the wrong life purpose, I'm open to allowing the Universe to guide me as I live into my life purpose.*

- ❖ *Even though my life purpose isn't good (or big) enough, I'm open to the possibility that my contribution is valuable, and this is what I'm meant to do.*

If this is a challenge for you and you want to use tapping to overcome this challenge, remember that a Specific or Open Choice may not be obvious to you at the beginning of the tapping. If your fear of taking an action is very high (a SUDS level of 8–10) you may not be able to craft a Choice Statement.

Use Simple Tapping first to lower your SUDS level to 7 or below before you try creating a Choice of either kind. If you try to create a Choice Statement while you are still working with a high SUDS level, your choice may not be the best one for you. You may find that you make different, more effective choices as your SUDS level drops. So be sure that you go through the process using the right choice for your SUDS level.

As a reminder, here are the guidelines:

SUDS level 8–10: Simple Tapping

SUDS level 6–7: Open Choice Tapping

SUDS level 5 or below: Specific Choice Tapping

Since the SUDS level is, by definition, subjective, these are only guidelines rather than hard and fast rules. You may try an Open Choice at a SUDS level 8, or do an Open Choice at a SUDS level 5. You can always do an Open Choice series whenever you're not yet sure what Specific Choice you want to make.

DECIDE WHAT YOU WANT (SUCCESS PRINCIPLE 3)

In order to go from where you are to where you want to be, you first have to know where you want to be. Many people feel unable to want things, or unwilling to admit to wanting things, because of messages that have made wanting "bad" or "wrong." These messages usually come from your parents, teachers, or other caregivers when you are young, and so have become part of your mental and emotional landscape without being examined or questioned.

If you're not aware of what you want, begin to identify preferences as you go through your daily routine. What would you prefer to wear, to eat, to read, to do? As you find yourself asking these questions, what thoughts and emotions occur for you?

- *I never get what I want, so why bother?*

- *It's selfish for me to consider my wants.*

- *My needs are not as important as the needs of* [my wife, my husband, my children, my parents, my boss, etc.].

- *I'll just be disappointed if I want things.*
- *It's not safe to want things.*
- *If I think about what I want, I'll do the wrong things or do what I shouldn't do.*

You may not even experience an emotion at all, just a blank feeling when you ask yourself what you want. In this case, your natural inclination to want things has been so shut down that you'll need to work on giving yourself permission, and making it safe, to want again.

Some reframes that may be helpful in getting you to want again include the following:

- ❖ *Even though I don't feel I have any preferences, I'm open to what it would be like to want things.*

- ❖ *Even though I'm not sure it's safe to want things, I'm open to looking at this issue.*

- ❖ *Even though I don't really want to want things, I'm open to seeing what's behind that feeling.*

Sometimes we fear that if we desire things, we'll be propelled into taking action that is scary. For example, if you find that you want a loving relationship and don't have one, you'll either have to explore beginning a relationship with someone new, or create change in an existing relationship that's not serving you. Sometimes it feels safer to deny that this is something you want, rather than face the actions that desire will demand of you.

Also, you may find yourself deciding what you want based on what you think you can have. You'll deny what you want if it seems it's too big or out of reach. After all, why want something just to be disappointed?

However, this approach ignores the important fact that your subconscious mind can help you as well as it sometimes stops you! When you create a vision of what you want, the subconscious mind will work to make that vision a reality. When you deny what you want, your subconscious continues to create what you already have.

Also, since the language of the subconscious mind is emotions and pictures rather than words, stating your preferences with no emotion behind them doesn't give the subconscious what it needs to work with. Also, stating your preferences with an invalidating thought or emotion behind them—for example, *I really want a new job in the arts, but there is no way I can get one that pays enough*—also interferes with your ability to get what you want.

Given all this, you'll need to:

1. Be willing to look at what you want (this may take tapping).

2. Identify what you want.

3. Identify any negative emotions or thoughts about wanting those things.

4. Tap to remove those emotions and thoughts that are limiting your dreams.

If you are afraid to want, use Simple Tapping on that fear. When your intensity is a 7 or below, then use an Open Choice to create the possibility of getting what you want, such as:

❖ *Even though I'm still afraid to look at what I want, I'm open to a new possibility.*

You'll also want to identify why you are afraid to look at what you want. Is it because you believe that you won't be able to have it, or because you believe that wanting is selfish? Both of these limiting beliefs can be addressed separately, then you can return to identifying what you want.

Little Voice Tapping can be particularly useful when you are working with strong "should," "ought to," and "you'd better" messages around wanting. Remember, the Little Voice is always trying to keep you either safe or happy, so tap continuously, and talk to it about supporting you in getting what you want rather than keeping you from acknowledging your true desires.

There may have been a time in your life when you made the decision *I'm never going to want anything again!* If you have a particularly unpleasant memory about wanting something, and being punished or disappointed, you can use Matrix Reimprinting to reduce the intensity of the memory or change the emotions in it altogether.

Now let's look at a new tapping technique that can give you a different access to clearing obstacles.

TAPPING TECHNIQUE: SENSATION TAPPING

If a thought gives you a sensation in your body, you can tap on the sensation, and often the thought will change. This method is particularly good for those who are kinesthetic, who feel things rather than, or in addition to, visualizing them. (**Note:** Watch the DVD section on Sensation Tapping for more information and examples.)

Step 1: Close your eyes, and begin Continuous Tapping. You'll keep tapping throughout the exercise. If you need to open your eyes to check these steps, that's fine. You can also have a friend read them to you one at a time.

Step 2: Focus on the issue that you're trying to clear, whether it's an emotion or a limiting belief. Notice any emotional reaction you have to it. Do you wince, feel fear, or feel as though you're lying? Also, notice any physical reaction that you have to it. Does your stomach feel uncomfortable? Do you purse your lips as though trying to hold the words in? Do you hunch your shoulders and try to hide?

Step 3: Evaluate the physical sensation on the SUDS scale. How intense is it? Perhaps you have more than one sensation. You could feel fear at a 4, but have a knot in your stomach that feels like a 6. If so, concentrate on the more intense sensation first.

Step 4: Focus on the sensation, and notice it without judgment. Don't try to get the sensation to go away; just notice it. Is it shifting as you continue to tap? Is it getting more intense; less intense;

moving to a different part of the body; or becoming a different sensation, such as tingling rather than pressure? Does it have a color or shape? Maybe you'll describe it as, "This red jagged ache in my stomach that's the size of a grapefruit."

Step 5: Keep noticing the sensation. It will probably be changing and shifting as you continue to tap. Continue to observe it, still without trying to change it. Sometimes this can go on for several minutes. You may shift through different physical sensations, such as aching, pressure, or tingling. It may change color, shape, or size if there is a visual element. It may also change location in your body, for example going from your chest to your stomach, then to your shoulders. Just keep observing.

Step 6: As you continue to tap, the intensity of the sensation will tend to diminish. Don't try to hasten this process, simply observe it. If it helps you stay focused on the sensation, you can give a running commentary of its changes.

Step 7: When the sensation seems to be gone, scan your body to see if any other uncomfortable sensation has come up. If so, repeat steps 3 through 6.

Step 8: If you are aware of a limiting belief that was feeding the sensation, check to see if you still believe it (i.e., if it still has any intensity).

SUCCESS STORY

Pamela writes: Rachel, a client who is a successful coach and healer, came from a very large family and had internalized the message *I can't want too much, there's never enough, and if I want too much I'll take away from other people, and that means I'm selfish and I'm a bad person.*

In working together, she identified a "want" that she had for a new office. However, every time she focused on that want, she experienced a "yuck" feeling with an intensity of 9.

We tapped on:

❖ *I can't think about that office.*

❖ *It just feels wrong.*

❖ *What if I'm disappointed?*

❖ *Either I won't get it if I want it, or if I do get it, it will be wrong somehow.*

❖ *And it would just be what I deserve.*

❖ *It's wrong to want that office.*

❖ *I'm in a bind because I do want that office.*

❖ *If I admit that I want that office, it won't stop. [Note: this is a change of aspect.]*

❖ *If I want that office, I'll become a wanting machine.*

❖ *And that's not spiritual.*

❖ *It's not spiritual to want all this.*

❖ *What if I'm here to want things?*

❖ *What if part of my journey is to want things?*

❖ *I don't believe that yet.*

At this point Rachel's intensity felt like it was increasing and she felt close to tears. I instructed her to tap without words, and she reported that some positive thoughts were beginning to be mixed with the negative thoughts. I asked her to focus on the negative emotions, and she reported feeling very strongly:

❖ *If I want that office, I'll get in trouble.*

❖ *I go numb when I think about wanting.*

We began using Sensation Tapping.

Pamela: Where is the numbness?

Rachel: It's around my face and mouth. It's covering my face.

Pamela: Focus on the numbness. Tell me about it. How big is it? What color is it?

Rachel: It's turning yellow. It's shrinking around my mouth.

Pamela: Clever numbness, covering your mouth. The edges, are they smooth or jagged?

Rachel: Smooth, egg shaped. The color and texture are changing. Now it's just at the corners of my mouth.

Pamela: Tell me more. *[A long pause, and lots of tapping without words.]* Focus on the numbness. You're wanting to pull away and look at something else.

Rachel: There's this part of me that's wanting to giggle. *[Rachel smiles.]*

Pamela: That's a big smile. You can move your mouth now! Say for me, "I want that office."

Rachel: I want that office.

Pamela: Does that feel congruent to you? Does that feel like a 10 to you? *[Note that with this question, we're using the truth meter (TM) scale, not the SUDS scale.]*

Rachel: It's an 8 now. But it was a 0 when we started. I do want the office now, and I'm not turning away from wanting it.

EXERCISE: CREATING AND LIVING YOUR VISION

Step 1: Create a vision of what you want in the following seven areas of your life: Financial/Wealth, Career/Business, Relationships, Health, Free Time/Hobbies, Personal Growth, and Contribution. You can write this in a journal, create a vision board, or create a goal list.

Step 2: For each part of your vision, ask yourself if you chose what you chose because it's truly what you wanted, or it's what you thought you could have. If it's what you only thought you could have, complete the statement: *What I really want is ____, but what I wrote down is different because I believe ____.* (For example: *What I really want is a thriving company with 50 people working for me, but what I wrote down is that I want a good job because I don't believe that I could run that big a company.*)

If you were at all challenged in creating the vision, because you didn't want to create a vision that you couldn't achieve, write that down to work on later.

Step 3: You should now have the first version of your vision and a list of limiting beliefs that kept your vision from being as big and exciting to you as it might have been. Take each one of those limiting beliefs and apply one of your tapping techniques such as SOS Tapping, Little Voice Tapping, or Sensation Tapping to transform that belief.

Step 4: Rewrite your vision to include your new, expanded desires.

ACT AS IF
(SUCCESS PRINCIPLE 12)

In shifting the established patterns of the powerful subconscious mind, one of the best ways to create new patterns is to actually experience them. We saw this working with the Matrix Reimprinting technique to heal the past, and you can also use this idea of experience to create your future. You can do this by role-playing; for example, have a "come as you will be" party, where you invite friends to come to a party and imagine that it is five years in the future. You and all the partygoers speak in the present tense about the wonderful things that are in your lives now, and what you've done and accomplished in the last 5 years. You can also create new mental patterns by acting on a daily basis as though you already have the things that you desire.

Both in the book *The Success Principles* and in other motivational works, the reframe for a limiting belief is usually given to you along with the empowering idea. This is incredibly valuable! It means that in many cases, you don't even have to figure out the reframe. You just have to tap in order to reduce your resistance to believing the reframe.

Of course, as you tap you may create other reframes and find other empowering beliefs, and that's wonderful. But even if nothing else occurs to you, you can use what's been given to create a reframe, and from that an Open or Specific Choice.

Let's use the ideas in Act as If (Success Principle 12) to show this. Consider: If you had accomplished everything that you wrote down earlier in your vision, how would you talk, act, walk, eat, live, and so forth?

Many people are uncomfortable with this because it feels fake to them. You may think:

- *This isn't me.*

- *It's arrogant to pretend like this.*

- *I feel uncomfortable, as though I'm lying.*

- *I can't be this way until I have these things.*

These thoughts usually come from one of two beliefs, either *I don't deserve to act like this,* or *I don't believe this is me, and I need proof to act like this.*

Let's look first at the belief *I don't deserve to act like this.* Ask yourself, "Why don't I deserve to act like this?" If the underlying thought is *I don't deserve to have this* (whatever it is that you wish you could have), you'll want to handle that the way that you would handle any limiting belief about yourself. If that's the case, review Success Principle 33: Transcend Your Limiting Beliefs in the beginning of Chapter 6 to replace that limiting belief with one that's more empowering.

More commonly, the answer will be *I don't deserve to act like this because I haven't earned it yet.*

To handle this limiting belief, you can create a setup statement that uses this reframe:

❖ *Even though I don't deserve to act like this, I'm open to the idea that I'm retraining my mind to become this person.*

You can use the above statement, or create a setup statement more specific for your situation. For example, if you wanted to be a musician, then you would create an Open Choice setup statement and Reminder Phrases such as the ones that follow. (Notice as you read that we're getting more flowing with the tapping phrases in this example. Rather than doing a negative, positive, then alternating round, the phrases just flow from negative to positive, ending in the Open Choice.)

If your feeling of "not deserving" is very strong, do some Simple Tapping to reduce your SUDS level to below 8 before using a Choice Statement.

Open Choice setup statement:

❖ *Even though I can't call myself a musician because I've only played the guitar for a year, I'm open to the possibility that I might make better progress when I claim that I am.*

Reminder Phrases:

❖ *I can't call myself a musician.*

❖ *I haven't been playing that long.*

❖ *I'm not good enough yet.*

❖ *How long do you have to play to call yourself a musician?*

❖ *Well, I know you have to be better than I am.*

❖ *I can't call myself a musician.*

❖ *If I'm not a musician, how will I ever learn to play the guitar?*

❖ *When do I get to call myself a musician?*

❖ *You have to have played for ten years and have performed at Carnegie Hall to call yourself a musician, right?*

- ❖ *What if I could be a musician now?*

- ❖ *What will open up for me if I claim that now? I'll prob-ably practice more; all musicians practice.*

- ❖ *It does feel more empowering to call myself a musician than to deny that I am.*

- ❖ *I wonder if I could call myself a musician.*

- ❖ *I'm open to calling myself a musician.*

When your resistance to your limiting belief is at a 5 or below, try a Specific Choice setup statement such as:

- ❖ *Even though I can't call myself a musician because I've only played the guitar for a year, I choose to create that I'm a musician, and live into that.*

Tap around the points, using similar Reminder Phrases to the ones above, and end with:

- ❖ *I choose to call myself a musician, and act that way.*

In this advanced tapping example, you see how tapping can quickly take you from a limiting belief to an empowering one. If your belief is that you need proof in order to "act as if," then you'll want to remind yourself of the power of training your subconscious mind. This success principle isn't about lying or deceit; it's about programming your reticular activating system (which we discussed in Chapter 4) to perceive opportunities and respond to situations as you will when you've actually reached your goal.

So rather than *I need to see it in order to believe it,* the truth is *I need to believe it in order to see it.*

Acting "as if" is not only a great way to train your subconscious mind to create the reality that you desire, it's also an excellent way to expose limiting beliefs so you can tap on them to release them!

SUCCESS STORY

Pamela writes: This story shows the use of humor in reducing intensity.

Sasha (not her real name), a successful personal coach, came to me because although she was very comfortable in one-on-one sessions, she was extremely nervous at the thought of presenting to groups. However, she wanted to start giving tele-classes (group training over the phone), and felt that getting over this fear so she could present comfortably would be better than "toughing through it." I agreed.

I asked if she had a particular fear of presenting to groups on the phone, or whether her fear was just groups in general. She felt that the fear was the same regardless of whether it was in person or on the phone.

I asked what, specifically, she was afraid of. She said, "I'm afraid that I'll make a mistake," "afraid that I'll appear incompetent," and "afraid that I'll look stupid." She rated the fear at an 8 intensity on the SUDS scale.

We initially did Simple Tapping:

❖ *I'll make a mistake.*

· ❖ *I'm afraid I'll look stupid.*

❖ *What if I forget what to say?*

❖ *I'll look incompetent.*

We did a complete round, using all points, including the finger points (which we mentioned in the section on Stealth Tapping in Chapter 2). Sasha reported that the fear had dropped to a 6, so we did another similar round.

At this point, Sasha reported that the fear had dropped to a 5. I told her that 5 was a great number, one where we could start playing a bit more. I said that I might use a little humor, and she thought that was a great idea.

Her setup statement used a variation of the Original EFT Affirmation:

- ❖ *Even though the world will end if I make a mistake in my teleclass, even though everything hinges on this teleclass, maybe even world peace, I choose to love and accept myself anyway.*

The Reminder Phrases were similarly silly:

- ❖ *I've got to do it right or the world might end.*
- ❖ *Everything depends on me being perfect.*
- ❖ *The fate of the world hinges on my perfect teleclass.*

At the end, Sasha was laughing and said that the fear was now at a 2 or 3. I asked her, if she had to guess, what was keeping the fear in place? She said that she was afraid that without the fear, she wouldn't adequately prepare for the teleclass. (**Note:** This is a great example of a change of aspect.)

She also reported at this point that something else was coming up—she was now feeling guilty that she had carried around this fear for so long, and it had kept her from doing group work and helping people in this way. She reported the emotion as "regret and sadness" with an intensity of a 6. Again, this was a perfect spot to use her variation of the Original EFT Affirmation.

Setup statement:

- ❖ *Even though I have this regret and sadness because I've had this fear for so long, I choose to love, accept, and forgive myself anyway.*

Reminder Phrases:

- ❖ *I should have gotten over this fear before this.*
- ❖ *Why didn't I get over it before this?*
- ❖ *I've been playing small.*
- ❖ *I could have done group work before this.*
- ❖ *I feel all this regret.*
- ❖ *I'm sad I didn't deal with this before.*

- ❖ *What if this was the perfect time for me to deal with the fear?*
- ❖ *What if I just wasn't ready before?*
- ❖ *What if I could trust that this is the perfect time for me to start giving teleclasses?*
- ❖ *What if now really is the perfect time?*
- ❖ *What if I could forgive myself?*
- ❖ *I choose now as the perfect time to start group work.*
- ❖ *I choose to forgive myself for my fear. I'm doing the best I can, and that's good enough.*

Sasha reported that the regret was completely gone at the end of the double round, and that the fear was still at a 2 or 3.

I asked her what she would really like to communicate to the teleclass participants, and how she would like to feel. She said that she would like to come across as warm, confident, caring, and positive.

We created a Specific Choice setup statement:

- ❖ *Even though I have to keep this remaining fear so I'll adequately prepare for the teleclass, I choose to consider that I could be warm, confident, caring, and positive instead.*

Reminder Phrases:

- ❖ *I have to keep the fear.*
- ❖ *I won't be prepared if I don't keep the fear.*
- ❖ *This fear is making sure that I will prepare.*
- ❖ *What if I don't have to keep the fear?*
- ❖ *What if I could prepare without it?*
- ❖ *What if I could prepare from a place of caring rather than fear?*
- ❖ *What if I could prepare from a place of confidence rather than fear?*
- ❖ *I choose to be warm, confident, caring, and positive.*

At the end of her session, Sasha reported that her fear was at a 1, and was quite happy with that level. I suggested to her that it might drop on its own to a 0 (hopefully setting her up to look for that if it should occur).

I asked her to visualize giving the teleclass, from setting it up to picking up the phone, talking to people, etc. She said that she felt a little nervous about the technology, but knew that she could walk through that with the help of a friend. She had no fear about the idea of speaking to the group, and recognized that was a different aspect from her discomfort with technology.

She expressed some concern that the fear might return, and I explained that in my experience, an additional aspect might surface, such as her discomfort with technology, but that usually the fears that were dissolved remained that way.

To keep her fear from spiking from any additional aspects that might surface, and from the "fear of the fear," I suggested that she tap every day until the teleclass using the following setup statement and Reminder Phrases:

Setup statement:

❖ *Even if I'm tempted to go into fear, I choose to focus on being warm, confident, caring, and positive.*

One negative round with the Reminder:

❖ *I might feel afraid.*

One positive round with the Reminder Phrase:

❖ *I choose to be warm, confident, caring and positive.*

Sasha reported that she felt confident about giving the teleclass, and when I checked in with her a week later, she was happily making final preparations with no return of the fear.

JUST LEAN INTO IT (SUCCESS PRINCIPLE 14)

Some people won't take a single step unless they can see the entire path. However, the path to greatness, or to living your dreams, is almost never clear-cut. So why not proceed? Why not begin to take actions towards your dreams, even if the whole picture isn't clear?

"Just lean into It" means getting into action, taking one step, giving it a try. It's the opposite of sitting back and contemplating while refusing to get in the game. And taking action can bring up fears.

One of the most common fears is *I'm afraid I'll fail if I go for what I want.* Given this fear, it's easy to procrastinate on taking any action. It's easy to come up with the excuse *I don't have it all planned out yet, so I shouldn't start* rather than moving ahead. After all, if you believed that you would succeed, wouldn't you be taking action now?

Once you confront your fear and eliminate it, leaning into it becomes much easier. So what, exactly, are you afraid of? Perhaps it's a belief such as one of these:

- *I'll look like a fool trying to do this.*

- *I'll feel like a failure if it doesn't work.*

- *Why would I succeed? I can't do what other people can.*

- *I'm afraid to start in the wrong way, and wreck everything.*

At this point, you're getting pretty experienced at looking at your fears. If your fear is intense, you'll want to use some Simple Tapping to bring it down. Then look at the underlying belief beneath the fear. Perhaps it's obvious, such as *I'll look like a fool trying to do this.* In that case, you can use SOS Tapping to reduce that fear.

Here's an example of what an SOS Tapping routine about this belief might look like.

First use Simple Tapping to reduce the fear of looking like a fool. (Continue until your intensity drops to 7 or below.)

Then create an Open Choice setup statement, and be open to the possibility that you won't look like a fool. At least, be open to the idea that looking foolish isn't fatal, and could very well be worth it if it means you can accomplish your dream. Examples of Open Choice setup statement include:

❖ *Even though I'm afraid of exposing myself to ridicule, I'm open to the idea that ridicule isn't fatal.*

❖ *Even though I'm afraid to try and fail, I'm open to the possibility that I can try until I succeed.*

❖ *Even though I'm afraid to fail because it means I'd have to give up on my dream, I'm open to the possibility that I may fail sometimes in the pursuit of my dream. I can still achieve success.*

After using the setup statement, remember to tap a Choices Trio (negative Reminder Phrase, positive Open Choice, then alternating). Continue until your intensity drops to 5 or below.

Then create a Specific Choice about how you'd like to approach this "leaning into it" action, how you'd like to feel and act. Some possible reframes include:

❖ *Even though I might look like a fool doing this, I choose to be proud of the fact that I'm moving in the direction of my dream.*

❖ *Even though I might make a mistake when I lean into it, I choose to consider that I'll never know what's possible if I don't take action.*

❖ *Even though I risk feeling like a failure if it doesn't work, the only way I'll succeed is by acting, so I choose to go for success rather than not acting to avoid failure.*

If your fear is *I'm afraid to start in the wrong way, and wreck everything,* ask yourself why you fear that. You may have a memory of having started something, or taken an action, and the outcome caused stress or trauma. If so, you'll want to clear that memory using Matrix Reimprinting.

Once you've cleared any memory that's related to that belief, check to see whether your fear about leaning into it has shifted. You may also have a limiting belief about yourself, your ability to take action, or what "always" happens when you take action that you'll want to clear.

BELIEVE IT'S POSSIBLE (SUCCESS PRINCIPLE 4) AND BELIEVE IN YOURSELF (SUCCESS PRINCIPLE 5)

Because the resistance to these two principles is so similar, we'll look at the two of them together. You've already worked on changing a number of limiting beliefs throughout this book. Believing in yourself is one of the most important empowering beliefs you can have, so let's look at and remove anything that stands in the way of that.

Look at the belief, *It's not possible.* Because we usually get what we expect to get, believing that something is possible gives tremendous power and momentum to the likelihood that it will occur. Studies in quantum physics have even shown that the expectation of the researchers can affect the outcome of an experiment. Whether this is because of neural pathways that we establish in our brains, a connection in the zero-point field identified in quantum physics, or simply the Law of Attraction, what we expect influences what we get.

If you're attempting something revolutionary, something that has never been done before, you can't know if it is possible, and you can't know that it's not possible. Just looking at the world around us gives you lots of examples. Most of our lives are filled with things that would have been judged impossible even 100 years ago, including computers, airplanes, television, artificial hearts, cell phones, space flight, and more. Yet in each case, someone was willing to try something that had never been done before, and ask, "What if?"

If you have a limiting belief that something you want to attempt or achieve is not possible, you'll want to remove that.

If you run into challenges trying to believe that it's possible, you may want to ask yourself if there is a downside to your believing that it's possible. For example, if it is possible for you to achieve a dream, will you be disappointed in yourself for not achieving it earlier in life? The fear of a disappointment like this may keep you from believing it's possible. You can remove that fear, and that judgment of yourself, and then work on the belief.

Next, you'll want to answer a very important question: "Why do I believe it's not possible for me to do this?" The answer to this question will be a limiting belief that you'll want to remove, and replace with an empowering belief instead.

But what if the answer to the question isn't a limiting belief, but seems to be a fact? For example, *It's not possible for me to succeed, because I'm dyslexic.* The fact that you have dyslexia is not a limiting belief; it's simply what's so.[9] However, the idea that you can't succeed if you're dyslexic *is* a limiting belief, and that's what you'll want to overcome.

According to Carol Dweck, the author of *Mindset,* studies show that those people who believe that they can always improve with hard work succeed far more than those who simply believe that they are talented or smart. Unfortunately, one of the messages that has been taught to us is the idea that if you are talented or smart, then hard work is not required for success. Therefore, those who believe that they have natural gifts are often burdened with a feeling that they *should* succeed, and that it should be very easy. When hard work is required, they feel like failures. This tends to cause people who think like this to avoid risks and not reach their full potential.

This doesn't mean that it's bad to think that you're talented or smart! But it does mean that if you have a belief in yourself that you can accomplish anything through hard work, regardless of how talented or smart you are in a given area, you are far more likely to succeed.

Reading success stories about other people can help you to train your mind to overcome these limiting beliefs. Because most success stories are written about people who started with some type of disadvantage, or triumphed against incredible odds, it becomes easier to believe, *If he can do it, so can I!*

You can collect stories like this to use as your reframes, and in your Choice Statements. *The Success Principles* is full of great stories that you can use as inspiration for your statements, as are all the *Chicken Soup for the Soul* books. Perhaps you even know someone yourself who has experienced that type of success.

In addition, you can use previous successes of your own to create a Specific Choice. For example, if you succeeded in school, sports, making friends, or a personal or work project, you can use that success.

❖ *Even though I don't believe I can succeed at this, I choose to remember that I succeeded in:*

- *getting through high school.*

- *having four close friends.*

- *graduating from college.*

- *getting that account.*

- *losing the first 20 pounds.*

Some people experience a completely different reaction to looking at and using success stories. If you see other people who have achieved what you desire, and you don't feel as though they are as smart, accomplished, or talented as you are, you may get frustrated and upset. This is the opposite of the belief, *I'm not good enough.* It's the belief, *I'm better than they are, so why have they succeeded when I haven't?* However, consider this interpretation: the Universe put these people in your life so that you could see that you *could* do exactly what you dream of! If they can do it, of course *you* can! Now go take 100% responsibility for your life, and create the life you want.

Installing a belief in yourself and your abilities is one of the most important things you can do for your success. Keep working at this one until you feel a 100% *yes* reaction to believing in possibility and believing in yourself.

EXERCISE: BELIEVING IT'S POSSIBLE, BELIEVING IN YOURSELF

Let's try an SOS Tapping technique. In this exercise, we'll be looking for two measures: (1) We want your feeling of *It isn't possible* to be a level 0 on the truth meter (TM) scale, which would mean "not true at all," (2) We also want stating your goal to feel 100% possible, to be a 10 on the truth meter (TM) scale.

The only reason that these two might be different is that you might have several different limiting beliefs about why your goal is impossible. Even if you bring the first one down to 0, your goal may still not feel 100% possible because there is another limiting belief in the way. When you clear all the limiting beliefs, then your goal will feel 100% possible, and new opportunities will open up that were not available to you before. During this exercise, we'll be working with the limiting belief, not the statement of your goal.

You'll want to work through this exercise with each limiting belief, one at a time. Don't try to work on all of them at once; you'll just sabotage your results. As you become more experienced, this exercise will take between 5 and 20 minutes to complete for each limiting belief, depending on how challenging they are to clear. Doing that several times is a very reasonable investment for the success of your goal!

Step 1: State your dream or goal as an affirmation, and be aware of any feeling of, *It isn't possible because . . .*

Step 2: Do Simple Tapping on your limiting belief if it's stronger than a 7. Otherwise, skip to step 3.

Step 3: If your limiting belief has a SUDS level of 7 or less, create an Open Choice setup statement. Here are some examples:

❖ Even though I don't believe it's possible to achieve my goal because _____, I'm open to allowing the Universe to surprise and delight me.

❖ Even though I don't believe it's possible because _____, I'm open to a creative new way to handle this situation.

❖ Even though I don't believe it's possible because _____, the world is filled with things that were once thought impossible. Maybe this will be another!

(Remember, each setup statement focuses on one limiting belief at a time. These are separate aspects, and should be treated separately.)

Tap a Choices Trio, skipping the alternating round if you find it's not necessary. Here are some possible Reminder Phrases:

Negative Round:

❖ I don't believe this is possible because_____.

❖ No one has done this before.

❖ I don't know that I'm smart enough to do this.

❖ Look at my track record.

❖ I've never created anything like this before.

Positive Round:

❖ Why wouldn't it be possible?

❖ Just because no one's done it before, doesn't mean it can't be done.

❖ I'm open to the possibility that I could do this.

❖ Everything seems impossible until someone does it.

❖ Why not me?

❖ I'm open to a surprising new way to do this.

❖ What if this is what I'm supposed to do?

❖ What if this is possible?

Step 4: If your limiting belief has a SUDS level of 5 or less, create a Specific Choice setup statement. Here are some examples:

❖ *Even though I still don't believe it's possible to achieve my goal because _____, I choose to consider_____.*

❖ *Even though I still don't believe it's possible because _____, I choose to remember my success at _____.*

Tap a Choices Trio, skipping the alternating round if you find it's not necessary.

Step 5: Assess your new SUDS level. If your limiting belief is not at a 0 intensity, repeat Step 4. Now evaluate your goal statement with the TM scale. Do you believe it's 100% possible, a level 10? If not, find the remaining limiting belief that is in the way, and repeat the exercise with that belief. Continue this until you believe 100% that your goal is possible, and that you can accomplish it.

If you are at a 0 SUDS level and a 10 TM level, great job!

BECOME AN INVERSE PARANOID (SUCCESS PRINCIPLE 6)

Do you believe that events in your life happen for your good, no matter how they may appear? That's being an inverse paranoid, which we discussed briefly in Chapter 4. Rather than believing that the world is "out to get you," you believe that it's working for your benefit.

Living this success principle gives you terrific practice in creating reframes. The better you get at creating reframes, the more effective and successful you can be. Each time you see something that seems like it is to your disadvantage, you can create an interpretation that makes that event, person, or circumstance be to your advantage instead.

So why is this a powerful success principle? Why bother to believe that events are all for your highest good? One reason to do so is that the belief causes you to constantly experience gratitude for everything in your life. Aside from the benefits of gratitude in harnessing the positive effects of the Law of Attraction, it just feels good.

Another reason is that living this principle helps you to "set your radar" for success. If you believe that every occurrence in your life has a benefit, you'll be looking closely for that benefit in the case of a situation that may at first seem unfortunate or negative. This means that you're constantly tuned in to the positive benefits in your life, and you're much more likely to see and make use of them.

Sometimes, though, it can be challenging to see the good in a situation, or to even believe it's there. You may ask *How can this possibly be for my benefit?* or you may have a belief *God is out to get me.* If those beliefs come up, you'll want to turn them around so you can take advantage of the opportunities in the situation.

The first step in this process is to work to remove the negative emotions such as anger, sadness, or frustration that may be present. It's hard to create the belief that something is for your benefit when you're furious about it.

You'll want to do the following SOS Tapping exercise if you don't, or can't, believe that the Universe is conspiring for your good. Perhaps you are challenged in believing this because an event happened that doesn't seem to be for your good, or because you look at historical events and think that the Universe is malevolent. We'll use the approach in the exercise that there is an event that doesn't seem to be for your good.

EXERCISE: BECOMING AN INVERSE PARANOID

Step 1: Evaluate your emotion and intensity about the event. If your SUDS level is an 8 or above, start with Simple Tapping to bring down the intensity of those emotions. You may very well be experiencing multiple emotions, so be open to tapping through each one. Often as you drop the intensity of one emotion, another will appear, which makes it seem like your intensity is not changing. However, remember that each emotion is a different *aspect*, and you'll need to work on each one separately.

Step 2: When your overall intensity is at a 7 or below (meaning you don't have any emotion with a higher intensity), create an Open Choice to bring possibility into the situation. Tap a Choices Trio. Possible setup statements include:

- ❖ *Even though I'm still angry about this situation, I'm open to seeing it in a way that empowers me.*

- ❖ *Even though I'm still so sad about this, I'm open to finding something positive in this situation.*

- ❖ *Even though I can't imagine feeling good about this, I'm open to the possibility that I could, even if I can't see it now.*

Step 3: As the intensity of your emotion about the event drops, you will begin to see some advantages in a situation, or you can create some empowering interpretations. You can then create a Specific Choice setup statement about those, such as.

- ❖ *Even though I'm still upset at losing my job, I choose to find an even better opportunity.*

- ❖ *Even though I'm still hurting because of the end of this relationship, I choose to allow the new space in my life to bring me something wonderful.*

Even when you remove all negative emotions, you may not be able to see the benefit of a situation yet. You can still create a Specific Choice that empowers you, such as:

- ❖ *Even though I'm still frustrated by the loss of this opportunity, I choose to become aware of all the benefits this situation brings to me.*

Tap a Choices Trio, then reassess your SUDS level. If it's not at 0, repeat step 3. Remember, you may need to do the entire exercise several times to cover all aspects of the event.

PEGGY'S STORY

Pamela writes: Peggy, an RN, came to me as a client, with a heart-wrenching story. She had been diagnosed with a rare form of lymphoma for which there was no cure. If she agreed to undergo a bone marrow transplant, she could expect to live for one to three years. She chose to have the transplant, and after one year came to me, full of anger, sadness, and upset about the disease. She had developed an ulcer, and every day lived in fear that the cancer would return.

We worked for two sessions, a total of almost four hours. We tapped on the anger first. When that diminished, the sadness was overpowering, and we tapped on that.

I asked Peggy at one point, "What could you feel other than anger and sadness?" She replied, "What is there to feel other than those things?"

As we continued to work, however, and the negative emotions diminished, new possibilities arose. Peggy created the possibility of "feeling calm and peace," and we used that as a Specific Choice when the intensities were low enough.

At the end of the four hours, all Peggy's negative emotions about her illness were gone, replaced by a feeling of calm and peace.

Here are Peggy's words from a few weeks after the session:

> Pamela guided me through the mechanics of EFT® and I began to replace all those feelings with hope and happiness for my current health. In one week I was able to discontinue the everyday use of the ulcer medication and my stomach feels great! I have a sense of peace regarding my disease.
>
> I can't say the cancer is gone, but I can now entertain a possible miracle . . . after all, why not? I'm worthy of a miracle!

Pamela's final note: This work took place five years ago. Peggy is already a miracle, having the longest remission on record for that particular type of cancer. She is now a Tapping Practitioner herself, specializing in helping people with diagnoses of cancer.[10]

KEEP SCORE FOR SUCCESS (SUCCESS PRINCIPLE 21)

An important element of goal setting is that the goal be specific and measurable—how much, by when. When you also keep track of the actions that you take that further these goals, in essence keeping score about your accomplishments and successes for each action, your "scorecard" can act as a motivator.

You can create a scorecard for every goal, project or activity that you engage in. Are you trying to increase the fun time in your life? If so, things that you might keep track of include your social engagements, or times that you play, act silly, or goof off. Are you trying to improve your relationship with a member of your family? Perhaps you want to track each time you two have a positive interaction, and each time you do something nice, supportive, or loving for that person. If you're in sales, you may want to tally the number of cold calls you do, or the successful sales conversations you have. Perhaps you want to track the number of days per week and length of time each day that you exercise.

When you consider keeping a scorecard, what comes up for you? Do you shy away from the idea of actually recording what you accomplished, and what you didn't? Does it feel like a burden rather than something to get excited about? Perhaps you feel trapped by the idea of keeping score or afraid you'll be shown to be a failure if you don't score high enough. A scorecard holds you accountable in a way that good intentions just don't do. That accountability can contribute tremendously to your success.

Here are some phrases that might indicate challenge with this success principle. Do any of them resonate with you?

❖ *Even though I don't want to see where I fall short . . .*

❖ *Even though I'm afraid I'll feel like a failure . . .*

❖ *Even though it's such a hassle to keep a scorecard . . .*

❖ *Even though it feels too confining, and I'd rather just live more organically and spontaneously . . .*

You can initially tap on these fears using Simple Tapping, then create an Open Choice out of any of them, or a statement that is more appropriate for you.

When the resistance to implementing this success principle has dropped to a 5 or below, you'll want to create a Specific Choice. One possible reframe for beginning to use a scorecard is that you'll get to see your progress and cheer yourself on. It's entirely possible that you're accomplishing more than you thought, but you haven't been aware of it. The scorecard will help with that. Also, if you find out that you're accomplishing less than you thought, you now have the awareness to change that. It's truly a win-win.

We'll use these ideas to create a Specific Choice, such as

❖ *I choose to use my scorecard to acknowledge and celebrate my progress.*

❖ *I choose to notice just how much I have been accomplishing.*

❖ *I choose to be grateful that I can now accurately see just where I can improve.*

ACTION STEP: KEEP SCORE FOR SUCCESS

Create your own tapping exercise based on this principle. What are the major challenges you face? How can you reframe them?

ACKNOWLEDGE YOUR POSITIVE PAST (SUCCESS PRINCIPLE 26)

Why is it so much harder to acknowledge our successes than our failures? There are two reasons, one neurological and one cultural.

Our brains are wired to pay more attention to negative emotions than to positive ones. Because of what psychologists call the negativity bias, negative emotions feel stronger to us than positive ones do, and we are more likely to remember them. From an evolutionary standpoint, this makes perfect sense. Thousands of years ago, a human's survival was much more likely if he remembered the horrible scare that he had with the saber-toothed tiger in a certain location. The brain could forget all the pleasant, non-traumatic experiences, because those didn't directly contribute to longevity. Since memories without strong emotions attached to them are not stored as long or as prominently, and because our negative emotions feel stronger to us than our positive emotions, we're more likely to remember our failures.

Also, from a cultural standpoint, we're often taught to ignore our accomplishments. Have you heard any of the following?

- *It's bragging to acknowledge your accomplishments.*
- *It's not right to toot your own horn.*
- *You don't want to be seen as arrogant.*
- *You'll get too big for your britches.*

Because one of the first things you'll want to do is to create a list of your past successes, let's first deal with the cultural messages against acknowledging your successes. In addition to the limiting beliefs mentioned above, you may also have thoughts such as

- *My successes aren't that big a deal.*
- *Anyone could do what I've done.*

You may want to ask a trusted friend about your successes. Chances are that they are more impressive than you're willing to admit, and having someone else echo this idea can help you acknowledge it. Even if it doesn't sink in emotionally, you can then use that acknowledgement as a reframe in a Specific Choice. Tapping is a great way to help acknowledgment sink in emotionally.

We suggest using Little Voice Tapping for these issues. Those voices inside that tell you not to acknowledge yourself (in whatever language they use) are just trying to keep you safe or happy. Explore the reason that these voices are sharing with you, be grateful for the intent behind what they are saying, and ask them to support you in a more positive and nurturing way.

That's helpful when you're working on the cultural voices, but how do we handle the way that the brain is wired? Just because we've been trained and conditioned to be this way, doesn't mean it has to stay that way! We've also seen in previous sections of the book that you tend to get what you expect. What will you expect if you're used to thinking only of your failures?

Just as you can set the preferences on your computer, or change the position of the driver's seat in the car, you're not stuck with the default setting. You can counter the brain's tendency to remember more negative than positive experiences with this simple exercise.

EXERCISE: ACKNOWLEDGE YOUR POSITIVE PAST

Begin Continuous Tapping. Bring to mind a specific success that you had. Create positive feelings around that success memory, such as gratitude, pride, satisfaction, or inspiration.

If you feel discomfort at focusing on your successes, notice your discomfort and continue tapping. Note the specific emotion that comes up. If the discomfort intensifies into a clear message, such as *It's arrogant to think about this,* switch to Little Voice Tapping and discuss that thought with your little voice. How is the little voice trying to protect you by not allowing you to acknowledge your successes? After completing the conversation, return to visualization and Continuous Tapping.

Magnify those positive feelings as much as you can. Visualize them surrounding you, penetrating every cell of your body, and radiating out into the world.

Do this for a few minutes every day, and you will begin to see yourself as much more of a success. You'll then feel more capable, take more action, and attract more success. You'll also have access to great reframes to use when working on overcoming your limiting beliefs.

SUCCESS LEAVES CLUES
(SUCCESS PRINCIPLE 9)

Do you have a dream? Do you want to have a business that you love; a new, exciting career; or a healthy, satisfying romantic relationship? Do you know how to achieve success in those areas? If not, are you taking action to learn how?

When you're trying to achieve success in a certain area, one of the best sources of information is from people who have already done what you want to do. If they have written books or developed educational programs, you can learn from them in that way. If they haven't, you could still interview them and ask for their insight into how you could proceed.

Resistance to this idea is often in the form of the fear of rejection. You fear asking for information from people you admire, or those whom you see as successful. You imagine that they will say no (which is possible), and that you will be humiliated in some way. You're afraid that you're not important, and that they will reflect that back to you.

Here's a reframe for this situation: If you recognize your value, your worth, then nothing that anyone else can do will make you feel unimportant or humiliated. (We've already dealt with the fear of rejection in other sections of this book, so you can also work with this fear the same way.)

Another reason that people don't seek out the clues to success is that one message in those clues is that success requires work and change. It doesn't have to require suffering, but work and change are concepts that leave many people uncomfortable. It's easier to dream of success and say "someday" than to research and discover exactly what is required.

When you think about researching what it would take to accomplish your dream, what comes up for you? It could be something like:

- *I don't know where to go for help.*
- *I can't ask for help.*
- *I don't want to look like I don't know what I'm doing.*
- *No one will want to talk to me.*

Another way in which people have recently begun to resist seeking out the clues to success has to do with information overload. It used to be that to obtain information you had to go to a library, bookstore, or college. Now there is a virtually limitless supply of information available on the Internet. But the best information still requires an investment of time and money. Instead of digging in deeply to study with a master in your chosen area, you may collect far too much varied free information, and then struggle just to process that information rather than charting a course from a mentor and taking action. Getting an overload of information is a terrific procrastination technique! The free information on the Internet is a great start—however, it is not a substitute for an organized educational system such as a book, program, or course; or interviewing someone in-depth on a subject.

Here's an exercise to identify what might be stopping you from implementing this success principle.

EXERCISE: COLLECTING THE CLUES TO SUCCESS

Begin Continuous Tapping. Visualize achieving your dream goal. You're running your business, or enjoying your relationship. Enjoy the feelings that come with this achievement.

As you consider your achievement, say to yourself, *In order to get here, I had to learn how to* _____. Finish this statement in as many ways as you can think of.

Look at your list, and as you continue to tap, ask yourself, *Who knows how to do this?* or *Who do I know who might know someone who knows how to do this?* Collect a list of names.

As you continue tapping, visualize approaching the people on the list of names. Will you call, e-mail, or send a letter? Will you ask someone for an introduction? What will you say? Some of your discomfort may diminish while you visualize and tap. You may also have limiting beliefs or fears that come up.

Write down any negative emotions or limiting beliefs that come up, and use the techniques that you have learned (such as

Little Voice or Simple Tapping) to work through each one until either the fear is gone, or the limiting belief has been replaced by a more empowering one.

Take action, and contact the people on the list!

CHAPTER CHECKLIST

I know the steps to creating a tapping routine.
I've tried Sensation Tapping.
I've done all the tapping exercises in this chapter.

◎　◎　◎

CREATING NEW HABITS FOR SUCCESS: TAPPING TO MAKE LIFE EASIER

DEVELOP FOUR NEW SUCCESS HABITS A YEAR (SUCCESS PRINCIPLE 34)

Remember the story of the rider and the elephant in Chapter 1? We discussed the idea that when the elephant (the emotional, subconscious part of the mind) is motivated, it's much easier to accomplish something. When the rider (the rational, conscious part of the mind) is trying to control the elephant, it's tiring for the rider, and willpower is exhausted very quickly.

One of the ways to make it much easier to accomplish your goals is to have the elephant trained to take actions that support them—in other words, to create habits so that you take action by rote, rather than effort. Any habitual action is much easier than one that's not. If you have habits that support your success, you're in good shape. If your habits sabotage your success, that's something you'll want to change.

Although creating the habits may take willpower, once they are in place they will be much easier. Scientific research indicates that in order to create a habit, you have to repeat an action for 25–30 days in a row without missing a single day. In order to not overwhelm yourself, just take on one new success habit every 13 weeks.

Most of the resistance to this success principle comes either from being unwilling to give up your sabotaging habits, or the fear that you'll try to do so and won't succeed.

Throughout this section, you'll create your own tapping routines, based on suggestions for each one of the success principles. This is an important step to take; it's essentially taking some of the "training wheels" off that we have used throughout the book to help you learn to tap. If you've done the exercises, you're now very familiar with SOS Tapping and Little Voice Tapping; you can base your own tapping routines on these methods. We'll do the first exercise for Redefining Time together, then you'll be getting more and more independent as this section progresses.

REDEFINE TIME
(SUCCESS PRINCIPLE 40)

In *The Success Principles,* Dan Sullivan's Entrepreneurial Time System was introduced. It divides all of your time into three kinds of days: Focus Days™, Buffer Days™, and Free Days™. Focus Days are days in which you spend at least 80% of your time operating in your core genius. (For example, for both of us—Jack and Pamela—a Focus Day is spent speaking, coaching, writing, editing, recording, or conducting seminars.) Buffer Days are days when you prepare or plan for a Focus or Free Day by learning new skills, locating resources, training support staff, or delegating tasks to others. Free Days extend from midnight to midnight and involve no work-related activity of any kind. A Free Day is for rest, fun, and recreation. Because we're discussing different kinds of days, we'll explore several different types of resistance.

EXERCISE: REDEFINING TIME

Some people can't have a Focus Day because they're doing too much activity that isn't in their core genius. For instance, if you're running a business but also answering all of the phone calls, sending all the e-mails, and running the errands, you're not spending much time doing what you do best. Yet the thought of delegating may bring up uncomfortable resistance.

How many Focus Days do you enjoy? What reaction do you have to the thought of increasing that number? It may be something like:

❖ *I can't afford to hire anyone, so I have to do everything.*

❖ *If I train someone to do what I do, they'll replace me.*

❖ *I don't have time to teach someone how to do it.*

❖ *People will be mad at me if I don't answer all my e-mails myself.*

All of these statements are based on a belief of *I can't, because* . . .

This is an excellent place to use the powerful questions *What if I . . . ?* and *How could I . . . ?* You can incorporate those questions into your Open Choice setup statements and Reminder Phrases. Here's one way to do so:

First, evaluate how strongly you feel about the *I can't*. This may be an emotion like fear, or it may just be a very strong belief that the *I can't* statement is true. Note your SUDS and TM levels.

If your intensity is an 8 or above use Simple Tapping first. When your intensity is at a 7 or below, use one of the following Open Choice setup statements, or make up a similar one:

❖ *Even though I can't _____ because _____, what if I could do that?*

❖ *Even though I can't _____ because _____, I'm open to how I could do that.*

❖ *Even though I can't _____ because _____, what would have to happen for me to do that?*

As you do a Choices Trio, use the "because" part of the setup statement for your negative round. Then use your Open Choice Statement, or *What if I . . . ?* or *How could I . . . ?* questions, for your positive round. Then, of course, you have your alternating round.

For example, your "because" Reminder Phrase might be:

❖ *I've never done it before.*

❖ *I can't afford to hire anyone.*

❖ *No one can do it as well as I can.*

❖ *I'll upset people.*

Your positive Reminder Phrases might be:

❖ *What if I could do that?*

❖ *I wonder how I could do that.*

❖ *I'm open to how I could do that.*

❖ *I'm open to a new perspective.*

Notice how strongly you feel about the *I can't*. It will usually be less strong than it was before.

Possible Choice setup statements include:

❖ *Even though part of me still believes I can't, I choose to consider that there is a way, even if I haven't seen it yet.*

❖ *Even though part of me still believes I can't, I choose to find the way that I can.*

❖ *Even though part of me still believes I can't, I choose to allow the answer to unfold.*

The objective of this tapping is not to immediately discover the answer to your question, although that sometimes happens.

The objective is to believe 100% that you *can* do what you previously believed you couldn't, even if the way is not yet clear. Once you believe that something is possible, you begin to see many possibilities that weren't available to you before.

Free Days will often give you that clarity. In order to function at your best, you need breaks that refresh your creativity, productivity, and motivation; and Free Days can give you those. Most people agree with this statement, yet still resist taking Free Days because of limiting beliefs such as:

- *I have too much work to do to take a Free Day.*

- *I don't have anything I need to do as much as work.*

- *I don't deserve to take days off until my business is successful.*

Sometimes these beliefs will diminish with some tapping and the reframe that Free Days actually increase productivity. For some people, however, there is a core belief that they don't deserve to have Free Days, that something horrible will happen if they take a Free Day, or that their worth comes from how hard they work (and Free Days diminish that worth). Usually beliefs like this are not conscious—the conscious mind knows that worth doesn't come from how many days one works—but emerge only after some tapping detective work.

You can use SOS Tapping for this. Remember to first use Simple Tapping to reduce your SUDS level to a 7 or below. If you feel panic about the horrible things that might happen if you take a Free Day, your Reminder Phrases could be:

- ❖ *I'll have to live under a bridge if I take a Free Day.*

- ❖ *No one will respect me if I take a Free Day.*

- ❖ *I'll feel worthless if I'm not working.*

When your SUDS level is a 7 or below, you create an Open Choice setup statement, such as:

❖ *Even though I can't take a Free Day because _____, I'm open to a new possibility about work and a Free Day.*

Then do a Choices Trio, using the "because" statement as your Reminder Phrase during the negative round, and your Open Choice Statement as your Reminder Phrase during the positive round. When your SUDS level is a 5 or below, create your Specific Choice setup statement and do another Choices Trio. Your setup statement could be something like:

❖ *Even though I can't take a Free Day because I have too much work, I choose to consider that I'll complete my work more quickly and easily when I take a Free Day.*

Reminder Phrases (negative round):

❖ *I have too much work to do to take a Free Day.*

❖ *I don't have anything I need to do as much as work.*

❖ *I'm just too busy for a Free Day.*

❖ *I don't need a Free Day as much as I need to work.*

Reminder Phrases (positive round):

❖ *What if I'm clearer and more productive after a Free Day?*

❖ *What if I have creative new ideas that allow me to work faster?*

❖ *Free Days are important for mental and physical health.*

❖ *I'm open to the idea that a Free Day is an important part of my productivity.*

Instead of doing SOS Tapping as we just described, you can try affirming the statement *I choose to schedule and enjoy Free Days,* and then use Little Voice Tapping to work with the objections that come up.

SUCCESS STORY

Carol told us that she runs a small business and felt like taking Free Days was absolutely impossible. She'd feel very uncomfortable if she even thought about scheduling one. She decided to use Little Voice Tapping to see if she could shift this, and here's what happened:

Carol: I choose to take and enjoy Free Days.

Little Voice: You can't do that. You have to work as hard as you possibly can in order to succeed and be respected.

Carol: And if I work 24/7, then I'll succeed and be respected?

LV: Well, no, it'll still never be good enough. But you have to try.

[Carol gives the voice a face, and it looks like her father.]

Carol: So no matter how hard I work, it'll never be good enough?

LV: No, but it's important to do your best.

Carol: Who told you that it would never be good enough? How do you know that?

LV: I don't know. It's just something I've always believed.

Carol: I have another idea. Let me show you something. *[Carol creates a visual picture of every human being, including herself, being divine and perfect just the way they are.]* If you don't have any reason for your belief, would you be willing to try a new one?

LV: Well, yes, but I still want you to be the best that you can be, and be respected and successful.

Carol: And I really appreciate that! I'm grateful that you've been working so hard to get me to be the best that I can be.

LV: [smiles, is pleased]

241

Carol: With this new image, can you see that being the best that I can be also might include the need for rest and recreation, so I become a well-rounded person, full of happiness and joy?

LV: Yes, I can see that.

Carol: So can you support me in taking my Free Days, and enjoying them?

LV: Yes, I can, certainly!

Carol: Thank you so much for your support!

Carol said, "At this point, I could feel almost a new, strong energy coming from the face/LV, and could hear him muttering about making sure I took my Free Days, which made me laugh. I knew that the LV would be almost militant in his insistence that I take and enjoy my Free Days, because that would make me the best person I could be."

WHY WE CLING TO OLD HABITS AND BEHAVIORS

When we look at changing something about ourselves, fear is often triggered. Sometimes the fear is hidden, and comes out as procrastination or another form of self-sabotage, and sometimes we're very aware of it.

One way to bring your fears out into the open is to ask the question *What might happen if I made this change?*

There are a number of reasons why people hold on to habits and behaviors that they know do not serve them. These include the following:

1. *I don't know who I'll be if I change.* (identity issues)
2. *It's not safe to change.* (safety issues)
3. *I'm not capable of change.* (limiting beliefs about ability)
4. *I don't know how to change.* (lack of knowledge issues)

These are general categories, so we won't tap directly on these limiting beliefs. Instead we'll look at specifically how these show up for you, and then tap on those particular issues. Often when you work on the specific belief, the general belief will collapse, either immediately or over time.

First you'll want to look at any perceived downsides to your changing your behavior, and establishing new habits, such as:

- *I want to lose weight, but I don't want to give up fast food.*

- *I want to quit smoking, but I don't want to lose my smoking friends.*

- *I want to spend more time with my family, but I'm afraid I won't get all my work done.*

- *I want to be more efficient, but I don't like organizational systems; they feel confining.*

We'll take each one of these general reasons, and see how it could show up in these specific issues.

1. IDENTIFY CONFLICTS

Sometimes when you think of changing or establishing a new habit, it could create a *conflict with your identity*. Your very self feels threatened. How can you create success, have a healthy body, become wealthy, or have a loving relationship, if you don't have those things now? If you do create them, who will you become?

If the vision of the person you know yourself to be doesn't have those things, it may feel like you literally will have to die to achieve those things. That can be very frightening! The truth is that small parts of you will die, or be eliminated, including your limiting beliefs and emotional responses that no longer serve you.

Notice as we proceed if you have any of these thoughts:

- *I don't know who I'll be if I achieve this.*

- *I'm afraid I won't be me if I do this.*

243

- *What if I don't like myself when I achieve these goals?*

- *Who will I be if I'm thin?*

- *I can't see myself as a nonsmoker.*

- *I see myself as a hard worker, and don't want to change that.*

- *I'm a creative person, so I'm not supposed to be organized.*

2. SAFETY ISSUES

There may also be fears involved, which creates the feeling that *it's not safe to change.*

Take a look at what you want to accomplish, and list the consequences, especially any negative consequences that you see. If these consequences cause you to feel unsafe or in danger, that's something that you can work on. For example:

- *If I lose weight, men will hit on me.*

- *If I become more successful, I'll be a target for criticism.*

- *If I make more money, my friends won't like me anymore.*

- *If I become more self-confident, I'll want to leave my marriage, and I don't want to think about that.*

- *I'm afraid that food won't be any fun anymore if I can't eat fast food.*

- *I'm afraid I'll lose my friends who smoke.*

- *I'm afraid my work performance will suffer.*

- *I'm afraid that I'll lose my creativity if I become more organized.*

3. LIMITING BELIEFS ABOUT ABILITY

If you have the belief *I'm not capable of change,* you may have some of these underlying thoughts:

- *I've never been able to control my eating successfully before.*

- *I've tried to quit smoking, and it just doesn't work.*

- *I'd be lost if I wasn't working all the time.*

- *I just can't make myself organized if I'm not.*

We looked at similar issues in exploring Success Principle 33: Transcend Your Limiting Beliefs. You may notice some thoughts such as:

- *I'm not capable of that kind of change.*

- *I don't deserve to have that much happiness.*

- *I shouldn't focus so much on myself and my own life.*

When you notice these types of thoughts, be aware that you're working with a very common limiting belief, and that it is only a belief. Like all beliefs, you can shift these with tapping, attention, and time.

4. LACK OF KNOWLEDGE ISSUES

If you have the belief *I don't know how to change,* you may experience thoughts such as the following:

- *I don't know what to do—I've always eaten fast food, it's convenient.*

- *I don't know which "quit smoking" system to use—will any of them even work for me?*

- *I don't know any way I could get my work done in less time.*

- *I can't think in organizational terms, so how could I do this?*

With some changes you try to implement, such as increasing your income or your time off, you may also have the limiting belief *I don't deserve to change.* If so, reread Success Principle 33: Transcend Your Limiting Beliefs in the beginning of Chapter 6, and work on that belief using the techniques described there.

In addition, when changing some habits, you may have to deal with the cravings for fast food, cigarettes, alcohol, or another item. Addictive habits such as these are caused by an attempt to soothe anxiety through a certain behavior. In order to remove addictions, you have to address not only the habit, but the underlying anxiety that is causing the habit. Otherwise you'll simply substitute one addictive behavior for another. (We could write an entire book on using tapping to remove cravings and addictions—but we have space for only a brief overview here. If you need support in this area, you may want to investigate one of the many tapping practitioners who specialize in this work.)

Once you identify the limiting belief that is keeping your habit in place, you can tap to remove that belief. If you find yourself saying, "*I just need to . . .*" in a way that suggests that just a little bit of additional willpower will solve the problem, it means you know what to do, but are experiencing resistance. Unfortunately, this situation often creates negative self-judgments, such as:

- *I don't know why I can't do it. I guess I'm just lazy.*

- *It's not that hard to do. I should have done it already.*

- *It would really require so little additional effort on my part. What's wrong with me?*

These self-judgments just compound the problem, because they support the mistaken belief that emotional resistance can and should be easily overcome with willpower. Instead, focus your attention and energy on removing the resistance using tapping, rather than beating yourself up for having the resistance.

As you examine your resistance to change, you may have to do some detective work to figure out what is causing it. While you don't have to do this, it may make it easier to see other perspectives and create Choice Statements. For example, don't stop at the statement *I don't want to give up fast food* but ask yourself why this is so. Your reasons might include:

- *It will be too inconvenient to eat healthy food all the time.*

- *I don't like the taste of healthy food.*

- *It's more expensive to eat healthy food.*

You can then create your Choice Statements to overcome these limiting beliefs. They might include:

- ❖ *Even though I was worried I'd be bored with my food, I choose to enjoy my new healthy diet.*

- ❖ *Even though I feared giving up cigarettes, I will love the energy I have when I'm a nonsmoker.*

As another example, suppose you believe, *I don't have time to create new habits.* You could ask yourself, *What will occur if I try to create new habits?* The answer might be, *I'll let something else slip* or *I won't be able to keep my obligations.* Those are fears, so that means that you believe it's not safe to change, and that something bad will happen if you do. You can approach these fears as you would tap on any fears, with any tapping technique you prefer.

EXERCISE: CREATING POWERFUL NEW HABITS

Choose a new habit you'd like to adopt. Be specific. For example, don't say "I'd like to eat more healthfully," say "I eat dessert no more than once or twice a week." (**Hint:** It is very powerful to do this step with a partner, even if the partner is establishing a different habit.)

Examine any resistance you have to creating the new habit first. Write down your challenges to committing to the new habit; which of the four categories do they fall in?

Create a tapping routine, using any technique you like, to eliminate your resistance to implanting your new habit. Some suggestions:

- SOS Tapping: Remove a limiting belief, create an empowering belief.

- Little Voice Tapping: Retrain your little voice to support you in this habit rather than resisting and telling you that you can't.

- Matrix Reimprinting: Consider this method if you have a memory that causes you to think that you can't succeed at establishing a new habit.

Setup statements that you could use in a tapping routine to overcome the discomfort of a new habit include:

- ❖ *Even though I don't want to get up and go exercise this morning, I choose to honor my commitment.*

- ❖ *Even though I don't have time to write that thank-you note right now, I'm open to how good expressing gratitude for that gift will feel.*

Committing to a new habit is not the same as actually *adopting* it. As you take action to create the habit, what do you notice? If new habits fail, it's usually for one of two reasons: either you forget to do the new habit, or you break your commitment because it's uncomfortable.

Be sure to record your progress with establishing your new habit!

SUCCESS STORY

David, a 60-year-old woodworker, knew that he needed to lose weight. Whenever he thought about doing it, his emotional reaction was *It will take all the fun out of life, I'll never be able to eat what I want again.* Although he intellectually recognized this reaction as overly strong, it continued to sabotage his efforts at eating a healthy diet.

He started with Little Voice Tapping, since the voice was so loud. He began Continuous Tapping, and envisioned the Voice as a little boy who was very upset with the idea of dieting.

LV: This won't be any fun. We'll never have fun again. I don't want to do this.

David: But I'd really like to look better, and I think I'd have more energy.

LV: But life won't be any fun at all!

David: Would you be willing to tap with me?

LV: [reluctantly] OK.

David: So tell me why life won't be any fun.

LV: It's always like this. I'm just not allowed to do anything that's fun. If it's fun, they want to take it away from me.

David: That doesn't feel fair, does it?

LV: No!

David: I appreciate you looking out for us to have fun, and making sure that life is fun. Thank you for that.

LV: [smiles]

David: What if there was a way for losing weight to be fun?

LV: That will never happen.

David: You do like going on adventures, don't you?

LV: Like going to cool places, trying new things? Yeah, that's fun.

David: What if we could experiment with food, just like experimenting with travel?

LV: I dunno. Maybe.

David: We could try new things that we've never had before. There are some things that we've been saying we didn't like for so long, I don't even think we know what they taste like.

LV: That might be true.

David: I'll bet we could find a way to make this fun. It would be a different kind of fun, much more adventurous.

LV: I like adventure!

David: Is part of the reason that you want to eat what you want because no one ever listens to you?

LV: Yeah.

David: Well, I'm listening now. And I'm happy to listen to you and get your help on all these new food adventures. Would you like that?

LV: I want to make sure you talk to me. It has to be fun.

David: OK, I'm relying on you to remind me to have fun with all the interesting new foods we're going to eat. Can you do that?

LV: Yes, I can.

David: Are you ready to go on this new adventure together?

LV: Yes, as long as I'm listened to and included.

David: Absolutely!

David began a new way of healthy eating, and found himself more open to new foods than he had been in the past. He immediately lost weight. Also, because of the conversation with the LV, he focused on creating more fun in his life, and found that food had decreased in importance for him. It had been a way of nurturing himself, and he found he could now choose new ways to nurture himself without food.

INQUIRE WITHIN
(SUCCESS PRINCIPLE 47)

We've spoken repeatedly about the power of the subconscious mind. What about the wisdom of the subconscious mind?

The connections and storage that are available to the subconscious part of the mind are much greater than those available to the conscious part. This is why you often can't remember details about a memory, but when something about an event triggers you, you'll remember details that you had forgotten. Those details were part of the vast territory of your subconscious mind.

In his book *Blink,* Malcolm Gladwell discusses the phenomenon of knowing a truth in an instant from a brief impression, even when we don't have the rational arguments to back up our knowing. Studies show that evaluations of teachers made by people watching just a few seconds of a videotape are astonishingly accurate in judging the effectiveness of the teacher. The same is true for people watching a few seconds of videotape of couples, and judging how long the relationship will last.[11]

Intuitive messages come through the subconscious part of the mind. Therefore, they may occur as pictures, as flashes of feeling or insight, or just a "knowing sense." Although words can also be involved, there usually won't be any reasons behind the words.

Learning to trust these intuitive insights is challenging for many people. Even for those who believe in the power of their intuition, it is sometimes more challenging to distinguish when a message is a true insight and when it's part of a fear, doubt, or limiting belief, since they all send us feelings and images.

One good test for whether something is intuition or fear is to examine how it makes you feel. Do you feel expanded and excited when you think of it? Or do you feel contracted and closed in? If it's the latter, it's probably a fear. You can then tap on the fear, and you'll get clearer intuitive messages.

Our intuition often leads us to expand, to take actions that will make us grow and give us what we are looking for. In those cases, it's more likely that fears will block our acting on our intuition.

How many times have you received a message to "go for it" with regard to some project or plan, and talked yourself out of it?

In that case, you can use tapping to overcome the fears about following your intuition. Since intuition by definition isn't rational, you may not be able to create a reasonable reframe about why you should do what you are intuitively guided to do. In fact, often intuition appears to us to recommend foolish or nonsensical actions. However, the more that you listen to your intuition and follow it, the more reliable it becomes.

Possible reframes for following intuition include:

❖ *Even though I'm nervous about acting on my intuition, I'm open to trusting the intuitive process.*

❖ *Even though acting on my intuition seems silly in this case, I choose to enjoy the experience of following my intuition.*

❖ *Even though I'm not sure I should act, because I don't trust my intuition, I'm open to accessing this source of wisdom in a powerful way.*

As with all tapping, these will be most effective if you're tapping on a specific instance in which you've gotten intuitive guidance and are debating whether or not to act on it.

If you don't trust your intuition in general, it can also be useful to tap to remove the limiting belief *I can't trust my intuition.* Remember to look for an event that may have caused you to have this belief, and clear any negative emotions around that event.

99% IS A BITCH; 100% IS A BREEZE (SUCCESS PRINCIPLE 35)

In the course of daily life, we're constantly asked to make decisions. It can be easy to become paralyzed by the sheer number of decisions and options in front of us. Success Principle 54: Keep Your Agreements, only hints at a way to decrease the pressure from this abundance of choices. When you keep your agreements, it takes some possible choices off the table. Of course, you do have to choose to make an agreement in the first place. This idea is more fully expressed in Success Principle 35: 99% Is a Bitch; 100% Is a Breeze.

Once you've made a commitment, constantly reevaluating whether or not you want to keep it today only takes more energy and introduces doubt in your life. Honoring your commitments and keeping your agreements clears your mind, reduces overwhelm, and makes life much easier.

What stops many people from being willing to make a 100% commitment is a fear that they will be trapped, or that they won't be able to respond to inner guidance. What if your inner guidance tells you that you're not supposed to keep a previous commitment that you've made?

One challenge with this situation is distinguishing between inner guidance and the sabotage of the ego. Is it really your inner guidance telling you not to work out today, or is your ego being lazy and trying to derail your efforts at improved health?

Making a 100% commitment actually helps this situation. When you're accustomed to operating from 100% commitment, you aren't constantly reevaluating based on the desires of the ego. This means that your inner guidance is clearer and more easily heard.

In any given situation, there are times when it may be appropriate to break a commitment. If you have a commitment to work out every morning, and one morning your child is injured and you need to take him to the hospital, you will probably make the choice to break your commitment to working out. These situations do not mean that you don't want to commit 100%. This means when you play big in life and make commitments, sometimes those will be challenged.

Examine any resistance you may have to this principle. If you're afraid you'll have to ignore your inner guidance, then build that into the commitment.

Here are some suggested reframes and tapping phrases that you could use. Create your own if none of these resonate with you.

The first example uses one negative and one positive Reminder Phrase. The second example has several different phrases. Do you prefer to repeat the same Reminder Phrase on every point, or use different phrases on different points?

Suggested Specific Choice setup statements:

❖ *Even though I'm afraid to commit 100% because I'll have to ignore my inner guidance, I choose to allow my guidance to support me in my commitments.*

❖ *Even though I'm afraid to commit 100% because I'll have to ignore my inner guidance, I choose to allow my guidance to help me design and deliver on my perfect commitments.*

Tap a Choices Trio to remove your fears, and create your new empowering belief. Reminder Phrases (negative round):

❖ *I'm afraid I'll have to ignore my inner guidance if I commit 100%.*

Reminder Phrase (positive round):

❖ *I choose to allow my guidance to support me in my commitments.*

Alternating round:

❖ **Top of the Head:** *I'm afraid I'll have to ignore my inner guidance if I commit 100%.*

❖ **Eyebrow:** *I choose to allow my guidance to support me in my commitments.*

❖ **Outside of Eye:** *I'm afraid I'll have to ignore my inner guidance if I commit 100%.*

❖ **Under the Eye:** *I choose to allow my guidance to support me in my commitments.*

❖ **Under the Nose:** *I'm afraid I'll have to ignore my inner guidance if I commit 100%.*

❖ **Chin:** *I choose to allow my guidance to support me in my commitments.*

❖ **Collarbone:** *I'm afraid I'll have to ignore my inner guidance if I commit 100%.*

❖ **Under the Arm:** *I choose to allow my guidance to support me in my commitments.*

Another possibility is that you may not want to commit 100% because you fear that you'll not be able to keep that commitment, and you'll feel like a failure. You could use the following reframe as your setup statement to overcome that fear:

❖ *Even though I'm afraid to commit 100% because I'll feel like a failure if I can't keep the commitment, I choose to play big and commit anyway.*

Reminder Phrases (negative round):

❖ **Top of the Head:** *I'm afraid I'll feel like a failure if I can't keep my commitment.*

❖ **Eyebrow:** *What if I commit, then I don't keep it?*

❖ **Outside of Eye:** *I'll really feel like a failure.*

❖ **Under the Eye:** *It would be easier not to make the commitment.*

❖ **Under the Nose:** *If I don't make the commitment, then there is no chance of being a failure.*

❖ **Chin:** *I just don't want to fail at this.*

❖ **Collarbone:** *It's easier not to commit.*

❖ **Under the Arm:** *I'm so afraid I'll look like a failure.*

Reminder Phrases (positive round):

❖ **Top of the Head:** *I may not fail if I don't commit, but I won't succeed either.*

❖ **Eyebrow:** *What if I commit and then only get partway to my goal?*

❖ **Outside of Eye:** *At least I'd be farther along than I am now.*

❖ **Under the Eye:** *I don't want to commit and then just do it halfway.*

❖ **Under the Nose:** *If I make this commitment, I want to go for it.*

❖ **Chin:** *If I don't make it, I'll work on that issue later.*

❖ **Collarbone:** *I can play full-out now.*

❖ **Under the Arm:** *The act of committing will give me extra strength to reach my goal.*

Alternating round:

❖ **Top of the Head:** *I'm so afraid I'll look like a failure.*

❖ **Eyebrow:** *I'm choosing to be powerful and commit.*

❖ **Outside of Eye:** *It's easier not to commit.*

❖ **Under the Eye:** *What if it's actually easier to commit?*

❖ **Under the Nose:** *I'm so afraid I'll look like a failure.*

❖ **Chin:** *I choose to use the power of commitment to get to my goal.*

❖ **Collarbone:** *There's always the possibility that I'll fail.*

❖ **Under the Arm:** *I choose to know that I can succeed, and I commit to it!*

CONSIDERATIONS, FEARS, AND ROADBLOCKS

As we've explored resistance to the different success principles, we've been looking at *considerations, fears,* and *roadblocks.*

Considerations are thoughts expressed by the negative voice in your head. As you state a goal, begin to take action, or contemplate implementing any one of the success principles, thoughts usually emerge such as:

- *You can't do that.*

- *That won't work because . . .*

- *You've always failed before.*

- *You'll have to work too hard to accomplish that.*

- *In order for you to do this, you'll have to _____ .*

Some of these are limiting beliefs, and some of them are neutral beliefs with negative emotions underlying them. Either way, you can use tapping to turn these around.

Considerations and fears work together—they are really two sides of the same coin. Fears are feelings that are there to protect you, to keep you safe. Occasionally you'll have a fear that doesn't seem to be attached to a thought. You may find yourself thinking *I'm afraid to do that, but I don't know why.* More often you'll have a thought attached to the fear, such as *I'm afraid to take action because I think I'll be rejected.* Considerations are the thoughts above the fears. When you examine considerations closely, you'll see that each has a fear behind it.

For tapping purposes, you can approach removing considerations and fears from either angle; that is, you can work by focusing on the fear, or you can focus on the limiting belief.

Roadblocks are external situations that appear to interfere with you achieving your goals. A roadblock might be a lack of resources, or a governmental rule that prevents you from doing what you wish to do. Many people think that they are encountering roadblocks when they are actually up against considerations.

For example, suppose you think *I have a roadblock of not enough money to achieve my goal.* That appears to be an external circumstance. However, could you earn the money, borrow it, or have it gifted to you? Most people say *I can't* or *I don't have* instead of *How could I?* In this example, the imagined roadblock of *I don't have enough money to achieve my goal* becomes a consideration of *I'd have to somehow find the money to achieve my goal,* bringing it much more into your control and within your power.

Even roadblocks which appear insurmountable can be overcome with a success-focused approach: a no-excuses, playing full-out attitude toward your goals. When you develop this mindset, the size of your challenges will seem to shrink considerably.

To begin this process, you can ask yourself these two questions:

What if I knew that there was a way to succeed?

If you know a puzzle is solvable, you will work on it longer than if you believe it to be unsolvable. Spend a few minutes visualizing your end result, without considering how it was accomplished. For example, your book became a bestseller, you achieved your ideal weight and health goals, or you married the person of your dreams. Feel the satisfaction, happiness, and pride of having achieved your goal. Now that you can see it as a possible, or even probable, reality, you'll feel more like putting effort into working on it.

What if the life of someone dear to me depended on my achieving this?

If the consequences of you giving up or failing were horrible to contemplate, you would truly play full-out.

You may need to take actions that are far outside your comfort zone in order to get around a roadblock. Or you may need to change the way that you think your goal or end result should look.

Another way to look at the process of overcoming considerations, fears and roadblocks is to ask yourself: "Is the best thing that will come out of this goal the *result* of achieving the goal, or *who I will become* in the process of achieving it?"

When you work toward any goal, you change. As you remove fears, overcome roadblocks, and change limiting beliefs to empowering ones, you become better able to succeed at anything you take on. With this reframe, all the challenges that arise for you are like the weights for the bodybuilder. The goal isn't to lift the weights, it's who the bodybuilder will become from lifting. And the weight isn't something to be avoided or complained about, it's what allows the bodybuilder to build his or her physique.

Certainly challenges will arise whenever you take on something new. But once you begin to contemplate a goal with this mindset, new possibilities occur that weren't available before. And with tapping to help you reduce the fears, reframe the considerations or limiting beliefs, and expand your thinking to include new options around the roadblocks, success becomes just that much easier.

PRACTICE PERSISTENCE (SUCCESS PRINCIPLE 22)

If you persist, your chances of success skyrocket. Why is it, then, that so many people give up after failing once, or a few times?

Failure can be disheartening. Some see failure as a sign that the universe is trying to get them to stop. But all successful people fail at some point. People who are not successful fail as well, obviously, but the difference is that they stopped trying, and never got to the success!

So how can tapping, or any technique, help you to practice persistence? In addition to using the ideas we talked about in the previous section on considerations, fears, and roadblocks, the key lies in reframing failure so that you aren't stopped by it, but instead proceed to try again.

When you hear the word "failure," what do you think? When you think about a previous event in your life that you've termed a failure, how do you feel? Do you believe that you've failed too many times, been turned down too often, or received too many rejection notices to persevere?

Are any of these thoughts true for you?

- *Why try? I'll only fail again.*

- *No one wants what I have to offer.*

- *No matter how hard I try, I just can't seem to do this.*

- *I've failed too many times.*
- *I don't have it in me to try again.*

The Success Principles is filled with stories of people who were rejected hundreds of times before they went on to be successes—including Jack when he was trying to publish *Chicken Soup for the Soul!* These stories may not entirely convince you to continue, but they make excellent reframes, and bring home the idea that "instant success" usually only comes after some amount of effort and failure.

Here are some reframes that you might consider:

- ❖ *I choose to consider that lots of successful people failed first, why not me?*

- ❖ *I choose to remember that even <u>Chicken Soup for the Soul</u> was rejected over 140 times.*

- ❖ *Some people don't want what I have to offer; what if others do?*

- ❖ *I choose to remember that just being persistent makes me a winner.*

With these reframes, you can work on this resistance using SOS Tapping, and it will be effective. Little Voice Tapping is also very useful, since after failure your subconscious is often trying to keep you safe, and will work to convince you that persistence isn't in your best interest. You'll need to work with the Little Voice to retrain it with the concept that having a new idea about failure and persistence can create even more of a feeling of safety than not trying at all.

SUCCESS STORY

Pamela writes: When I was launching my first big business coaching program, I did a series of joint calls with other coaches, talking about my program and inviting people to participate. I wanted 50 people to enroll. Although thousands of people listened to the calls, I only had 16 people signed up for the program nine days before the first class. I felt very much like a failure, and like I had missed something critical that I should have done.

I did Simple Tapping on my disappointment, and my feelings that I had failed.

I then used some Specific Choices, including:

❖ *Even though I feel like I failed in this launch, I choose to look at how much I've learned.*

❖ *Even though almost none of those people liked what I had to say, I choose to acknowledge how accomplished I've gotten in sharing my message.*

❖ *Even though it feels like I've failed, I'm open to an exciting possibility.*

At the end of my tapping, rather than feeling defeated, I was feeling open to possibility.

That night, a friend mentioned an advertising campaign on the web that she was impressed with. It was a series of informative videos. I watched the first one and thought, *Would this work for me?* I immediately put together a four-part video series that I created at home in two days, and sent the videos out via e-mail to the thousands of people who had listened to the calls.

Within five days, I had almost 100 people signed up for the program. It was my first big program, and it led to my business crossing the million-dollar mark only 15 months later . . . all because I chose to practice persistence and eliminate my feelings of being a failure.

CHUNK IT DOWN
(SUCCESS PRINCIPLE 8)

In order to complete any project, you have to perform a number of tasks. However, many people go to work on a project by trying to tackle the entire project at once, or they procrastinate about starting because it seems too overwhelming. Breaking your project down into action steps, or "chunking it down," allows you to organize your project so it's not so overwhelming, and gives you a schedule to commit to. It just makes sense, yet some people resist chunking it down because they have a limiting belief about their ability to organize and schedule, or fear that a plan will trap them in some way.

Let's look at the process of chunking it down, and work on any resistance you may have to this success principle. First you'll need to determine all the action steps within a project, then turn those action steps into a to-do list, then schedule your to-do list. These may bring up thoughts such as:

- *I don't know what all the action steps are.*

- *I'm afraid I'll be overwhelmed if I lay it all out.*

- *I'm afraid I'll miss a step.*

- *I'm not that organized.*

- *I've never been good at scheduling.*

- *I'm afraid I'll schedule something and won't finish it in time.*

- *I don't want to be trapped by a plan. I want the project to flow more organically.*

Before you read the following reframes, why not try to come up with some of your own? Imagine that you're talking to a friend who is expressing these blocks. What would you suggest to him or her?

If you're feeling a lot of emotional intensity around this, you'll want to do some Simple Tapping to bring it down. Then you can either use the reframes or work with Little Voice Tapping if you hear a voice trying to keep you safe (and small).

Here are some possible reframes, written as Open or Specific Choice Statements:

❖ *Even though I don't know what all the action steps are, I'm open to starting to lay things out.*

❖ *Even though I'm afraid I'll be overwhelmed if I lay it all out, I can tap on the overwhelm, and it will be good to know what I'm facing in my project.*

❖ *Even though I'm afraid I'll miss a step, I choose to trust the process.*

❖ *Even though I'm not that organized, I choose to find a creative, effective way to do this.*

❖ *Even though I've never been good at scheduling, I choose to remember that I've learned other skills; perhaps I could learn this one.*

❖ *Even though I'm afraid I'll schedule something and won't finish it in time, I choose to see that as an opportunity to improve my scheduling skills.*

❖ *Even though I don't want to be trapped by a plan, and I want the project to flow more organically, I choose to start with a plan that I can always modify as I go.*

Once you've removed your resistance, you can chunk down your big project and get it done!

COMMIT TO CONSTANT AND NEVER-ENDING IMPROVEMENT (SUCCESS PRINCIPLE 20)

In order to commit to improvement, you first have to acknowledge that there is something to improve, and that you are capable of improvement. Although they have the same root, let's look at each of these separately.

Remember the concept of fixed and growth mindsets? With a fixed mindset, if you are smart or talented, success should be easy; and if you fail, it proves that there is no hope for you. You're just that way, not smart or talented enough. With a growth mindset, there is always room for improvement; success is based on how hard you work rather than talent; and failure is a tool that shows you where to focus your work, not an indicator of how you will always be.

With a growth mindset, these two ideas—that there is something to improve, and that you are capable of improvement—are givens. They are part of the mindset.

You may be unwilling to admit that there is something to improve, because you're worried about the consequences of that admission. If you admit that you don't have the perfect job, or the perfect marriage, what will follow from that acknowledgment? You may fear that dissatisfaction could cause you to pursue uncomfortable actions such as looking for a new job or a new spouse. Although this may happen, it is also possible that acknowledging that there is room for improvement, taking responsibility, and beginning to work on it completely revitalizes the situation.

More common is a frustration such as, *I'm not improving fast enough,* or *I'll never be good enough.* (We've looked at that in Chapter 5 with Success Principle 16: Be Willing to Pay the Price.)

TAPPING TIP: USE LANGUAGE THAT TRIGGERS YOUR EMOTIONS

When you're tapping, it's vital to use language that accurately reflects your emotional state. If you try to be polite or politically correct, you'll cut yourself off from the emotional energy that you're trying to clear.

This may mean that you use profanity, or strong images such as *I'd like to wring her neck* or *I want to kick him in the butt.* Don't censor yourself from using that language if that's what comes to mind when you're tapping.

Notice in the next success story that Rose used strong language about herself very effectively.

SUCCESS STORY

Rose was a healing practitioner who wanted to build her practice, but felt that she had a block to making more money. After thinking about it, she realized that her extended family shared a belief that rich people are greedy. Because she and her husband had an adequate income, more than many of her family members, she felt uncomfortable with the idea of trying to earn more money—it felt greedy to her, even though consciously she thought it was perfectly acceptable that she earn more.

She measured her emotional belief that it was greedy to want to earn more at a 7, so she tapped using Open Choices:

❖ *Even though it feels greedy to want more money, I'm open to a new way to look at this.*

❖ *Even though I feel like I'm a moneygrubbing bitch for wanting to earn more, I'm open to a new way to look at this.*

Reminder Phrases included:

❖ *It feels so greedy!*

❖ *I feel like a bitch for wanting that money.*

❖ *Only horrible, greedy people want more money.*

After a few rounds of tapping her belief that she was greedy had dropped to a 3, so she switched to a Specific Choice:

❖ *Even though I still feel greedy for wanting more money, I choose to take good care of my family this way.*

She used a Choices Trio, tapping first the negative (*I still feel greedy*), then the positive (*I choose to take good care of my family*) and then alternating them.

After she ceased to feel greedy, she realized that she was also concerned that she would be pressured to give away her extra earnings to her extended family should she make more. Although she was excited about making more for her immediate family, she didn't want to feel pressured to give, and recognized this as an important block.

This is a fairly complex belief to work with, because it's composed of the thoughts *They will pressure me to give them money and they'll make me feel guilty if I don't do that* and *I'm worried they won't speak to me if I don't give them money*. These are two separate aspects.

Rose used the setup phrase:

❖ *Even though they'll pressure me to give them money, and I'm afraid I'll feel guilty, I choose to take responsibility for my feelings.*

She also used lots of different Reminder Phrases, including:

❖ *I'll feel so guilty.*

❖ *They'll want me to share what I've worked hard for.*

❖ *They'll make me feel so guilty.*

As the fear diminished over several rounds, Rose shifted to:

❖ *I choose to take responsibility for my feelings.*

❖ *No one can make me feel guilty if I don't choose to.*

The fear that her extended family wouldn't speak to her had diminished after working on the first issue, but was still at a 3.

❖ *Even though I'm still a little worried that they won't speak to me, I choose to stand firm in my commitments to myself and my immediate family.*

Reminder Phrases included:

* *What if they don't speak to me?*

* *That would make me sad.*

* *It's not my responsibility to give them money I make.*

* *I'm worried they won't speak to me.*

* *I can choose to be loving, and still spend my money the way that I want.*

At the end, Rose felt very excited about the possibility of earning more money in her business, and felt completely in integrity with doing that. She no longer felt concerned about her extended family. She has since significantly increased the success of her business, and her income.

TAPPING TIP: BE A DETECTIVE

How do you really know what's stopping you? Sometimes you have so many reasons why you "just can't do it" that it's hard to be clear on what's actually stopping you.

When you have a thought that stops you from taking action, you can use this process to both get to the underlying issue and to remove it. Very often we rationalize, meaning we create reasons that aren't the real ones, about why we behave the way that we do.

If you think about why you are resistant to doing something, you may come up with the real answer, or you may not. For example, if you decide to schedule time to clean up your office, and you think *I have more important things to do,* that will interfere with your cleaning. But is that the real reason, or is it an excuse that your subconscious is putting up in order to keep you from feeling anxiety associated with letting clutter go? Tapping can help you figure out the answer.

One way that tapping can help is simply the process of evaluating your SUDS level. As you become experienced in asking yourself "How intense is this emotion?" you'll notice that the rationalizations don't have the emotional intensity behind them. Also, when you get used to tapping and speaking freely, rather than repeating the same Reminder Phrase over and over again, you'll start voicing the real reason that you're stopped.

TAPPING TECHNIQUE: FREE-ASSOCIATION TAPPING

Free-Association Tapping can bring many of the same benefits as journaling. It can be helpful, although not necessary, to record what you're saying as you do this process in case you want to refer back to it.

Start by identifying the action that you're resistant to taking, and why you believe you don't want to take that action.

Tap the first point, and state the resistance you have to taking the action before you. Then tap the next point, and begin to explain why you have that resistance.

Say one sentence per tapping point, then move to the next point as you continue to talk. You can also repeat your original resistance statement.

After some time, you may notice your reason for resistance shifting. Allow all the thoughts and emotions that you may be experiencing to surface as you speak. Like Firm Stand Tapping, you won't necessarily clear all the issues that you uncover, because you're not focusing on and evaluating your SUDS level, nor are you making sure to clear each aspect completely. However, as you do this process more often, it will become easier to get the deeper messages from your subconscious about what is truly stopping you. You can then use the other tapping techniques to clear the issues that you've uncovered.

SUCCESS STORY

Rita, an attractive single woman in her 50s, was reluctant to date, although she felt as though she wanted a romantic partner in her life. Her initial resistance to dating was that she didn't have enough time, but she decided to do some Free-Association Tapping to see if there were additional issues.

She tapped with the Reminder Phrases:

- ❖ *I don't have enough time to date.*
- ❖ *I'm really too busy with my work.*
- ❖ *I suppose I could make time.*
- ❖ *But what if I had a date that I didn't enjoy?*
- ❖ *That would feel like a waste of time.*
- ❖ *If I did meet someone nice, that would really take up my time.*
- ❖ *Do I actually want a partner?*
- ❖ *It might be nice to have someone in my life.*
- ❖ *Partners can be very demanding, though.*
- ❖ *What if my partner started interfering in my work?*

(At this point Rita realized that she had a strong belief that a partner would try to prevent her from working, just as her father had prevented her mother from working.)

- ❖ *This feels so true to me, that a partner would stop me.*

Rita then stopped the Free-Association Tapping. She recognized that although part of her believed emotionally that a partner would try to stop her from working, rationally she knew that it didn't have to be that way.

This old emotional belief brought up the fear that she would be forced to choose between her work and her partner, and possibly lose a valuable relationship in order to continue her work, which would be very painful.

She rated her belief that a partner would try to stop her work at an 8. So she started with Simple Tapping, with the Reminder Phrases:

❖ *If I have a partner, he will try to stop me from working.*

❖ *He'll be so upset at how important my work is to me.*

❖ *We'll argue about it.* [At this point her intensity was at a 10.]

❖ *It will be so painful.*

❖ *I don't want to have to choose between work and a partner.*

❖ *I just want to be able to do my work.*

❖ *Why can't I do my work and be loved, too?*

❖ *I'm so afraid of the pressure from this partner.*

❖ *I'm afraid my partner will try to stop me from the work I love.*

❖ *I don't want to be stopped.*

❖ *I don't want to have to choose.*

Rita reevaluated her intensity, and found it was now a 6, so she began SOS Tapping. She created the Open Choice setup statements:

❖ *Even though it still feels like a partner would try to stop me, I'm open to the possibility that it doesn't have to be that way.*

❖ *Even though I have this old belief that a partner would try to stop me, I'm open to the idea that there are lots of people with close partners doing work they love.*

After several rounds of tapping, the strength of her belief that a partner would stop her was a 3. She realized that the belief was still there because she doubted her ability to attract a partner who would respect her work. She created several Specific Choices to address this concern:

❖ *Even though I'm still a bit afraid that a partner might try to interfere with my work, I choose to consider that I can find a partner who is perfect for me.*

❖ *Even though some partners might try to interfere with my work, I choose to trust myself to find a partner that will support me in doing what I love.*

❖ *Even though it's possible I might make a mistake in choosing a partner, I choose to trust the Universe to bring me the perfect partner who supports my work.*

After several rounds of tapping using the Choices Trio Method, Rita no longer feared attracting a partner who would stop her, but instead was excited about the possibility of having someone in her life who would support her and her work. When she looked at her willingness to date, she found that she no longer experienced any resistance to the idea of dating.

STAY FOCUSED ON YOUR CORE GENIUS (SUCCESS PRINCIPLE 39), BUILD A POWERFUL SUPPORT TEAM AND DELEGATE TO THEM (SUCCESS PRINCIPLE 41), AND HIRE A PERSONAL COACH (SUCCESS PRINCIPLE 45)

How much do you delegate in your life? If you are an entrepreneur, manager, or CEO, you probably delegate to some extent. However, everyone can benefit from the concept of delegation; if you want to be truly successful, you'll need to raise delegation to an art form.

If you grew up in a home where your family did all the work yourselves, the concept of hiring household help may seem strange to you. You may fear looking arrogant or like a spendthrift if you hire assistance. You may also worry about it not being done as well as you would do it.

Perhaps you are concerned about your ability to run a support team, or feel overwhelmed by the thought of trying to manage others.

Many times, others can do something better than we can, especially if the task is not our core genius. Even if it's not done as well as you might do it, the slight improvement in quality that your efforts might add isn't worth it. It doesn't make up for the fact that you are costing yourself time that you could be spending to bring yourself more joy, such as time with your family, or costing yourself money if you're not working in your area of expertise.

This is a great opportunity to use Firm Stand Tapping. Create a statement about delegating that is empowering, even if you're not comfortable with it yet. Then alternate between all the reasons that you can't delegate and that statement.

For example:

❖ *I choose to delegate and focus on my genius for the good of everyone, including myself.*

❖ *It feels arrogant to have others do my grunt work.*

❖ *I choose to delegate and focus on my genius for the good of everyone, including myself.*

❖ *I don't believe anyone will do as good a job as I will.*

❖ *I choose to delegate and focus on my genius for the good of everyone, including myself.*

❖ *I feel intimidated by the idea of managing others.*

❖ *I choose to delegate and focus on my genius for the good of everyone, including myself.*

As you continue this process, and it may take a number of rounds, some of the objections will begin to fall away and will no longer be issues for you. At some point in this process, one or possibly two of the objections to delegating may feel like they aren't shifting. Stop and switch to SOS Tapping around those issues.

If your concerns about delegating are financially based, you may also have those same concerns about hiring a coach. However, no athlete or athletic team would try to win a competition without the support of a coach. Now that coaching has expanded into the business and personal realm, having a coach is a way of life for the truly successful.

The statement *I can't afford it* may seem to be a fact, rather than a belief. However, believing that you only have access to a certain amount of money, or that there is only one way to acquire what you want, are very limiting beliefs. This is particularly true when you're talking about an investment such as a support team or a coach, rather than just a personal expenditure.

If this is an issue for you, you'll want to do two things. First, you'll want to deal with any emotions or secondary beliefs about not being able to afford support. If you feel inadequate or feel like a failure because you don't believe that you can afford help, you'll want to tap on those feelings first.

Second, when there is no emotion beneath the statement *I can't afford it,* you'll want to open yourself to possibility in this area, and an Open Choice Statement is a good way to do that. You might use the statements:

❖ *Even though I think I can't afford it, I'm open to a way to find the money.*

❖ *Even though I believe I can't afford it, I'm open to a surprisingly creative way to get what I need.*

❖ *Even though I still think I can't afford it, I'm open to the Universe providing a solution to this situation.*

Tap a Choices Trio using one of these setup statements, or create a setup statement and Reminder Phrases of your own. When you remove the phrase *I can't afford it* from your vocabulary, and substitute a more empowering phrase, such as *I easily and consistently acquire what I need to succeed,* you'll find yourself attracting and keeping far more money.

EXERCISE: BUILDING MY ULTIMATE SUCCESS SUPPORT TEAM

If you feel that your team is complete now, and that there is no one else you need, do some Free-Association Tapping on what it would mean to have more support in your life. You may find that you're blocking even the idea of support because you don't feel you can get it.

Identify where in your life or business you could use more support. Do you need personal help? Could you use help with your kids? Do you need the guidance and support of a coach, mentor, or other support professional? Do you need to bring on new staff or additional administrative help? Make a list. Don't skimp on the list; put everyone on it you'd like, even if you don't think it's possible.

As you review the list you've created, write down the "stopper" next to each role, person, or title—what is it that stops you from having that person on your team? Is there a fear that you can't ask? Is it the belief that you can't afford help?

Build a tapping routine around each stopper. Each one is a fear or limiting belief, and you can use any of the tapping techniques you've learned so far to transform them.

KEEP YOUR EYE ON THE PRIZE (SUCCESS PRINCIPLE 27)

It's easy to have your focus settle on the negative occurrences, thoughts, and feelings that you experience, and it can take training and practice to keep your attention on the positive. Activities like keeping a Daily Success Focus Journal as described on pages 206–207 in *The Success Principles* can help. Doing an evening review, where you look back at the day and ask where you could have performed in a manner more in alignment with your values and goals, can also help. However, an evening review can also turn into an opportunity for you to criticize and denigrate yourself, which doesn't support your success.

Let's look at how to do an evening review with tapping so that it becomes even more powerful.

TAPPING TECHNIQUE: TAPPING EVENING REVIEW

There are two parts of the Tapping Evening Review. The first part deals with your view of other people, and the second with your view of yourself.

Part 1: As you look back at your day, ask yourself *Is there anyone I interacted with today that I still feel upset, angry, or irritated with?* If you find any of those emotions present, you'll want to tap for that irritation. You can use any of the tapping techniques to do this, although Simple Tapping or SOS Tapping are your most likely choices.

If you had an interaction with someone with whom you have long-standing issues, you'll want to schedule some time to clear those issues, perhaps using the Tapping Forgiveness Process.

Part 2: As you look back at your day, ask yourself *Is there any way that I responded or interacted that is not in alignment with my commitments and goals?*

Tap to remove any upset or anger you have with yourself about how you behaved. You may want to use an Acceptance Choice, or you may want to use the Tapping Forgiveness Process for yourself. The Original EFT Affirmation, and its variations, can be useful in this case.

When your upset with yourself is less than a level 5, you can create a Choice Statement. Ask yourself *If I had it to do over again, what would I do differently?*

Here's an example of a Tapping Evening Review from Pamela:

I answered the question in Part I with: *I'm still upset that Bill told me he's going to be late with that shipment.* Since the intensity was at a 7, started with an Open Choice:

❖ *Even though I'm upset at Bill, and I don't know how I'll handle that late shipment, I'm open to somehow turning this into something good.*

Examples of just a few of the Reminder Phrases:

❖ *I'm upset at Bill.*

❖ *Why is he late?*

❖ *He had plenty of notice.*

As the intensity dropped, I realized that I needed to find a new supplier. The intensity of the upset shifted to 3.

❖ *Even though I'm still a bit upset at Bill, I choose to be grateful for the realization that I need a new supplier.*

Examples of just a few of the Reminder Phrases I used:

❖ *I'm still a bit upset at Bill.*

❖ *It's too bad he just can't deliver.*

❖ *It's exciting to think about finding a new supplier.*

❖ *I choose to find someone who really meets my needs well.*

I became calm now about Bill, and felt grateful. Since I had tapped earlier in the day for another upset, I felt warm and grateful toward all the other people I had interacted with. Continuing to review my day, I realized that I was also upset at myself for overindulging in a heavy afternoon snack. My upset was at an 8, so I started with Simple Tapping.

Examples of just a few of the Reminder Phrases:

❖ *Why did I do that?*

❖ *I feel like a pig.*

- ❖ *What's wrong with me?*
- ❖ *I know better than to eat like that.*
- ❖ *That doesn't support my goal of maintaining my health.*
- ❖ *I really need to do better.*

After several rounds and a few minutes, the intensity dropped to a 4.

I created the Specific Choice setup statement:

- ❖ *Even though I'm still upset that I chose that snack, I choose to remember this and make better choices next time.*

Reminder Phrases:

- ❖ *I'm still upset.*
- ❖ *I can make better choices.*
- ❖ *I'd like to accept myself.*
- ❖ *I'm still not happy with myself.*

After a few rounds, I started putting in positive Reminder Phrases:

- ❖ *I will remember this feeling, so I don't do it again.*
- ❖ *I choose to stock up on healthy snacks to make it easier for myself.*
- ❖ *I choose to know that I can consistently make better choices.*

I continued with my review, and realized that I had not made a call I had committed to making. I felt a bit guilty, about a 3. I created the setup statement:

- ❖ *Even though I feel guilty for not making that phone call, I choose to do so tomorrow.*

Two rounds of tapping removed the guilt. Afterward, I found no more upsets. While using Continuous Tapping, I acknowledged the positive in my day, offering gratitude for each good thing that happened.

CHAPTER CHECKLIST

I know the four reasons that we cling to old habits and behaviors.

I have done the tapping exercises.

I know the difference between considerations, fears, and roadblocks.

I have committed to doing the Tapping Evening Review for a week.

9

FINANCIAL SUCCESS: TAPPING FOR MONEY AND PROSPERITY

DEVELOP A POSITIVE MONEY CONSCIOUSNESS (SUCCESS PRINCIPLE 56)

Money is a topic that causes most people some kind of emotional distress. It is the number one cause of divorce, and an overwhelming number of people don't feel they have enough money. With all this emotional drama, it's no surprise to find that the area of money is one in which most people feel their success is blocked in some way.

Let's look at how money beliefs show up in your identity, your view of spirituality, your relationship to others, and your beliefs in your own ability and worthiness. In this chapter, we'll explore many limiting money beliefs, and give you powerful reframes for changing your money consciousness. However, you'll need to do the tapping to completely embrace these powerful reframes. Without the tapping, it's only in your head, not in your heart, and you won't take effective action towards your money goals.

There are two general processes that can help you develop a positive money consciousness. First, you'll need to identify any limiting beliefs that you have about money. You'll want to deeply explore how you feel about money, write down your beliefs, and then ask if those beliefs serve you. If the beliefs aren't serving you, meaning they aren't supporting your conscious goals and dreams, you'll want to tap on them. That's primarily what we'll be doing in this section.

Second, you'll want to identify any incidents from your past that caused you to make a decision about money. For example, perhaps you spent a lot of money when you started a hobby, and then didn't pursue it. Or you may have put money into an investment or business and didn't get the return that you expected. Matrix Reimprinting is a great technique to use to clear emotions you may have about the decisions you made in the past, and emotions from past events that are keeping you from earning, receiving, or keeping more money.

When removing limiting beliefs about money, you'll want to ask yourself how this belief has served you in the past. For example, negative beliefs about rich people can take the pressure off you to succeed and thrive. If you believe, for example, that it's dangerous to be too visible or wealthy, or that you have to work too hard to be wealthy, it will support a belief such as *I don't want to be rich anyway, because rich people are greedy.*

These kinds of limiting beliefs can keep you safe, which is the job of the subconscious mind. You'll want to note these beliefs as well, because clearing them is essential to installing the new beliefs that support your goals.

MONEY BELIEFS ABOUT OTHERS

Most of us grew up with attitudes about people who have money. Consider whether any of these statements feel true to you:

- *Rich people are greedy.*
- *Rich people don't care about others.*
- *If you're rich, you must be dishonest.*
- *Rich people don't really earn their money.*
- *Rich people are fakes.*
- *Rich people are mean snobs.*
- *Rich people only care about money.*
- *Rich people aren't spiritual at all.*

You may believe some of those statements consciously, or you may intellectually know them to be false, but have an emotional belief that they are true. Either way, if you have negative emotions about rich people, you're unlikely to become one. Even if it's not a goal of yours to become wealthy, if you have a negative image of wealth, you may constantly struggle with money and finances.

MONEY AND SPIRITUALITY

Limiting beliefs about money not being spiritual are closely related to beliefs about rich people. Do any of these statements feel true to you?

- *It's not spiritual to want money.*
- *It's wrong to ask for more than I need.*
- *It's not spiritual to ask for money.*
- *Spiritual people don't think about money.*
- *I can't be spiritual and wealthy.*
- *If I focus too much on money, I'll lose my spiritual focus.*
- *Money will corrupt my spirituality.*

There are many societal and religious messages that link spirituality with poverty, so it's very common to have these sort of limiting beliefs, particularly if you had a strong religious or spiritual upbringing. If you consider, however, that everything is energy, then money is just another form of energy. It can be used to benefit people, or it can be used to harm. One phrase we love to share is that *Money is a magnifier: If you're greedy and mean-spirited, money will make you more so. If you're generous, spiritual, and compassionate, money will make you more so.*

One common reason that people hold on to beliefs like these is that it gives them an excuse for a lack of success in business or financial areas. Consider these beliefs instead:

- *I can treat money as a spiritual practice.*

- *I'm open to finding a way to enhance my spirituality through money.*

- *I can do more spiritual good in the world as a wealthy person.*

Although these may seem challenging or even shocking, try using them as Open or Specific Choice Statements, and combine them with your limiting beliefs for a powerful tapping experience. For example:

- ❖ *Even though I can't be spiritual and wealthy, I'm open to finding a way to enhance my spirituality through money.*

- ❖ *Even though I'll lose my spiritual focus if I think too much about money, I choose to find a way to treat money as a spiritual practice.*

MONEY AND YOUR IDENTITY

One of the challenges in changing your income level is that you may have an identity that is linked with a certain income level. This may be why 30% of all lottery winners file bankruptcy within five years. If your family was poor or working class, you may have difficulty identifying yourself as wealthy. Do any of these feel true to you?

- *My family has never been wealthy; we're just not cut out for it.*
- *I can't imagine myself doing what wealthy people do.*
- *I'd be a traitor to my people if I became wealthy.*
- *I'd feel uncomfortable in fancy places.*
- *I'm just a "jeans and T-shirt" kind of person.*

Our concept of ourselves, and of wealthy people, can be almost funny at times. Pamela reports that one of the blocks that she had to wealth was that she believed that wealthy women always wear high-heeled shoes. Since she dislikes high heels, she subconsciously felt that she could never really fit in with the wealthy. Once she got clear on that belief, it was a simple matter to tap away the belief that she wouldn't fit in with wealthy people, and tap on the possibility of being wealthy (and wearing whatever kind of shoes she wanted to wear).

MONEY AND WORTHINESS

If you have low self-esteem, you may not feel that you deserve to make or receive more money. If you've lost money in the past through a failed business venture, bad investment, or simple irresponsibility, you may have a belief that you shouldn't get more money because you'll just waste it. Or you may feel that there are people who need the money more, and if you get more, you'll be taking it from them. This just isn't true.

One important reframe to consider is that when you have money, you get to decide what to do with it. You can spend it, save it, invest it, or contribute it. Your ability to influence and benefit the world increases as the amount of money you have increases. Do you have any of these limiting beliefs?

- *I'm not worthy of receiving more than I do.*
- *I don't deserve to make more money.*
- *I'm not worthy of being wealthy.*
- *I don't deserve to be rich.*

One way to work with this type of belief is to make a list of what you will do when you have a specific amount of money. When you plan for more money, you attract it to you. Also, having a plan makes it more likely that you will use your money responsibly and in accordance with your values.

CREATING A MONEY "WHY"

When you have a compelling reason behind an action that you're taking, you're much more motivated to take that action. A compelling reason that gets you emotionally engaged, rather than being a "should," will be much more motivating. Remember the rider and the elephant? You want your elephant, your emotional subconscious, to be supporting your compelling reason.

THE MYTH OF SECURITY

Saying "I want a million dollars" without having a compelling reason gives you no emotional support for that goal. Most people who claim to want a certain amount of money are usually looking for security, which is a "why" that will not support you. Any amount of money can be lost, as so many lottery winners can attest. And many people with millions of dollars in the bank do not feel secure. Instead, you may wish to cultivate a feeling of "financial serenity," which is the feeling that you always have enough, and that you always have the ability to create all the money that you need and want.

Perhaps you'd like to have a certain type of home in a certain location. Perhaps you'd like to contribute to good causes. What type of lifestyle would you like to live, and how much money would it take to live that lifestyle?

EXERCISE: CREATING A MONEY "WHY"

Create a list of what you'd like to do with money. Include any physical items, such as homes, cars, and boats; and any lifestyle changes, such as travel or training. Include investments, such as retirement accounts and portfolios. Include contributions to non-profits, religious organizations, friends, and family.

As you make the list, notice what thoughts or emotions come up for you. Perhaps you think:

- *I don't really need that. Perhaps I shouldn't list it.*

- *It wouldn't be right for me to have things this nice.*

- *I'll never be able to come up with that much money, so I won't put that on the list.*

When you find yourself thinking those thoughts, make a note of them so that you can tap on them later. This is *very* important. If you're shying away from the things that you want because of feelings of guilt, unworthiness, or inability to receive them, you will sabotage your success.

Create an SOS Tapping routine (or any other tapping technique) to clear the doubts, concerns, or challenges that you have with your list. You've already created the Reminder Phrases. Start with Simple Tapping if you need to, then when the intensity is 7 or lower, you can create Choices.

List your SUDS level separately for each challenge. After you tap on the first one, the SUDS level may shift on the other challenges, or new challenges may appear that weren't there at first.

Here are some suggestions for setup statements that you can use:

- ❖ *Even though I don't know how I'll be able to afford that, I choose to allow the abundance of the Universe to support me.*

- ❖ *Even though I don't think it's right to want so much, I choose to consider that I deserve to ask for what I want.*

❖ *Even though I'm hesitant to put something on the list that I don't think I can get, I choose to allow the Universe to surprise and delight me.*

Complete your list of money "whys," then create a list starting with: *I am so happy and grateful that I receive* [list all your items].

Read the list aloud frequently, at least once a day. If you feel any emotions other than joy, gratitude, and expectation, tap on those emotions.

A BIG MONEY "WHY"

When Jack and Mark Victor Hansen created *Chicken Soup for the Soul* they created what they called a "2020 vision": to sell 1 billion Chicken Soup books and raise $500 million for charity through tithing a portion of all their profits by the year 2020. To date, they have sold more than 400 million books in 47 languages, and contributed tens of millions of dollars to charity.

TO SPEND MORE, FIRST MAKE MORE (SUCCESS PRINCIPLE 60)

There is an enormous difference in the money mindset of entrepreneurs and employees. An employee, who is used to a fixed paycheck, will look at something and say, "I can't afford it." On the other hand, an entrepreneur will look at the same thing and ask, "*How* can I afford it?" The entrepreneur is accustomed to thinking of money not as a fixed sum, but as something that can be increased at will.

Do you have an employee mindset or an entrepreneurial mindset?

Many people want the advantages of more money, but won't put in the effort to earn it. It takes time, effort, commitment, and sometimes a monetary investment to run a business (even a part-time one), but the rewards can be huge. If you're already in business for yourself, but have a belief that you can't make more than a certain amount in your business, you've created your own self-limiting cage.

When you think about making more money, what comes to mind? It may be something like:

- *That's too much work.*

- *I don't know how to do that.*

- *I don't know anything that people will pay me for.*

- *It's not possible to make more money doing what I do.*

- *It's greedy to want more money than I have now.*

- *I don't want people to think it's all about the money.*

- *No one in my family has ever earned that much money.*

- *My friends won't like it if I get rich.*

If you're content with the amount of money you have, that's fine. But if, like most people, you'd like more, you'll need these beliefs:

- *It's okay to have more. It's not greedy, unethical, betraying my family, or taking from others for me to have more money.*

- *It's possible to have or earn more. I have the ability to create additional income.*

Some very powerful reframes to support the first belief include the fact that many wealthy people are very generous, giving millions or billions to charity. Also, if you're a generous person now, you can do far more good with more money than with less.

One thing we always teach our students is *If you're poor, the good that you can do is limited to your physical presence.*

To support the second belief, you might have to do some thinking or research. How could you make more money? There are many possibilities such as the Internet, network-marketing companies, or starting your own company from a skill that you have.

If you have a limiting belief about your ability to earn money, or learn new things, work on that belief as you did in Chapter 6 with Success Principle 33: Transcend Your Limiting Beliefs.

Because money is such an emotionally charged issue for most people, limiting beliefs about money could fill an entire book. If your definition of success includes more money, you'll want to explore your money beliefs and change those that don't empower you.

YOU GET WHAT YOU FOCUS ON (SUCCESS PRINCIPLE 57), PAY YOURSELF FIRST (SUCCESS PRINCIPLE 58), AND MASTER THE SPENDING GAME (SUCCESS PRINCIPLE 59)

The final section of *The Success Principles*, "Success and Money" has an enormous amount of great suggestions, information, and resources for managing your money, investing, and spending wisely. However, many people read good information like this and don't act on it. The reasons include:

- *I don't know what to do first.*

- *I'm not good with numbers.*

- *I don't have enough money coming in to make it worth managing.*

- *I don't want to know what I'm spending my money on.*

- *The idea of learning all that financial stuff is boring.*

In order to have more money, you'll need to start taking action to become fiscally responsible. One way to overcome these limiting beliefs is to use the technique we discussed in Chapter 5 in Success Principle 13: Take Action. You begin by determining one action that you can take.

Here's an example. Suppose that the action you are taking is to figure out your net worth. This is actually a project, with several actions. To do that, you may need to do these steps and more:

- Assemble all bank records.

- Find out amount in retirement accounts.

- Look up current value of portfolio.

- Call to get remaining balance on outstanding loans (mortgage, car, credit cards).

- Get appraisals of properties you own.

- Consult with a financial advisor.

When you look at this list, can you schedule these items? Are you motivated to do them, or do you shrink from the project? Perhaps you're feeling:

- *This feels overwhelming.*

- *I don't want to know my net worth; it will be embarrassing.*

- *This is too much trouble.*

- *What good will this do anyway?*

- *I'm too busy to waste time with this.*

If you're unwilling to take this on, then just saying "I should" probably won't get you there. Instead, consider the following possible reframes, given here as Choice Statements:

- ❖ *I choose to know this is my first step on the way to wealth.*

- ❖ *I'm excited about becoming knowledgeable about my finances.*

- ❖ *I choose to measure my net worth, so I can follow its increase.*

Create your own tapping phrases that you can work with so that you are willing and eager to be in control of your money.

EXERCISE: SUPERCHARGING YOUR MONEY BELIEFS

This is an exercise that cannot be done in a single day. Most people have far too many limiting beliefs about money to clear so quickly. Instead, set aside time in your schedule to work on these regularly. You may want to have one day a week that is "Money day," or you may want to devote 15 minutes every day to transforming your money beliefs.

Read through the following list of limiting beliefs about money. You can also add other limiting beliefs that we've mentioned in this section. By each one, note how true it seems to you, using the truth meter level.

- *People in my profession don't make much money.*
- *It's too hard to make it in this economy.*
- *Rich people have no souls.*
- *You can't be rich and spiritual, too.*
- *You're a better person if you work hard.*
- *Wealthy people are just showing off.*
- *Rich people are all crooks.*
- *You have to have a good education to make money.*
- *Rich people are either born that way or are very lucky.*
- *Money corrupts the soul.*
- *Money doesn't grow on trees.*
- *Our people have always been poor but honest.*
- *I don't belong in fancy places.*
- *I can't see myself doing the things I want to do.*
- *I'll lose my friends if I make more money.*
- *I'll be corrupted if I make more money.*
- *I was never meant to be wealthy.*
- *My family will try to take it if I make more money.*

- *If I make more money, I'll just waste it.*

- *I can't see myself as a rich or successful person.*

- *Expensive things are just a waste of money.*

Pick one belief from the list with a TM level greater than 0, and create a tapping routine from it. The belief will become your Reminder Phrase.

When you are ready to create your Open Choice Statement, or Specific Choice Statement, ask yourself these questions:

- *Is this true in <u>every</u> single case?*

- *Can I find any exceptions to this idea?*

- *How is this belief holding me back or limiting me?*

- *What would I like to believe, if I could?*

Create a new empowering belief to replace the old belief. For example, you may start with *I can't see myself as a rich or successful person,* and in the process of tapping, create the Choice *I choose to know 100% that I can be rich and successful.*

Finally, create a new list of these empowering beliefs. Read it once a week, or more frequently.

CHAPTER CHECKLIST

I've created my money "why."
I've done the "Supercharging Your Money Beliefs" exercise.

SUCCESS STORY

Gail used a combination of Little Voice Tapping and Matrix Reimprinting in this interesting case. She writes:

One of my ultimate life goals is to earn over a million dollars a year. However, I found that every time I tried to sit with this goal in order to really create an image in my mind of how it will look and feel, I found myself wincing inside. Something was clearly out of alignment. Part of the discord came from the limiting belief that I'd have to work 24/7 to accomplish such a goal. But I sensed something deeper so I just started tapping.

> *Self:* I joyfully earn over a million dollars a year. *[said several times all while tapping on my collarbone point]*
>
> *[An objection eventually came forth. It was another voice or an inner feeling.]*
>
> *Voice:* No, you don't belong in that group.
>
> *Self:* That's interesting. Why don't you feel I belong?
>
> *Voice:* Those people are free to do anything they want. You aren't. You're not good enough to play in that world.
>
> *Self:* Where did you learn this?

Then I found myself as a very young child, perhaps around eight years old. It seemed to be shortly after my mother had really let me have it for something I had done that she didn't approve of. My father had died when I was six and my mother was bound and determined that I grow up well. Once I identified the situation, I froze the scene and entered the room so I could chat with my younger self. She knew who I was immediately.

> *Self:* You look upset, as though you feel trapped.
>
> *ECHO:* I am. She tells me what I can do. Only that. Anything I do on my own is *wrong* and bad. She can't stand me when I do things on my own.

Self: I know this is going to be weird, but can you tap on yourself the way I'm tapping while you tell me about it?

ECHO: Yes.

Self: Great. Go on.

ECHO: She is the boss of everything. She knows and dictates everything I can do. I'm in big trouble if I do anything on my own. She attacks me every time.

Self: That sounds awful. But I have an idea. Would you like to hear it?

ECHO: Sure.

Self: What if we bring Dad back and tell him how you feel?

ECHO: That would be great!

Self: *[I brought Dad into the room.]* Keep tapping and tell him exactly what you told me.

ECHO: Dad, she is the boss of everything. She rules everything I can do. *Nothing* I do on my own is okay. To her, it's not alright for me to do anything unless she says it's okay. Everyone else can do things, but not me. I'm not good.

Dad: What? Are you crazy?! You're brilliant! *[big smile]* You're awesome, and you can do anything you put your mind to.

ECHO: Really?

Dad: Absolutely! You're amazing! Look, your mom really means well. She just isn't going about it the right way because she's afraid and no one ever taught her. She's only doing what she thinks is right. Don't pay any attention to all that stuff. You can do anything. Trust yourself. I know I do! I'm so proud of you. I know you can be great at whatever you do.

ECHO: Oh Dad, I'm so happy to hear you say this. I love you so much.

Dad: I love you, too.

At this point my Dad faded away and I was left sitting with the child. She felt so much better. She was released from my mother's grasp and free to fully express herself for the first time ever. I left her playing with her friends and feeling free to just be who she's meant to be. It was awesome!

Now I feel that my goal of making a million dollars a year is completely within my reach . . . and that I'm totally worthy of it. Hooray!

NEXT STEPS

Although this is the end of the book, it is not the end of your journey. As you continue to live the success principles, additional challenges will come up. You can use the techniques that we've outlined here to work through and overcome these challenges.

The good news is that challenges come up when you're stretching and growing. When you reach for new levels in your life, your relationships, your career or business, and your health, it's natural to encounter resistance and challenges. So pat yourself on the back when they show up, because it's usually a sign that you're playing big.

We'd love to have you work with us to spread these techniques and ideas to empower others. If you'd like to join us, or for more information about tapping, including lists of practitioners, please visit: **www.TappingIntoUltimateSuccess.com**.

QUICK REFERENCE GUIDE

Success Principles:
- Experience Your Fear and Take Action Anyway (Success Principle 15)

Chapter 3: Overcoming Limiting Beliefs

Tapping Techniques:
- Open Choice Statements
- Specific Choice Statements
- SOS Tapping

Tapping Exercises:
- Creating a Growth Mindset
- Putting SOS Tapping Into Action
- Embrace Change with SOS Tapping
- Tell the Truth Faster with SOS Tapping

Tapping Tips:
- Getting Specific
- Skipping Steps or Rounds

Success Principles:
- Embrace Change (Success Principle 31)
- Tell the Truth Faster (Success Principle 50)

Chapter 4: Foundations for Success: Responsibility and Forgiveness

Tapping Technique:
- Acceptance Choice

Tapping Exercises:
- Take Responsibility in Order to Learn
- Take 100% Responsibility for Your Life
- Eliminating Complaining with SOS Tapping
- Tapping Forgiveness Process
- Overcoming Resistance to Forgiveness with SOS Tapping

Success Principles:
- Take 100% Responsibility for Your Life (Success Principle 1)
- Complete the Past to Embrace the Future (Success Principle 29)

Chapter 5: Accelerating Success: Tapping for Action and Results

Tapping Techniques:
- Continuous Tapping
- Little Voice Tapping
- Visualization Tapping
- Firm Stand Tapping

Tapping Tips:
- The Truth Meter (TM) Level
- Using Humor and Exaggeration in Tapping

Tapping Exercises:
- Enjoying the Journey
- Asking for What You Want

Success Principles:
- Release the Brakes (Success Principle 10)
- Transform Your Inner Critic Into an Inner Coach (Success Principle 32)
- See What You Want, Get What You See (Success Principle 11)
- Be Willing to Pay the Price (Success Principle 16)
- Take Action (Success Principle 13)
- Unleash the Power of Goal Setting (Success Principle 7)
- Ask, Ask, Ask (Success Principle 17)
- Reject Rejection (Success Principle 18)
- Exceed Expectations (Success Principle 24)

Chapter 6: Healing the Past:
Removing the Triggers that Slow Your Success

Tapping Technique:
- Matrix Reimprinting

Tapping Exercises:
- Clearing the Past with Matrix Reimprinting
- Saying No to Create Freedom
- Speaking Impeccably to Create Power
- Cleaning up the Incompletes

Success Principles:
- Transcend Your Limiting Beliefs (Success Principle 33)
- Keep Your Agreements (Success Principle 54)
- Use Feedback to Your Advantage (Success Principle 19)
- Face What Isn't Working (Success Principle 30)
- Just Say No! (Success Principle 42)
- Speak with Impeccability (Success Principle 51)
- When in Doubt, Check It Out (Success Principle 52)
- Clean Up Your Messes and Incompletes (Success Principle 28)

Chapter 7: Creating the New You:
Tapping for Empowerment and Transformation

Tapping Technique:
- Sensation Tapping

Tapping Exercises:
- Creating and Living Your Vision
- Believing It's Possible, Believing in Yourself
- Becoming an Inverse Paranoid
- Acknowledge Your Positive Past
- Collecting the Clues to Success

Success Principles:
- Be Clear Why You're Here (Success Principle 2)
- Decide What You Want (Success Principle 3)

- Act as If (Success Principle 12)
- Just Lean Into It (Success Principle 14)
- Believe It's Possible (Success Principle 4)
- Believe in Yourself (Success Principle 5)
- Become an Inverse Paranoid (Success Principle 6)
- Keep Score for Success (Success Principle 21)
- Acknowledge Your Positive Past (Success Principle 26)
- Success Leaves Clues (Success Principle 9)

Chapter 8: Creating New Habits for Success: Tapping to Make Life Easier

Tapping Techniques:
- Free-Association Tapping
- Tapping Evening Review

Tapping Tips:
- Use Language That Triggers Your Emotions
- Be a Detective

Tapping Exercises:
- Redefining Time
- Creating Powerful New Habits
- Building My Ultimate Success Support Team

Success Principles:
- Develop Four New Success Habits a Year (Success Principle 34)
- Redefine Time (Success Principle 40)
- Inquire Within (Success Principle 47)
- 99% Is a Bitch; 100% Is a Breeze (Success Principle 35)
- Practice Persistence (Success Principle 22)
- Chunk It Down (Success Principle 8)
- Commit to Constant and Never-Ending Improvement (Success Principle 20)
- Stay Focused on Your Core Genius (Success Principle 39)

- Build a Powerful Support Team and Delegate to Them (Success Principle 41)
- Hire a Personal Coach (Success Principle 45)
- Keep Your Eye on the Prize (Success Principle 27)

Chapter 9: Financial Success:
Tapping for Money and Prosperity

Tapping Exercises:
- Creating a Money "Why"
- Supercharging Your Money Beliefs

Success Principles:
- Develop a Positive Money Consciousness (Success Principle 56)
- To Spend More, First Make More (Success Principle 60)
- You Get What You Focus On (Success Principle 57)
- Pay Yourself First (Success Principle 58)
- Master the Spending Game (Success Principle 59)

GLOSSARY

Acceptance Choice: a Choice Statement with the format, *Even though I feel* [this emotion], *I choose to accept myself and my feelings.*

acupoints: a term from Chinese medicine, denoting electrically sensitive places on the body. Tapping focuses mostly on eight tapping points on the body (from the top of the head to under the arm). A few acupoints on the hand, such as the Karate Chop point, are sometimes used. (see: *Stealth Tapping*)

alternating round: tapping the eight acupoints while saying a negative phrase at the first point, a positive phrase at the second point, a negative phrase at the third point, and so on.

aspect: one part of a problem. (ex: *The fear of flying has many different aspects, such as fear of confined spaces, fear of being out of control, and fear of crowds.*)

belief: a thought or idea considered to be true.

Choices Method: a tapping technique that uses positive affirmations in both the setup statement and Reminder Phrases to install new empowering beliefs. Many of the positive affirmations begin with the words, *I choose.*

Choice Statement: a setup statement that begins with the words *I choose . . .*

Choices Trio or **Choices Trio Method:** a tapping series consisting of a setup statement and three rounds of tapping: a negative round, a positive round, then an alternating round.

Continuous Tapping: a tapping technique in which the eight main acupoints are tapped in sequence, but for a much longer period of time than in Simple Tapping (often a minute or more). No setup statement is used, and a single point is tapped for as long as it takes to visualize an event, explore a physical sensation in the body, or hold a conversation.

ECHO: Energy Conscious Hologram, the term used to refer to the "younger self" in the Matrix Reimprinting technique.

EFT: Emotional Freedom Techniques, the tapping technique created by Gary Craig.

emotional mind: subconscious mind; the source of emotional beliefs.

energy meridians: the pathways of life force that flow through the body, according to Chinese medicine. They are used in acupuncture as well as in tapping. Tapping's full name, Meridian Tapping, borrows from this concept.

Firm Stand Tapping: a tapping technique that alternates an affirmation with the resistance to the affirmation. It is particularly good for identifying all aspects of an issue.

fixed mindset: a belief that a person has a certain set of abilities and that these cannot be substantially changed.

growth mindset: a belief that a person can always change, grow, or improve.

inverse paranoia: the belief that the universe is conspiring for one's benefit.

Karate Chop (KC) point: an acupoint on the side of the hand. It is tapped whenever a setup statement is spoken.

Little Voice Tapping: a tapping technique in which a conversation is held with a part of the personality that may be sabotaging your success out of fear or the desire to protect you.

Matrix Reimprinting: a tapping technique characterized by visiting a scene from one's past, effective for healing the past and defusing painful memories.

Meridian Tapping: the full name of the tapping processes discussed throughout this book. Usually referred to merely as "tapping."

negative round: tapping the eight acupoints while repeating a negative Reminder Phrase.

NLP: Neuro-linguistic programming, the science of modeling the patterns of human behavior.

Open Choice Statement: a Choice Statement with an affirmation that invites creativity rather than specifying a certain outcome. (ex: *I choose to be open to a new idea.*)

Open Choice Tapping: a tapping series consisting of an Open Choice setup statement and three rounds of tapping using the Choices Trio Method (negative round, positive round with Open Choice Statements, alternating round).

Open Choices: statements or questions, used in the Choices Method, that invite creativity and openness rather than specifying a certain result. (compare: *Specific Choices*)

Original EFT Affirmation: The affirmation used in the setup statement of original EFT. It is: *I deeply and completely love and accept myself.* It is used in a setup statement like: *Even though I* [state your issue], *I deeply and completely love and accept myself.*

positive round: tapping the eight acupoints while repeating a positive Reminder Phrase (often phrased as a Choice Statement).

Psychological Reversal: a state of self-sabotage.

rational mind: one's conscious mind.

reframe (noun): an interpretation that produces empowering thoughts.

reframe (verb): to construct a new belief or interpretation that produces empowering thoughts.

Reminder Phrase: a statement of the problem, issue, or challenge. The Reminder Phrase is repeated as each acupoint is tapped.

reticular activating system (RAS): a part of the brain that controls conscious focus, and allows one to filter out stimuli. Essentially the gatekeeper that controls what is perceived by the conscious mind.

round: the act of tapping once through all eight acupoints from the top of the head down to under the arm.

Sensation Tapping: a tapping technique that focuses on physical feelings in the body, rather than thoughts or emotions.

series: a setup statement and all the rounds that follow.

setup statement: a combination of the problem, and an affirmation, in the format of: *Even though* [I have this problem], *I* [affirmation]. During a series, the setup statement is repeated three times while tapping the Karate Chop (KC) point.

Simple Tapping: a tapping technique in which the eight main acupoints are tapped in sequence while the problem or challenge is voiced. (see: *Reminder Phrases*)

SOS Tapping: a tapping technique combining Simple Tapping, Open Choice Tapping, and Specific Choice Tapping.

Specific Choice Statement: a Choice Statement that specifies a certain outcome or desired emotional state, such as: *I choose to feel calm and confident.*

Specific Choice Tapping: a tapping series consisting of a Specific Choice setup statement, and three rounds of tapping using the

Choices Trio Method (negative round, positive round with Specific Choice Statements, alternating round).

Specific Choices: statements, used in the Choices Method, that specify a certain result. (compare: *Open Choices*)

Stealth Tapping: a method of tapping using finger points rather than the eight main acupoints of the body, with the objective of not being noticed. You can view a diagram of the finger points on page 26 in Chapter 2.

success principles: a set of ideas and instructions designed to accelerate happiness and achievement.

SUDS scale: Subjective Units of Distress, the scale that measures the intensity of emotion from 0–10, with 0 meaning "neutral" and 10 meaning "extremely intense." This number is one's SUDS level, which is used to track progress while tapping.

Tapping Forgiveness Process: a seven-step system for removing anger and other negative emotions surrounding a person or event, to reach a state of peace.

tapping phrases: a general term referring to both Reminder Phrases and setup statements.

truth meter scale: also known as the TM scale. Used to rate how strongly true a belief feels to a person. It ranges from 0–10, with 0 meaning "not true at all" and 10 meaning "completely true." This number is one's TM level.

Visualization Tapping: a tapping technique that involves no words, but instead tapping on visualized images or events.

ENDNOTES

1. The metaphor of the rider and the elephant comes from social psychologist Jonathan Haidt.

2. Chip Heath and Dan Heath, *Switch: How to Change Things When Change is Hard* (New York: Broadway Books, 2010).

3. Robert O. Becker and Gary Selden, *The Body Electric* (New York: Harper Paperbacks, 1998).

4. Dawson Church, Ph.D., *The Genie in Your Genes* (Fulton, CA: Energy Psychology Press, 2008).

5. For more detailed information on Choice Statements, including the official Choices manual, please visit **www.masteringeft.com**.

6. Carol S. Dweck, *Mindset: The New Psychology of Success* (New York: Ballantine Books, 2006).

7. Lisa S. Blackwell, Kali H. Trzesniewski, and Carol S. Dweck (2007), "Implicit Theories of Intelligence Predict Achievement Across an Adolescent Transition: A Longitudinal Study and an Intervention," Child Development, 78, 246-263.)

8. See her book *Loving What Is: The Four Questions that Can Change Your Life* (New York: Three Rivers Press, 2003), or visit her website at **www.TheWork .com**, where you can download numerous free resources and worksheets.

9. Tapping has also shown impressive results in reducing the effects of dyslexia.

10. See **www.JoyAfterCancer.com** for more information about Peggy's work.

11. Malcolm Gladwell, *Blink* (New York: Back Bay Books, 2005).

ACKNOWLEDGMENTS

This book is the result of the combined efforts of many people. We would like to acknowledge the following people:

Roger Callahan, the author of *The Five-Minute Phobia Cure,* who first applied tapping on certain acupuncture points to eliminate fears, phobias, and addictions. Jack started successfully using the five-minute phobia cure more than 15 years ago in his workshops and trainings.

Next are Patricia Carrington and Gary Craig, who took Callahan's work and simplified and evolved it, and then worked diligently to get it out to the mainstream and the masses. Without their pioneering work, none of what we do would be possible.

Dawson Church, the new pioneer in clinical EFT, whose tireless work is proving the scientific validity of tapping. He was kind enough to consult on this book regarding why tapping works.

Nicholas Ortner for originally coming up with the idea of writing a book that would use the power of tapping to overcome and release the most common emotional blocks and limiting beliefs that surface when one begins to apply the principles of success to one's life. Nicholas wrote what might be considered the first draft of this book and simply offered it up as a gift to the work after interviewing Jack for the brilliant movie *The Tapping Solution*, which he and Jessica Ortner produced. He has also been more than generous with his time and resources in helping us get this book into the hands of the tapping community.

Martin Laschkolnig from Austria, who selflessly drafted a second version of this book, and who is responsible for first introducing Jack to EFT (Emotional Freedom Techniques) and tapping. Martin has also taught tapping in several of Jack's Breakthrough to Success trainings in both the United States and Germany.

Russell Kamalski, the acting Chief Operating Officer of the Canfield Training Group, who caught the vision of this book and helped the people at Hay House catch that same vision.

Patty Aubery, the President of the Canfield Training Group, who makes sure that the business side of things run smoothly so that Jack can focus on the creative and transformational side of things, and who is always there with an open heart and a loving hand when it is needed.

Veronica Romero, Jack's executive assistant, who made sure Jack had time to do this work, and who tirelessly typed copy and entered edits to our drafts over the course of the year it took to complete this book.

Lisa Williams, Jesse Ianniello, Andrea Haefele, Sam Chillingworth, Teresa Collett, Alice Doughty, and Katie Roth of Jack's staff, who supported this project in so many different ways as this book was being produced and now distributed across the world.

Margaret Lynch and Eleanore Duyndam, two tapping visionaries who supported Pamela in getting her early tapping work into the world.

Denise Haney, Pamela's business manager, who worked through the book for Pamela, fixing details to allow the vision to shine through.

Our brave DVD tapping volunteers: Liz, Kathy, Dina, Marisela, Eleanore, Erin, Bob, and Steve who gave us their vulnerability and authenticity, and demonstrated powerful transformation.

David Babb, for the beautiful tapping points illustrations in the book.

Louise Hay, the founder of Hay House, for having the vision to create such a wonderful publishing company that is dedicated to the evolution of consciousness and the transformation of how we live our lives.

Reid Tracy, President and CEO of Hay House, for his business acumen in the publishing field and for his belief in us and our work.

The dedicated staff at Hay House for their brilliant editing, graphics, PR, and marketing support in getting this work into the world.

Inga Canfield and David Woodworth, our wonderful, loving, and supportive life partners, for so graciously giving us the freedom and the time away from them that was required to complete this book.

We love and appreciate you all!

◎　◎　◎

ABOUT THE AUTHORS

For information about Jack Canfield, please visit:
www.JackCanfield.com.

For information about Pamela Bruner, please visit:
www.MakeYour SuccessEasy.com.

For more information about tapping, including lists of
practitioners, please visit:
www.TappingIntoUltimateSuccess.com.

◎ ◎ ◎

HAY HOUSE TITLES OF RELATED INTEREST

YOU CAN HEAL YOUR LIFE, the movie,
starring Louise L. Hay & Friends
(available as a 1-DVD program and an expanded 2-DVD set)
Watch the trailer at: **www.LouiseHayMovie.com**

THE SHIFT, the movie,
starring Dr Wayne W. Dyer
(available as a 1-DVD program and an expanded 2-DVD set)
Watch the trailer at: **www.DyerMovie.com**

◎

*THE TAPPING SOLUTION: Finally Move Past Recurring Negative
Patterns Around Health,* by Nick Ortner

POWER VS. FORCE: The Hidden Determinants of Human Behavior,
by David R. Hawkins, MD, PhD

THE REAL RULES OF LIFE: Balancing Life's Terms with Your Own,
by Ken Druck, PhD

*SUCCESS INTELLIGENCE: Essential Lessons and Practices from the
World's leading Coaching Programme on Authentic Success,*
by Robert Holden, PhD

YOU CAN HEAL YOUR LIFE, by Louise L. Hay

All of the above are available at your local bookstore,
or may be ordered by contacting Hay House (see next page).

◎

We hope you enjoyed this Hay House book. If you'd
like to receive our online catalog featuring additional
information on Hay House books and products, or if you'd
like to find out more about the Hay Foundation, please contact:

Hay House UK, Ltd.,
292B Kensal Rd., London W10 5BE • *Phone:* 0-20-8962-1230
Fax: 0-20-8962-1239
www.hayhouse.co.uk • **www.hayfoundation.org**

Published and distributed in the United States by:
Hay House, Inc., P.O. Box 5100, Carlsbad, CA 92018-5100
Phone: (760) 431-7695 or (800) 654-5126 (760)
Fax: 431-6948 or (800) 650-5115 • www.hayhouse.com

Published and distributed in Australia by: Hay House Australia Pty. Ltd.,
18/36 Ralph St., Alexandria NSW 2015 • *Phone:* 612-9669-4299
Fax: 612-9669-4144 • www.hayhouse.com.au

Published and distributed in the Republic of South Africa by:
Hay House SA (Pty), Ltd., P.O. Box 990, Witkoppen 2068 • *Phone/Fax:*
27-11-467-8904 • www.hayhouse.co.za

Published in India by: Hay House Publishers India, Muskaan Complex,
Plot No. 3, B-2, Vasant Kunj, New Delhi 110 070 • *Phone:* 91-11-4176-1620
Fax: 91-11-4176-1630 • www.hayhouse.co.in

Distributed in Canada by: Raincoast, 9050 Shaughnessy St.,
Vancouver, B.C. V6P 6E5 • *Phone:* (604) 323-7100 • *Fax:* (604) 323-2600
www.raincoast.com

◉

Take Your Soul on a Vacation

Visit **www.HealYourLife.com**® to regroup, recharge,
and reconnect with your own magnificence. Featuring
blogs, mind-body-spirit news, and life-changing
wisdom from Louise Hay and friends.

Visit **www.HealYourLife.com** today!